AMERICAN MOTORS CORPORATION

THE RISE AND FALL OF AMERICA'S LAST INDEPENDENT AUTOMAKER

BY PATRICK R. FOSTER

motorbooks

First published in 2013 by Motorbooks, an imprint of
Quarto Publishing, 400 First Avenue North, Suite 400, Minneapolis, MN 55401 USA

All photographs are from the author's collection unless noted otherwise.

Motorbooks titles are also available at discounts in bulk quantity for industrial or sales-promotional use. For details write to Special Sales Manager at 400 First Avenue North, Suite 400, Minneapolis, MN 55401 USA.

To find out more about our books, visit us online at www.motorbooks.com.

ISBN-13: 978-0-7603-4425-5

Library of Congress Cataloging-in-Publication Data

WWW.MOTORBOOKS.COM

Foster, Patrick R.
American Motors Corporation : the rise and fall of America's last independent automaker / by Patrick R. Foster.
p. cm.
Summary: "Patrick Foster's American Motors Corporation: The Rise and Fall of America's Last Independent Automaker is the definitive history of the AMC corporation. Featured vehicles include the Rambler, Javelin, and more, as Foster walks the reader through not only the history of an American classic, but a history of the automotive industry itself as it evolved through emissions restrictions and the gas guzzlers of the 80s and 90s." Provided by publisher.
ISBN 978-0-7603-4425-5 (hc w/flaps)
1. American Motors Corporation--History. 2. American Motors automobiles--History. 3. Automobile industry and trade--United States--History. I. Title.
HD9710.U54A652 2013
338.7'6292220973--dc23

2013014304

Editor: Darwin Holmstrom
Editorial Assistant: Madeleine Vasaly
Assistant Managing Editor: Caitlin Fultz
Design Manager: Cindy Samargia Laun
Designer: Mary Rohl
Layout designer: Erin Fahringer
Cover designer: Kent Jensen

On the front cover: Photo © Dave Wendt 2013

On the back cover: In February 1965 AMC introduced its new sporty car, the Marlin. The Marlin was a bigger version of the Tarpon concept and was built on the Classic chassis rather than the American's. This move took it out of the pony car segment and practically insured that the car would never sell in decent volume. Only 10,327 Marlins were produced for 1965.

On the frontis: The 1955 Nash Statesman featured all-new styling with controversial inset headlamps.

On the title page: Jeep Corporation became a part of American Motors at the beginning of the 1970 fiscal year. Shown here are two limited-edition Jeep CJ-5 Renegade II's.

Printed in China

10 9 8 7 6 5 4 3 2

DEDICATION

I'd like to dedicate this book to all the men and women of American Motors Corporation, especially my friends Bob Nixon, Vince Geraci, Jim Pappas, Bob Bristow, Bill St. Claire, Gerry Meyers, George Maddox, Roy Lunn, Allan Kornmiller, Jack Carroll, Phil Lundy, Joe Cappy, Bill Chapin, Chuck Heide, Larry Hyde, Miller Johnson, Chuck Jones, Ron Konopka, Eric Kugler, Bill McNealy, Cruse Moss, Dale Dawkins, W. Paul Tippett, Bob Thomas, Richard Boch, Howard Turtle, Tom Hale, Jack Wildman, Carol Card, D. Dean Greb, Ken Siroonian, John Sanderson, and Brenda Martin.

You and I will always remember American Motors as a special place, an exciting and liberating place in which we all struggled to keep the company alive and vibrant.

I'd also like to remember those AMC friends I've known who helped me over the years and who have now passed on to a greater existence: Roy D. Chapin Jr., George and Lenore Romney, Bill Reddig, Ed Anderson, Charl Greene, Bob Loudon, Jim Alexander, Chuck Mashigan, Carl Chakmakian, John Conde, Bill McGaughey, Evelyn Ay, and Dick Teague.

Last but not least I'd like to thank Frank Peiler and John Biel of *Collectible Automobile* magazine for loaning me pictures of the 1979-1982 AMC production cars.

CONTENTS

	Introduction	8
CHAPTER ONE	1986: The Crucial Year	10
CHAPTER TWO	1954–1957: A New Company is Born	14
CHAPTER THREE	1958–1963: The Rambler Takes Off	46
CHAPTER FOUR	1964–1967: Things Go Wrong	72
CHAPTER FIVE	1968–1969: Chapin at the Wheel	94
CHAPTER SIX	1970–1974: A New Generation	108
CHAPTER SEVEN	1975–1977: The Game Changes	132
CHAPTER EIGHT	1978–1982: The French Connection	152
CHAPTER NINE	1983–1984: The Comeback	176
CHAPTER TEN	1985–1987: The Final Struggle	190
	Index	205

INTRODUCTION

AS I WRITE THIS AMERICAN MOTORS has been officially out of business for 26 years. It doesn't seem possible that so much time has passed since America's "Last Independent" was still a part of corporate America, still listed on the New York Stock Exchange, still talked about and written about in the daily newspapers—that so much time has passed since last we test drove a new AMC car. It doesn't seem possible that it's been 26 years since the closing of so many AMC dealers, and the morphing of others into Jeep/Eagle franchises. For many of us the sadness still lingers.

The Hudson Jet was a compact car that Hudson introduced in hopes of breaking into the territory of the so-called low-priced three. But the Jet proved a flop because of too high a price tag along with styling that few liked. In an easier sales climate it probably would have sold better, but 1954 was a tough year to try to compete with the Big Three.

1

1986
THE CRUCIAL YEAR

IT WAS THE FALL OF 1986, and Roy D. Chapin Jr. was worried. For some days now he had been hearing rumors that American Motors was for sale. As a former CEO and chairman of the board, current board member, and still a leading stockholder, he knew the idea hadn't been discussed by the board of directors. But AMC had a majority owner who could negotiate a sale without consulting the board: French automaker Régie Renault. Chapin decided to talk with the French executives who represented what had become AMC's largest stockholder. His question: Was AMC about to be sold? Despite reassurances from the Renault executives, Chapin walked away still feeling uneasy about the future. But he had Renault's word that no sale was planned, and that would have to do.

One of the rarest AMC muscle cars: the 1971 Hornet SC 360. Here we see three fine examples.

Roy D. Chapin Jr., former chairman of the board of American Motors and still a board member in 1986, was concerned about rumors he had heard that AMC was about to be sold by majority stockholder Renault. However, French executives assured him the company was not for sale.

American Motors Corporation was an old company, with roots in the industry that went back even earlier than the date in March 1902 when the original Rambler automobile was introduced by the Thomas B. Jeffery Company to enthusiastic reviews. The early Rambler quickly gained a reputation for quality and reliability, and it ranked up there in sales with the top sellers, at least initially. But Thomas B. Jeffery and his son Charles, owners of the company, never sought the title of world's largest car company. Instead, they preferred to earn their living building smaller quantities of high-class, medium-priced cars they could be proud of. Let the others follow the volume route; they would build at a pace that ensured top quality.

After Tom Jeffery passed away, Charles took over the company. He later decided for the 1914 model year to rename the product the Jeffery, in honor of his late father. Then in 1916 Charles Nash, former president of General Motors, purchased the Jeffery company and renamed the firm. His Nash Motors Company quickly grew into one of the leading independent automakers in the United States. In 1937 Nash merged with Kelvinator to form the Nash-Kelvinator Corporation, and in 1954 that company merged with the legendary Hudson Motorcar Company, founded in 1909, to form American Motors Corporation. Since that time, AMC had experienced good times and bad and had managed to survive in the intensely competitive U.S. automobile market.

In 1978 AMC formed a strategic partnership with French automaker Renault, in which the French company purchased a small percentage of AMC in exchange for cash that it needed to fund product development. The arrangement was never meant to lead to a merger, and it worked well for a short time. But over the ensuing three years, as AMC's fortunes and working capital fell, Renault ended up owning a commanding share of American Motors and began calling the shots regarding products that would be offered. It was not an ideal situation for AMC by any stretch of the imagination, but its directors could at least be proud that they had kept the old company afloat. And the company was still somewhat autonomous from Renault. It was still, the directors believed, an independent auto company. It was America's last independent.

Roy D. Chapin Jr. knew all of this, and he also knew the French executives who were reassuring him that no sale of AMC was in the works. Chapin fervently hoped that was true, for this was a company worth saving as an independent. It had seen ups and downs before, and it had survived. This was a company with a proud history.

Here we see the 1957 Nash and Hudson senior cars on the assembly line.

2

1954–1957
A NEW COMPANY
IS BORN

IN RETROSPECT, IT WAS SIMPLE TO SPOT. The slow but steady process of erosion would have been easy to see if anybody had bothered to look. In America before World War I, there had been literally hundreds of independent automakers, those smaller companies that were not part of General Motors, Ford, or, later, Chrysler. The independents had a mixed history back then; some, like Willys, Auburn, Studebaker, Franklin, Hudson, Packard, and others had thrived. But most, like Knox, Brush, Thomas, Riker, and so many others, faded away by the time World War I arrived. After the war, the ranks of the independents were enlarged by newcomers like LaFayette, Cord, Graham-Paige, Rockne, and a good number of others. And 1925 saw the birth of what became a new giant company, Chrysler Corporation. But then the Great Depression killed off many more independents, including some of the greatest names in the business: Peerless, Marmon, and even the mightiest of them all, Duesenberg. By the early 1930s the ranks of the independents had dwindled to the dozens rather than the hundreds or thousands. It was a simple process of purging, Darwinism, survival of the fittest, whatever you want to call it. The heyday of the independent was slipping away.

By the time World War II arrived, very few of the old companies were left. Thankfully, the war helped save a struggling Willys-Overland, Bantam, and Graham-Paige from bankruptcy and helped strengthen the other companies that had benefited from money pouring into corporate coffers as a result of lucrative war production contracts. By the time the war ended, the lineup

Hudson dealers had the exclusive Hudson Italia sports coupe to offer for 1954, and it was a very pretty car indeed. But a high price and doubts about Hudson's ability to survive in the marketplace made the Italia a hard sell. Fewer than 30 were built, making it a highly desirable collector car today.

of major independent car companies had shrunk to Packard, Nash, Studebaker, Hudson, and Willys-Overland. Little Crosley still produced its tiny economy cars, and Checker still made its sturdy cabs in small numbers, and Graham-Paige, though it had halted production, was making plans to reenter the passenger car market. It soon teamed up with the Henry J. Kaiser interests to start a new company, Kaiser-Frazer.

From 1946 to 1953 the auto industry, and the automotive independents in particular, enjoyed incredible demand and lush profits. No U.S. auto production had occurred from mid-January 1942 until August 1945, and America's roads were clogged with older cars that had too many miles on them. Americans had plenty of money to spend, so even though the companies were producing warmed-over 1942 models, buyers lined up to purchase them. Once civilian production resumed, automakers could sell every car they could build. Getting enough raw materials was a problem, but selling the end product wasn't. New model introductions helped keep demand high from 1949 to 1952, and by that point, the Korean War had begun, and it, too, kept demand high. It wasn't until 1953 that demand began to be influenced strictly by ordinary market forces.

But in late 1953 a young Henry Ford II decided he'd had enough of Chevrolet being the top-selling car in the country. He vowed to have Ford retake the number-one spot or kill

When Hudson and Nash merged in 1954, George W. Mason, CEO of Nash-Kelvinator and one of the smartest men in the automobile business, became the president and CEO of American Motors. Mason had been the architect of the merger, and he had big plans to merge operations to improve amortization and lower costs.

The most popular and coveted product of the new American Motors Corporation was the four-door Rambler station wagon, seen here in Custom trim. The trademark dipped roofline was designed by Bill Reddig, assistant director of styling. He also suggested including the small roof rack as standard equipment, feeling it improved the looks.

the company trying. He began shipping thousands of new cars to his dealers, often ones they had never ordered, and told them to sell them quick because more were on the way. And they were; Henry's factories were spitting out new Fords at a furious pace. Chevrolet was not about to take this sitting down, so it began building and shipping new cars to its own dealers, and the great sales battle of 1953–1954 was on.

It was an epic struggle. All through 1954, the two giant automakers battled for supremacy. But while they fought each other, the independent makers became collateral damage; they simply couldn't compete at that intensity, and their sales dropped like stones. The numbers show it: In 1953 Nash sold 137,507 cars. In 1954 that dropped to 82,729. Studebaker dropped from 161,257 to 95,914 cars. And mighty Packard suffered a sickening drop from 71,079 to just 38,396 cars. Hudson dropped from 66,797 to 35,824. Poor Kaiser-Frazer sold just 10,012 cars for the year. Meanwhile, Ford sales jumped up from 1,116,267 to 1,400,440 units, though in the end Chevrolet still beat that by some 17,000 cars. It had been a whirlwind year—and it nearly destroyed the independents.

The big 1954 Hudson Hornet was America's stock car champion, having dominated NASCAR racing since 1951.

By early 1954 each of the remaining independents realized it needed to merge with some other company to survive. Each needed to create new products, but the cost of tooling and dies had skyrocketed after the war. The Big Three could afford the cost because they spread the expense across their several brands, using shared body shells. The independents needed to be able to do the same thing—to spread their tooling costs over a larger number of cars than in the past—and the only way to do that was to share body shells with another firm. There was no magic in this; for years, GM, Ford, and Chrysler had built numerous cars on one or two bodies. Pontiac usually shared its basic body with Chevrolet, while Olds and Buick were platform mates. It was the most economical way to produce vehicles.

A comparison illustrates the problem. Packard, Nash, and Hudson together marketed only eight series of cars, yet required five basic body shells. In contrast, Ford made seven series of cars from just two basic shells, and GM produced fourteen series of cars from just four body shells. The cost of tooling for each basic body shell was enormous and had to be distributed over a great many vehicles.

In addition to the exorbitant cost of tooling, the number of dealers selling independent brands had taken a marked decline. The combination of a weak used-car market in 1953 and 1954 (due to the fact that in many cases it was cheaper to buy a new car than a used car) and the sales decline caused by the Chevy-Ford sales war had devastated dealer networks at each of the independents. Fewer stores meant still fewer sales. The situation soon became critical.

Kaiser and Willys-Overland were the first to join together, in 1953, when Kaiser bought the operating assets of Willys-Overland and formed a new affiliate called Willys Motors.

Left: The lowest-priced big Nash was the Statesman, seen here in its four-door sedan version. (A two-door Super sedan was also offered, along with higher-priced Custom models.) For 1954 Nash senior cars offered the recessed grille shown here as well as increased horsepower in most engines.

Below: Seen here in August 1954 is George W. Mason. Small duck paperweights decorate his desk; Mason was one of the founders of the conservation organization Ducks Unlimited, and duck hunting was one of his passions. Unfortunately for this great man, he had less than two months to live when this photo was taken.

Meanwhile, the remaining Little Four automakers investigated the possibilities of merging with one another. Packard, beginning to hemorrhage money, looked into merging with Hudson, Studebaker, Nash, and Kaiser-Willys. Nash, which had been solidly profitable in 1953 and continued to be until the second quarter of 1954, looked into merging with Packard and Hudson. Studebaker claimed it was above the fray, but it, too, was bleeding capital and began talks with Packard.

The president of Nash-Kelvinator, George W. Mason, was one of the smartest men in the auto industry. He'd been shrewd enough to foresee the coming showdown and had been trying since at least 1946 to convince one or more of the other independents to join forces with him. Hudson and Packard both turned him down flat. He looked at Studebaker but concluded that the firm was too entrenched in South Bend,

Indiana, and might fight any attempt to move production to another state, a likely eventuality in any merger scenario.

Then in June 1953 the weakest of the bunch, Hudson, which would announce a loss of more than $10 million for the year, asked Mason if they could talk. The company was bleeding to death and might not last another year if things didn't improve. Hudson president A. E. Barit met Mason June 16 in room 2607 of the Book-Cadillac Hotel in Detroit. Before the end of the meeting, they shook hands on an agreement in principle to join forces. By the end of the year, the merger of the two firms was well under way, though it would take several more months to work out the details, especially the valuation of assets.

Once Hudson was on board, Mason made another attempt to convince Packard to merge, meeting with its board of directors in early 1954. He had his public relations people make up a flip chart illustrating the many advantages of the union and took it to Packard for a formal presentation. Packard's president, James J. Nance, was interested in the possibilities and might have agreed to the merger but for one holdup: the question of who would be the top man running the new corporation. Nance, despite his near-total lack of experience in the auto industry, somehow felt he was the most competent man for the job. Mason, who had run Nash-Kelvinator successfully for nearly 20 years, couldn't allow that. Mason's offer was to have himself at the helm, with his executive vice president George Romney serving the same position in the new firm and Nance assigned to be vice president in charge of the Packard/Clipper division. A defiant Nance refused even to consider such a plan; he had to be the top executive or it was no deal. After Mason gave a full presentation to the full Packard board, Nance talked the directors out of accepting Mason's offer. Instead, he would merge the company with Studebaker, which had the highest unit volume of all the independents and whose management had already indicated that they would step aside and let Nance run the show.

One of the better-looking cars of the 1950s was the big Hudson Hornet, shown here in the Hollywood Hardtop body style. The big Hudsons were overengineered and overbuilt, which made them costly to produce but gave them long life and relatively trouble-free operation.

It was time to do or die. Each of the independents was being hammered by losses, and they could wait no longer. After tough final negotiations between Nash-Kelvinator's Mason and Hudson's A. E. Barit—Mason said, "I have dealt with tough traders before but this Barit has a heart of stone!"—the two companies merged effective May 1, 1954. The particulars of the merger were that Nash stock became AMC stock on a one-for-one basis, whereas Hudson shareholders traded in three shares of Hudson stock for two shares of Nash stock, which then was turned in for AMC stock. Barit had gotten the best deal he could, considering that his company was on the ropes and he held no high cards in the negotiations. Mason himself came up with the name for the new company: American Motors Corporation. It had a nice ring to it.

It was the biggest merger in the history of the auto industry to that point, easily dwarfing the union of Willys and Kaiser the year before. The new company had 40,000 employees, 10,000 dealers, and two distinct brands of cars; along with Nash's extensive appliance operations, Kelvinator, Leonard, and ABC; plus Ranco, Inc., the world's largest producer of temperature controls for the auto and appliance industries. Over the span of more than half a century, the two companies combined had sold more than $10 billion worth of merchandise—more than 6 million automobiles, more than 10 million appliances and commercial products, more than 68 million automatic temperature controls, and a billion dollars of defense material. The new firm had 58,000 stockholders, plants in five states and 44 cities throughout the world, and distributors in more than 100 countries. It also had one of the best management teams in the business.

The new American Motors was the fourth-largest car company in America. The company stated in its first annual report: "The merger was consummated to achieve economies

Introduced in early 1954 as the Nash Metropolitan, a version of this car was given to Hudson dealers to sell right after the merger. The only differences between the Nash and Hudson versions were the grille badge and possibly the hubcaps. Shown here is the Nash version. Metropolitans could get upwards of 40 miles per gallon of fuel, yet were smooth-riding and comfortable to drive.

in manufacturing, tooling, and overhead expenses, and advantages in selling, which neither company could obtain alone."

George Mason was recognized by many in the industry as a farsighted, even visionary, leader, a man who was a pioneer in small cars and who'd built Nash up from a small company to a large, important one. His executive vice president, George Romney, was young, lean, and athletic, a combination of ambition and energy. Dealers who met him came away impressed at his intensity and intelligence. Romney was a first-rate executive.

When the merger came together, A. E. Barit retired from active management, taking a seat on the board but having no real power, thank goodness. His tenure at Hudson had seen an almost unbroken decline in the company's fortunes. Once one of the biggest producers in the country, Hudson was now very much a junior partner in American Motors. One Hudson executive who came with the merger was Roy D. Chapin Jr., son of one of the founders of Hudson, whose family owned a large

Above: After months of negotiations and working out details of the merger, Nash and Hudson joined forces to create American Motors effective May 1, 1954. Shown here, left to right, are A. E. Barit, president of Hudson; George W. Mason of Nash; and Mason's executive vice president, George W. Romney. In time Romney would succeed Mason as the head of AMC.

Right: One of Nash's most popular models in 1954 was the Rambler four-door sedan, seen here in Super trim. The four-door Ramblers rode a 108-inch wheelbase, 8 inches longer than the two-door Ramblers, and were much roomier inside. Families loved the compact exterior size of the Rambler and appreciated the exceptional fuel economy it delivered.

The Nash-Kelvinator headquarters building in Detroit, seen in this November 1953 photo, became the headquarters for the new American Motors Corporation in May 1954. The building in front with the large tower is the actual headquarters. The large building stretching out behind it is the massive Kelvinator factory.

amount of Hudson stock. Chapin came in as assistant treasurer but also held a seat on the board, a result of the large holdings (now in AMC stock) that his family owned.

The structure of the new company was simple. There were four main divisions: automotive, which included Nash and Hudson; Kelvinator; Export and Subsidiaries; and Hudson Special Products, which handled military production. Within the automotive division, the sales functions of the Nash and Hudson car divisions would remain separate, but it was vitally important that automobile manufacturing be consolidated as quickly as possible.

Mason and Romney wanted Hudson because the two product lines were very similar, so sharing a common body shell would be relatively easy. ("You can't do that with a Studebaker," Romney once commented to a reporter.) Besides, Hudson had a fairly large dealer network, and the two men expected to distribute the Rambler through both organizations, which had the very real potential to make the Rambler a high-volume product.

From October 1, 1952, to September 30, 1953, which coincided with Nash's fiscal year, the two companies combined had sold 237,108 cars to their dealers. American Motors would continue to use Nash's October–September fiscal year, and its goal was to consolidate production and increase unit sales from that dismal number.

Because the merger took place in the middle of the 1954 model year, both companies had already launched their new products. Hudson had its big step-down Wasp, Super Wasp, and Hornet and its Jet compact, all of them powered by six-cylinder engines. From 1951 to 1954 Hudson had dominated NASCAR racing, but that success hadn't been able to halt its steady sales decline. Now in 1954 Hudson sales were in free fall.

Left: The 1955 Nash Statesman featured all-new styling with controversial inset headlamps.

Right: Nash was one of the pioneers of air conditioning in cars and homes and played it up often in their advertising. Here we see an air-conditioned 1954 Ambassador crossing the Arizona desert.

Over at Nash, sales of the big Ambassador and Statesman, compact Rambler, and sub-compact Metropolitan were doing a little better than Hudson's, but these, too, were in a sharp decline. The only products that seemed to be selling well were the four-door Rambler sedan and station wagon models.

As a first step toward integrating the product lines, Hudson dealers were quickly given a Hudson version of the 1954 Metropolitan to sell. The only difference was in the grille badge and hubcaps—the whole thing was a barely disguised Nash, but it gave the Hudson salesmen another product to sell. Meanwhile George Mason had ordered his styling chief, Edmund E. Anderson, to begin designing a new Hudson senior car lineup based on the Nash body shell. One of the chief designers on the project was Allan Kornmiller, who later recalled, "I was told to have engineering send two body shells to the styling studio, where I was to design the 1955 Hudson Hornets and Wasps." It was critical that the new cars be ready for 1955 introduction; Hudson sales were collapsing faster than Mason had expected, and the need to consolidate production onto one basic shell was severe.

For the balance of the 1954 model year, Hudson and Nash continued selling their separate lines. The Hudson Hornet and Wasps shared the same body shell and were very much alike save for wheelbase (Wasps had a 119-inch wheelbase; Hornets, a 124-inch) and interior trim. Power-wise, the Hornet was king, propelled by its big, powerful 308-cubic-inch six. Wasps and Super Wasps had more modest sixes powering them and were priced lower. Hudson even brought out a lower-priced version of its Hornet, called the Hornet Special, to try to grab a few more sales; it helped, but in the end it couldn't turn the tide. Hudson also had its limited-production Italia sport coupe, a sharp car handmade in Italy, but it was pricey and the company had fewer than 30 built.

The real problem in Hudson's lineup was its lowest-priced car, the Jet series. The Jet had been introduced as a 1953 model, and it was, for lack of a better term, a sales disaster. Only 21,000 were built for 1953, and for 1954 only about 14,000 would be produced. Hudson had expected to sell many more than that, and because it hadn't, the company had to adjust its amortization schedules to fit reality. The Jet's failure was a big part of the reason Hudson was losing so much money.

At Nash, the situation was similar. Its big six-cylinder Ambassador and Statesman models were selling at much-reduced rates. Rambler sales were also lower, though its very profitable four-door models were holding up fairly well. Sales of the Metropolitan were exceeding expectations, but then again, expectations had been rather low to begin with. The company claimed that the Metropolitan, introduced in early 1954, was being sold on a "market-test" basis.

The Nash Statesman competed with the Hudson Wasp, while the Ambassador competed with the Hornet. Jet and Rambler were in competition with each other too, but Mason had no intention of keeping the poor-selling Jet in the lineup. He had refused to absorb its losses and decided to end production as soon as he reasonably could. There would be no 1955 Jet.

Nash also had a high-priced sporty car to sell for 1954, the beautiful Nash-Healey, offered in coupe and convertible styles. Seen here with actor William Holden, who drove one in the movie *Sabrina*, the Nash-Healey racked up an enviable racing record at Le Mans.

Like Hudson, Nash had a specialty car, also handmade in Italy. The Nash-Healey was one of the first postwar sports cars and was powerful and extremely attractive. Priced in the stratosphere, it attracted diehard sports car enthusiasts and had established an enviable racing record at Le Mans.

The 1954 model year ended up being a disaster for the independents. On October 1, 1954, a struggling Studebaker merged with Packard, so all the major independents were now teamed with a partner.

All this time, design chief Ed Anderson and his assistant Bill Reddig had their designers hard at work on the next new Nash and Hudson models for 1955. The 1955 Nashes were mostly already designed, so the company would be able to roll them out at introduction time with little difficulty. But work was still proceeding on the new Hudsons. In addition to sharing the same shell as the Nash, the new Hudson would integrate the 1954 Hudson gauge cluster into the instrument panel—no easy task because the two weren't compatible. But

Above: The Hudson Jet was a compact car that Hudson introduced in hopes of breaking into the territory of the so-called low-priced three. But the Jet proved a flop because of too high a price tag along with styling that few liked. In an easier sales climate it probably would have sold better, but 1954 was a tough year to try to compete with the Big Three.

Right: Two of the best stylists in the business— Bill Reddig, left, and Ed Anderson, right—were, respectively, assistant director of styling and director of styling at American Motors. Both former Nash men, they set up the styling department GM-like, with separate Nash, Hudson, Rambler, and Interior studios.

Hudson had something like 30,000 gauge clusters still in stock, and Mason wanted to use them up. Allan Kornmiller came through with a neat design.

The decision was made in May 1954 that all car production would be consolidated into the existing Nash plants in Kenosha and Milwaukee, Wisconsin, and El Segundo, California. The surplus Hudson plants would be sold. Mason planned to hold on to the Hudson body-making plants and equipment because of a deal he made with Packard. Mason and Romney knew they need a V-8 engine for their big cars but were hesitant to tool up for one because of the great expense. They cut a deal to buy V-8 engines and Ultramatic transmissions from Packard. In exchange, Packard would purchase parts from American Motors in dollar quantities at least equal to what AMC was paying. Mason and Romney called this concept 'reciprocity' and had conceived of the idea a few years earlier. With it, the independents could enjoy greater production volumes even without a merger. After signing the agreement, Romney and Mason moved on to other problems.

The engine deal was consummated late in the 1954 model year, and that timing caused a major delay in introducing the new 1955 cars because the body shell and assembly process had to be changed to fit the big Packard engine. The new V-8 Nashes would not be ready until the end of the year. The all-new Hudsons would be similarly delayed. Both lines of cars finally reached production in December 1954, but line speed took a long time to reach normal production rates because of the difficulty of integrating three lines of cars—Nash, Hudson, and Rambler—into one assembly line. Eventually the decision was made to set up a separate line for the Ramblers, and a wartime plant was converted for that purpose.

George Mason never got to see the new Hudsons and Nashes coming off

Top: A midyear addition to the option list on Ramblers was the Fashion-Tone paint combination shown here on the Rambler Country Club hardtop. Bright, contrasting colors made these cars real standouts. Ramblers had open front wheelwells for 1955.

Bottom: Following the death of George Mason, George Romney was elevated to chairman, president, and CEO of American Motors. Romney was placed in a difficult situation. The Chevy-Ford sales war of 1954 had weakened Nash and Hudson before the merger, and the aftereffects were still pulling down AMC sales. Romney would have to work hard to try to save the company.

the assembly line. On Sunday, October 3, 1954, Mason returned home to Detroit from a fishing vacation in Wyoming. That evening he was stricken with abdominal pain and taken to Detroit's Harper Hospital. He was in bad shape at first. George Romney visited him at the hospital on Monday and Tuesday morning, and Mason was very ill and not lucid. However, by Tuesday afternoon he was improving, and Romney was able to talk with him. When Romney visited him again on Wednesday, Mason was even better, so Romney sat and talked business with him. The two men discussed a sales executive Romney wanted to hire for the Nash Motors division to replace sales VP H. C. Doss, who was against the company's small-car program. They also talked about concerns that Packard thus far wasn't honoring the reciprocity agreement they'd made; no orders had come in for purchases of body stampings from American Motors. On Thursday, Mason was even better when Romney visited him again.

Mason seemed to be on the road to recovery, but his health took a sharp turn for the worse late Thursday evening, and on Friday, October 8, 1954, he died at 11:45 a.m. His pancreas had ceased functioning, and he had contracted pneumonia. Romney got the call from the hospital while in the company's styling studios. He put the phone down, said a silent prayer for Mason, and went to tell his fellow executives.

When the board of directors met to discuss what to do about replacing Mason, a great deal of discord arose. The controversy was about whether Romney should assume all Mason's responsibilities. There wasn't any argument about Romney taking over *some* of the responsibilities; after all, Mason had obviously been grooming him for that. But several board members felt Romney was too young and inexperienced to take over *all* Mason's responsibilities and titles: chairman of the board, CEO, president, etc.

"The question wasn't whether or not I'd succeed Mason," Romney recalled in later years. "It was would I succeed him as president but not chairman, or chairman but not CEO, and so forth. They wanted [vice president] A. M. Wibel, a very capable man and former Ford executive, to take over some of Mason's titles because he was older and had more experience. It was one of my hardest jobs convincing the board that that would be a mistake, and to appoint me as Mason's complete successor. I talked with them about my concepts. You see, the basic difference between Mason and me was that he visualized the Rambler as a

Left: The Rambler Fashion-Tone color scheme was different on four-door sedans and wagons. This Rambler was photographed in front of AMC's headquarters in Detroit. The script above the front door of the building bears an old Lord Kelvin saying: "I've thought of a better way."

Right: The Hornet four-door sedan for 1955 was built on the basic Nash body but had its own unique styling. Interestingly, the grille and front end motif were very similar to what Hudson's own stylists had proposed for a future facelift. One of the chief stylists on the 1955 Hudson was Allan Kornmiller.

Top: It took a while to integrate Hudson production with Nash and Rambler, but it was eventually done and cars began rolling off the lines. This photograph illustrates the various engines waiting to be joined with their respective bodies on the assembly line. In time, Rambler production had to be moved to its own assembly building.

Bottom: The Hudson Rambler four-door Cross Country station wagon for 1955. The Hudson Rambler series replaced the former Jet and was much more popular. Rambler sales were beginning to grow with the addition of the Hudson sales network behind it.

The beautiful 1955 Nash Ambassador Country Club hardtop was offered only in Custom trim, as was befitting for a high-end car like this. The contrasting white top really adds to the beauty of the car. Note the inset headlamps and delicate running lights set in the front fenders.

supplemental line to the Nash and Hudson cars and I had become convinced that Rambler was the car of the future."

After a great deal of discussion and a lot of salesmanship on his part, Romney was able to convince the board. The day after Mason's funeral the board gave him what he'd asked for, electing him chairman, president, and chief executive officer of American Motors and giving him all Mason's other titles: chairman of Redisco, Kelvinator's finance arm; board member of both Redisco Canada Ltd. and Kelvinator Ltd. of Great Britain; director of Kelvinator of Canada; and director of American Motors of Canada Ltd.

There has been speculation that Romney was able to influence the 1955 model lineup when he took over, but in reality it was too late to change anything. George Mason is the man to credit or criticize for the 1955 product line because he approved each car months before his death.

American Motors was a sickly company by October 1954. The seemingly unending sales battle between Chevy and Ford was still going strong, sucking away sales from the independents and causing massive losses. By now even Plymouth had become involved, and American Motors was hemorrhaging cash. It was going to take a lot of work and more than a bit of luck to turn things around. One of the first steps Romney took was to broom out some of the older executives who were against the Rambler and to hire Kaiser-Willys executive Roy Abernethy to become sales manager. Abernethy was the person Romney had discussed with Mason in the hospital. He was known as someone who knew how to work with dealers, and he professed to be a small-car enthusiast.

If Romney had any doubts about AMC's future, he didn't show it. In a family newsletter dated October 16, 1954, he wrote: "We are very optimistic about our program for the coming year and are not at all interested in merger with Studebaker-Packard. Our company is much stronger. We have $116 million in working capital as compared to their $85 million and we have $416 million worth of assets as compared to their $254 million. As a result we have exploded the idea that Nance of Packard is the logical man to head up a combination of the two companies and that it is necessary for the two companies to merge. . . ."

Romney's mention of Packard president James Nance was a strong indication of the rapidly deteriorating relations between the two men. When Mason first proposed merging with Packard, Romney had been upbeat about having Nance on board because Packard would have been a great addition and under the proposed Nash-Packard merger as Mason had developed it, Nance would have been vice president in charge of the Packard-Clipper division, and Romney would have continued as executive vice president of the corporation . . . and thus Nance's boss. But Nance rejected that setup, believing he should be appointed both president and CEO of American Motors. Ever since the Nash-Hudson merger, Nance had been saying some nasty things about Romney behind his back. Romney later recalled: "Not long after American Motors was formed, Nance starting telling newsmen that 'Romney is a neophyte. He was just there to hold Mason's briefcase.' He said that he [Nance] would scoop up American Motors before the end of the year. Things like that." For Romney, it was too much to stomach gracefully. Hostility was growing between the two men, but since the two companies had gone their separate ways, it didn't appear that it would cause any real problems.

The press hounded Romney with questions about whether or not he would merge AMC with Studebaker or Packard. They pointed out that Studebaker had high volume production and Packard had prestige.

The lady hitchhiking in this photo had better watch out; the driver of that pretty 1955 Hudson Hornet is a real wolf! American Motors' ad agency thought up this humorous photo, but we can't find any evidence that they actually used it anywhere. It's a bit risqué for the era.

Top: AMC president George Romney had his public relations people put together an exhibit to illustrate the many facets of American Motors. The display showed the various factories AMC owned in the United States and around the world, as well as the many businesses it was in, such as automobiles, appliances, temperature controls, and financing.

Bottom: Here's something you don't see every day: a rare Nash Canadian Statesman four-door sedan. The senior Nash cars built for Canada wore Canadian name badges alongside the usual model identification, giving Canadian buyers greater pride of ownership.

Romney pointed out the basic wisdom of the AMC merger. He realized that merging Studebaker and Packard together would cause problems; because the two lines were so dissimilar, building them on one body shell and in one factory would be difficult. Certainly it couldn't be done until a whole-sale redesign was completed, and that would take a minimum of two years. Beyond that was the fact that Studebaker had the highest costs in the industry, a thoroughly spoiled union, and a spirit of antagonism between labor and management. He was simply not interested in Studebaker, and by the time that company had teamed up with Packard, there was no hope of the four companies ever getting together.

Still, at many press events toward the end of 1954, the question would come up as to whether AMC was going to merge with Studebaker-Packard. Romney usually managed to avoid the issue, always saying that no negotiations were in place for any additional mergers. But he also made sure to mention that he had a product reciprocity agreement with S-P that would provide both companies with many of the benefits of a merger—better use of their facilities, greater sales of components, reduced overhead—without actually having to merge. However, when pressed at one meeting to talk about the products S-P was buying from AMC, Romney was stuck, and he tried to dodge the question because the truth was that Studebaker-Packard had not purchased anything of real value from AMC, just some minor items that engineers termed "five- and ten-cent parts." The large orders for body stampings were not coming. Thus, as American Motors was shelling out millions of dollars for Packard engines and transmissions, that company was not bothering to honor the agreement it had signed.

This was verified in early October when two AMC executives returned from a meeting at Packard with word that the vice president in charge of Packard manufacturing did not recognize any corporate obligation to buy from American Motors. Romney was incensed. Then, on October 22, mere weeks after Mason's death, Romney learned that Packard had taken an option to buy a body manufacturing plant from Murray Corporation. That meant that Packard would never become a purchaser of body panels from AMC as both he and Mason had expected. Angry, Romney called Nance's office but found he couldn't get through; Nance's gatekeepers were on duty. So Romney sent a telegram to Nance's home, which read: "Believe consummation of the deal with Murray as it is reported to us would be contrary to the spirit, contractual, and moral obligations of your current understandings with us. . . . Believe you and I should meet and discuss entire situation."

Amazingly Nance replied to Romney's urgent communiqué by *letter*. He denied any wrongdoing. A clause in the contract stated that "Packard shall be the sole judge of whether products offered it by AMC can be purchased by Packard . . . on a competitive and advantageous basis." It was a standard loophole both Mason and Romney were aware of but did not believe Packard would actually utilize. After all, the two companies had an *understanding* on the need for reciprocity. . But Nance had since become convinced that he was doing AMC a favor in selling them drivetrains and that AMC needed him more than he needed them. There was no doubt about this attitude; in his letter Nance stated that "we regret that our company name was used in a discussion with the press of a reciprocity agreement."

For their part, S-P executives claimed they had asked for quotes on body parts but that the resulting estimates were higher than they could buy the parts elsewhere. This may have been true, but it overlooked the fact that AMC was paying a premium for the Packard engines and transmissions, some $200 more than if they had produced those components themselves.

Romney next tried to get one of Nance's top men to acknowledge the reciprocity understanding. After talking by phone with a Studebaker-Packard vice president, a conversation in which he pleaded his case, Romney hung up, turned to a companion, and said, "That fellow just lied to me three times in that one conversation. You just cannot do business with someone who lies."

Left: The handsome gentleman in the suit is styling director Ed Anderson, pictured along with his secretary Carol Card, a longtime AMC employee. The landmark 1956 Rambler was designed under Anderson's direction, and it saved AMC from almost-certain bankruptcy.

Right: Vice president Jack Timpy was one of the few Nash executives Romney kept on after George Mason died because he was one of the few men who believed in the Rambler's potential to become a volume car. Timpy came up with the volume investment fund program to reward dealers for Rambler sales.

The relationship between Nance and Romney was beyond salvation. A furious Romney called in his vice president of engineering, Meade Moore, and ordered him to begin designing a new line of V-8 engines for American Motors' cars. It was going to cost the company $10 million at a time when it was short of cash, but Romney was determined to sever all relationships with Nance and Studebaker-Packard. From that point forward, AMC would go it alone. In time, Packard's engine plant and all its brand-new automated machinery would be sold for scrap metal.

For AMC, fiscal 1954 came to an end on September 30, 1954. Results were about what might have been expected; in the most competitive year since the Great Depression, the new American Motors Corporation posted an operating loss of more than $22 million, which was reduced to a net loss of $11,071,237 after application of an $11,590,000 tax credit, made possible by Nash-Kelvinator's record of good profits in prior years. The cost of accelerated amortization of tooling, cancellation of purchase commitments (mostly related to Hudson), and other nonoperating charges amounted to $9,156,026 after a tax credit of $5,700,000. This was charged against an $11 million reserve set up specifically for this purpose using earnings from prior years retained in the business. By the time all the additions and subtractions were made, AMC had net working capital of $82 million—good, but down substantially from the beginning of the fiscal year.

The operating loss came as a result of the sharp drop in car sales. The separate companies had sold 237,108 cars in fiscal 1953, which was not a great year. But for 1954 this dropped to 135,794 units, an unmitigated disaster. The only good news was that the Big Three's sales war was now over, and 1955 was shaping up to be a very good year for the industry.

George Romney firmly believed 1955 was going to be a much better year for AMC. For one thing, his tooling costs would be cut nearly in half because of the combined tooling program he'd initiated. In addition, car sales and appliance sales had both been on the upswing toward the end of fiscal 1954, and it looked as though business conditions were returning to normal. AMC had an all-new line of big Hudson automobiles, a revamped line of senior Nash cars, a new V-8 engine, and some noticeable restyling of the Rambler series. Rambler prices were among the lowest in the industry—the two-door Rambler Deluxe was the lowest-priced family sedan on the market, and AMC even covered the import market with its little Metropolitan, which was the second-best-selling imported car after Volkswagen. In 1955 the Met would take more than 11 percent of the import market.

Left: When the 1956 Rambler made its debut, Super and Custom model trims emphasized the so-called basket-handle C-pillar. Although buyers loved the Rambler's overall styling, the basket-handle trim received a good share of criticism, so the company pushed through a midyear redesign of the Custom trim.

Right: Although at first glance this looks like a 1957 Rambler, it is in fact a 1956 Rambler Custom model with the revised side trim. This style proved more popular than the others, and a slightly different version was adopted for 1957. The Super trim for 1957 was also changed to deemphasize the basket-handle roofline.

For a time, Boch Motors out in Massachusetts was the largest Rambler dealer in the world and sold an amazing number of Ramblers. This scene from 1956 shows a complete front row of Rambler wagons, which were the most popular Ramblers. Note the car on the roof of the building.

The senior Nash line for 1955 received new front-end styling that was quite unusual. The headlamps were moved from the front fenders to the grille, Nash-Healey-style, and the front fenders retained their controversial enclosed front wheels, albeit this year they were modified to show more wheel than before. The front fenders themselves leaned forward, shark-like, and featured delicate fender lamps on the leading edge. Side trim was a simple chrome molding on the character line running from the front wheel to the back of the car. It was a very clean look, but one that took some getting used to. Although by the sixties most cars would carry their headlamps in the grille area, in 1955 it was curious-looking.

The Hudson big cars were all-new, built on the existing Nash body shell. The styling was quite attractive, and looked very much the way Hudson had envisioned a facelift of the old product. The grille was a near copy of what the Hudson stylist's had planned for 1955. The new Hudson's were slightly smaller than the old, and weighed less. The Hornet series offered either the old 308 six or the new Packard-sourced V-8 engines, while the Wasp came now with a slightly more powerful version of the old Jet six. The Jet, of course, was history, replaced by an extensive lineup of Hudson Ramblers.

The Rambler lineup for both Nash and Hudson was identical. Part of the original product plan was for Hudson dealers to get a restyled version of the Rambler, something made to look distinct from the Nash product. But in the end the excessive cost of styling two versions, along with the need to bring the Rambler into Hudson showrooms as quickly as possible,

This lineup of two Nashes, a Rambler, and a Hudson, all 1956 models, is getting ready to partake in one of the numerous fuel economy runs that American Motors participated in during the 1950s and 1960s.

meant that the two divisions would share the same product. Apart from badges and hub-caps the Nash and Hudson Ramblers for 1955 were identical. Even the prices were the same.

The Rambler series began with a low-priced two-door sedan priced at $1,550 and topped out with the Custom four-door Cross Country station wagon tagged at $2,055. In between were hardtops, two-door wagons, and four-door sedans. It was a complete line-up, offering more choices than in the senior car lines.

The Metropolitan lineup consisted of two cars, a Met hardtop priced at $1,445, and a convertible at $1,469. As in 1954, the 1955 Met was sold in Nash and Hudson versions.

Early in the model year, with sales going slowly and little hope in sight, Romney made a momentous decision. Faced with the need for new products, he realized he had only enough funds to redesign one series—either large cars or the Rambler. Historically, big cars provided better sales and higher profits, but his big cars were trending downward in sales and his Rambler was doing a little better. Styling chief Ed Anderson had his team working on new senior cars as well as an all-new Rambler for 1957. Romney, after considerable dis-cussion, decided that the Rambler was the product to emphasize. And because time was running out he ordered that the new 1957 Rambler be moved up for introduction as a 1956 model. It would cost an extra $5 million of AMC's rapidly depleting cash, but it was needed now. Romney worried 1957 might be too late.

Since 1954 AMC's dealers had been hard hit by the drastic drop in sales, and many were on the verge of going out of business. To strengthen his dealer network at this crucial time and help keep them solvent, Romney and vice president Jack Timpy came up with the Dealer Volume Investment Fund. Under this plan, all Nash and Hudson dealers received a bonus on each Rambler they sold. The bonus was $30 per car for the first 25,000 cars, $40 for the next 25,000, and $55 per car for more than 55,000 units. For Nash and Hudson senior cars, the bonus began at $50. The program helped push Rambler sales up to more than 73,000 units, and over a two-year period it pumped $7 million into dealers' hands, strengthening the network's operating capital and helping many dealers weather the storm. Yet even with this help, the dealer network would fall from 2,800 dealers in 1954 to 1,900 by 1956.

Sales results for 1955 were not very good. The company produced a total of only 153,522 Nash and Hudson cars, up from 1954 but not nearly enough. The company's breakeven point by then was just under 200,000 units, and until sales reached at least that number, losses would continue. American Motors reported another loss, this time a net total of nearly $7 million after a tax credit of $9.7 million. Working capital fell to $62.4 million. Romney put the best face possible on the situation when he stated, "1955 was primarily a year devoted to laying the groundwork for re-establishing American Motors' earning power under the competitive conditions existing today."

One bright light: In the final seven months of fiscal 1955, when all models were available and in full-scale production, 109,068 cars were produced, compared with 58,147 in the same period a year before. That was a gain of 87.6 percent.

So 1956 held a lot of promise. Not only were sales trending upward, but an all-new Rambler was debuting, and it was a beauty. Designed by a team of stylists under Ed Anderson and Bill Reddig, the new Rambler, though still compact, looked much larger and more modern than it had before. The lines were smooth, and the slab sides allowed for much larger interior space. Both the windshield and rear window were wraparound, and glass area all around was greater, giving a bright, airy feel to the interior.

Engineering-wise the Rambler was also a winner. The former flathead six was replaced by a new overhead valve version of the same mill, with 33 percent more power and reportedly improved fuel economy. The standard manual steering was so light that one road tester stopped the car to check under the hood; he swore it felt like power steering! Seats were wide and comfy, the instrument panel was a beauty of design, and overall styling was unique and extremely well done.

The new Rambler was well received by the press. They liked its looks, interior

Seen at the 1956 Chicago Auto Show is the Hudson display of new cars. In the forefront is a Rambler four-door hardtop, and the rest of the visible cars include a Hudson Hornet Hollywood and two Rambler station wagons. It was a strong lineup and should have sold better than it did.

Top Left: The Nash Ambassador Country Club hardtop for 1956. The new styling features this year were larger running lamps up front and new, taller rear fenders with lollipop taillamps. Side trim was also new.

Top Right: The Nash Statesman Super four-door sedan for 1956. The side trim was the lower molding from the Ambassador and the two-tone color scheme consisted of a main body color with a contrasting color for the roof. The Statesman was a lot of car for the money but found few buyers.

Above: Midyear changes to the 1956 Nash senior line included this new look for the front end. The extra moldings on the front fenders are highlighted by contrasting paint, which carries over to the rest of the front sheet metal around the grille. Called the Bold Look, it came first to Ambassador Customs but eventually was added to all senior models.

space, ease of handling, and power. *Car Life* magazine said its performance was better than competing six-cylinder cars and almost as good as other makers' V-8 models. They also complimented its ride, calling it "one of the best-riding cars in the industry, regardless of wheelbase or price."

The Nash Ambassador and Statesman received minor styling and engineering changes—nothing of great consequence. The senior Hudsons, though, got a complete facelift, this time by independent stylist Richard Arbib. The so-called V-line styling was controversial from the first, and the public was, at best, apathetic toward it.

The big problem now facing AMC was money. The company was running out of cash. AMC needed to renew its credit lines with the banks and insurance companies that financed the company just when it was at its lowest point. In July 1956 Romney met with the financial people and spoke to them of AMC's future product plans and his plan for getting the company back into profitability. He spoke about the Rambler's future as a "basic volume" car, how it was different and better than Big Three cars, and how AMC had the compact-car segment all to itself. Getting financing was difficult, but Romney pulled it off. The same group of financiers had recently met with Studebaker-Packard and turned down their request for money. But Romney had a clearer product picture; he was much more convincing than Nance was, and in the end the bankers approved new financing arrangements for AMC. The company got a lower credit line than was asked for—$45 million versus $73 million—but it was enough to get by. "Believe me, it was blue sky," recalled VP Roy D. Chapin Jr., "because we didn't have a thing in the book to justify it." One important advantage to the new agreement was that it lowered the minimum working capital provision to $42 million; it had been $55 million.

AMC sales for 1956 were bad. By midyear Romney was burning through AMC's cash at a frightening pace. He ordered more cuts. Gifts of watches and clocks for employees with 30 years of service were delayed, offices were cleaned only every other day, and the company garage stopped giving free gas and service to executives' cars. Cutting every budget to the bone, sheet toilet paper replaced rolls, zone managers were ordered to economize on hotel stays, and a less expensive contract for design services was negotiated with Italian designer Pininfarina. Romney had Jack Timpy sell AMC's two company airplanes; Romney and his top executives voluntarily also took pay cuts of as much as 35 percent.

To instill a sense of urgency in the troops, Romney had buttons and signs made up that read *L.B.C.*, which stood for "Let's Be Competitive," but many workers thought it stood for "Let's Beat Chevrolet." Each employee was asked to contribute suggestions on how to make his or her job more efficient.

Costs were cut still further. To save cash, AMC resigned from the National Association of Manufacturers, and the company's advertising agency, Geyer, was required to start paying rent for the space it occupied at AMC headquarters; previously it had been provided free. Romney ordered the consolidation of all car manufacturing in its Kenosha plants, selling the El Segundo, California, car factory for $3 million and the Hudson body plant in Detroit for $2.1 million. Stock in AMC's Ranco Inc. division, the world's largest maker of temperature controls for appliances and cars, was sold for $10.6 million. All this cash flowed into AMC's coffers in hopes it would stave off the seemingly inevitable collapse.

Through such harsh cost-cutting, Romney was able to reduce AMC's breakeven point to fewer than 150,000 cars a year. Now all he needed was to increase automotive sales while trying to keep afloat in an intensely competitive marketplace.

By mid-1956 Romney decided that when the time came to redesign the Nash and Hudson big cars, they would have to be built on the basic Rambler shell with an extended wheelbase, rather than having their own big-car platform. He told his styling team to drop the plans they were working on for all-new big cars and focus instead on designing their re-placements around the Rambler. Bill Reddig came up with some very handsome designs for

This is the Rambler Custom sedan for 1957. Compare the side trim with the midyear 1956 model shown earlier and you can see the difference easily. Appearance-wise, the Rambler was little changed, but this year offered a 250-cubic-inch V-8 as an option.

Top: The Hudson senior line for 1956 got a complete facelift, and it was quite controversial. Although many writers have blamed Ed Anderson for the styling, the fact is that Anderson's choice was overridden by management and this design, by independent stylist Richard Arbib, was chosen instead.

Bottom: The fastest production American sedan for 1957 was the fabulous Rambler Rebel. A limited-production car—only 1,500 were produced—it was powered by the big 327-cubic-inch V-8 used in the Nash Ambassador and Hudson Hornet. This photo was taken at Daytona Beach during Speed Week. The Rebel was America's first true muscle car.

the Ambassador and Hornet that each had unique styling and didn't look at all like the Ramblers they were based on; they had fins out back and long, highly styled front ends.

But AMC faced another big problem: a hostile takeover attempt by the most feared corporate raider of the day, Louis Wolfson. The book value of AMC stock by mid-1956 was more than $20 a share, but it was trading around $6, making it a prime target for a takeover. In addition, it had accumulated more than $33 million in tax losses that any raider could use to offset profits from a merger with another company.

Romney agreed to meet with Wolfson. Although Wolfson believed Romney to be out of his depth, in truth the two men were evenly matched. Both were relatively young, hard driving, and fiercely ambitious. The talks started out on a strained note, but before long they were at a more relaxed tone. Wolfson explained that he now owned 200,000 shares of AMC stock and had bought it with the idea of liquidating the auto division. He claimed to have received requests from several stockholders to move in and take over management of AMC, but said he would not do so without first meeting and talking with Romney. After a lengthy discussion, Wolfson's view was that Romney was sincere and honestly trying to save AMC. Wolfson said he was trying to decide whether he should use the $8 million in cash he had on hand to buy more AMC stock, beginning a push to take control of the company or invest it in another enterprise. Romney went into a frank and earnest explanation of the plans he'd laid out for American Motors. He admitted to Wolfson that the auto division was the one running up the heavy deficits; the appliance division was solidly profitable. But he didn't want to sell Kelvinator and lose those profits, and he didn't want to see the auto division liquidated because he felt he could turn it into a major profit maker. By the end of the meeting the air was cleared, and Wolfson decided to forgo buying up the stock for the time being. In the November board meeting of American Motors, the directors met and discussed Wolfson's position and ideas and unanimously agreed to oppose any effort by him to take control of the company.

Success didn't come in 1956. Wholesale sales of cars to AMC's dealer group were 126,575 units, down quite a bit for the year despite all the new product news. A big part of the problem was the 1956 Rambler; by moving it up a year earlier, the company ran into problems trying to ramp up production to a profitable pace and missed the market. Quality problems were rampant that year. The company reported an operating loss of $31 million, with a net loss of $19,746,243. Working capital dropped to $54.6 million.

The business outlook for 1957 wasn't good, either. The senior lines were being consolidated into just two cars, the Hudson Hornet and Nash Ambassador, each offered in Super or Custom trim. They would all have the new AMC 327-cubic-inch V-8, and Nash would have new frontal styling, but other than that the cars were carryover. The 1957 Rambler would have revised trim, a new optional 250-cubic-inch V-8, built by AMC, and a limited-edition Rebel model, but not much else. The Metropolitan was essentially unchanged.

The company had purchased the rights to build the Mighty Mite, a mini-Jeep-style military vehicle, but ran into problems when the army criticized its foreign-sourced engine. This year AMC had developed its own air-cooled V-4 engine in hopes of eliminating this one drawback that seemed in the way of a lucrative military contract. The U.S. Navy and U.S. Marines were now testing the Mighty Mite.

Years earlier Romney had proposed having introductory shows for its employees, and once he took command he made sure that was done. With the disastrous 1956 model year coming to an end, it seemed more important than ever to take his

This lovely lady shows off the handsome taillamps of the 1957 Rambler and Rambler Rebel. According to the license plate, this particular car is a Rebel.

Right: Midway through 1956 came this Nash Ambassador Special. Powered by the same 250-cubic-inch V-8 engine as the Rambler and Hudson Hornet Special, the Ambassador Special was primarily a high-value car, but buyers failed to respond to it and few were produced.

Below: Also midway through the 1957 model year, American Motors introduced a new Hudson Hornet Special, built on the shorter Wasp body and powered by the new 190-horsepower, 250-cubic-inch AMC V-8. The Specials were well priced but failed to attract many buyers.

message to the workers, to help shape their attitudes and to get them to become part of a team working for a common goal. At a mass meeting at the Kenosha Lakeside Stadium on the night of Friday, September 14, Romney came with a special message for his employees.

He spoke of the mistakes that had been made within the company and the opportunities lost, and he made sure management took its share of the blame. He told the employees that no one could be accountable for their future except themselves, and he included management in that assessment. He spoke of the many quality problems with the 1956 cars and read from letters he received from dissatisfied owners.

After explaining how the company was able to refinance itself successfully with the banks and insurance companies, Romney gave the employees a frightening vision. He firmly stated, "We cannot have, and I want to emphasize this, because it is vital to every one of us, we cannot have another year like 1956 in 1957 and survive. We cannot. We must correct our own internal weaknesses."

But he made sure to add that he was not looking for anyone to blame:

"Let's analyze the past, see what our mistakes have been, and let's correct our weaknesses, but let's live for the future and forget the past from any other standpoint." He quoted Emerson: "There is no defeat except from within. There is no insurmountable barrier save our own inherent weakness of purpose". He told them "The differences between success and failure or mediocrity are small. The difference between a championship team in the National League is going to be the difference of a game or two. The first champion race horse to win $1 million only beat the next best horse that year by a nose or a length in the 13 races they were in. But the difference was the difference between a million dollars for the winning horse and $75,000 for the second horse, a difference of 13 times. The United Airlines crash in the Wyoming Mountains just a year ago killed 65 people because of a difference of 55 feet. They hit a 12,000-foot peak 55 feet from the top. Fifty-five feet would have saved 65 lives. The difference between success

Top: For 1957 the Nash line was reduced to just four models, all of them Ambassadors. Shown here is the Ambassador four-door sedan in Super trim. Custom trim was also available. This year, all Ambassadors were powered by AMC's new 327-cubic-inch V-8, which delivered an impressive 255 horsepower and outstanding performance.

Bottom: Note the new grille, quad headlamps, and open-front wheelwells on this gorgeous 1957 Nash Ambassador Custom Country Club hardtop. The model was also offered in Super trim this year.

AMC vice president and former Hudson executive Roy D. Chapin Jr. and the 1957 Rambler Custom station wagon, one of the models that was leading AMC's midyear recovery. Chapin would go on to become AMC's chairman in 1967.

and failure or mediocrity is small. If we fail to meet our challenge and opportunity, it will not be because of others. I want to emphasize this point. If we fail to take advantage of our opportunity, it will not be because General Motors has prevented us from doing it. It won't be because Ford prevented us from doing it. It won't be because Chrysler has prevented us from doing it. *It will be because we ourselves have prevented ourselves from taking advantage of our opportunities.*"

During the 1957 model year sales started off a little better than before, and with each month came better results. By May 1957 Romney felt certain that AMC was coming out of the woods. The financial press didn't know it, however, and continued to write disparaging articles about AMC. During September 1957 financial columnist Sylvia Porter wrote several stories that cast a poor light on AMC. She even reported that American Motors was looking into selling the Rambler operation to Chrysler. This astonishing idea had actually been discussed earlier between Romney and Wolfson, along with a handful of Wolfson's closest associates. When Romney saw it reported in the newspaper, he angrily accused Wolfson of leaking the information. Wolfson shot back that he had leaked no such information and that Romney should take his words back. Romney refused to retract, again stating that the information was known only to Romney, Wolfson, and his associates and therefore had to have been leaked by one of them. Neither man would give in.

Days later, AMC's Vice President of Communications Bill McGaughey, who knew Sylvia Porter fairly well, asked where her information had come from, because Romney had always denied that any such plan was in place or had even been discussed. Porter told McGaughey that she had been on vacation in Florida, sunning herself on

the beach, when she overheard a few men who were conversing near her. It turned out that the men were Wolfson's associates and that they were talking about a last-ditch proposal by Romney to sell the Rambler to Chrysler. When McGaughey asked, Romney reluctantly admitted that the story was true. "I felt I had to protect the stockholders interests," he said. In the end, it didn't matter; Chrysler wasn't interested in buying Rambler.

Ultimately, the threat from Louis Wolfson, though potentially catastrophic for American Motors, never amounted to anything more than that: a threat. Wolfson came in as the big bad wolf about to devour little AMC, and George Romney simply outmaneuvered him, stalling Wolfson long enough for AMC to become healthy again. America's most feared raider was beaten by a rookie automotive president.

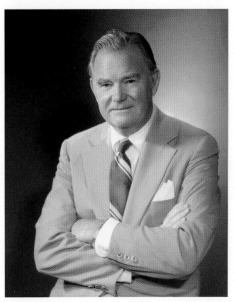

Above: The Hudson Hornet for 1957 received only minor styling updates. This was the last year for the Hudson nameplate in America, just as it was the final year for the Nash brand. From 1958 onward, the company would focus its efforts on the Rambler.

Left: Vice president Bill McGaughey was in charge of company communications and executive development. He had worked at the Automobile Manufacturers Association with George Romney prior to joining Nash in 1952. He continued on with AMC once Nash merged with Hudson.

Despite all of the hard work and cost-cutting, American Motors was not able to produce a net profit for 1957, instead reporting another year of loss, this time of $11.8 million. Working capital fell to $46 million. But things were looking up. The automotive division had been in the black for seven months of the fiscal year and was improving daily. Rambler sales for the fiscal year were up 30 percent over the prior year. The turnaround was under way. What it might lead to, if indeed anything at all, no one could truthfully tell.

What a happy day! A young couple at their local Rambler dealership picks up a new Rambler Classic. There were literally hundreds of thousands of scenes like this across America in 1962 as Rambler sales continued their upward climb.

1958–1963
THE RAMBLER TAKES OFF

AMERICAN MOTORS WAS CLEARLY ON THE UPSWING, but its demise had been a very near thing. At times AMC seemed to manage to hold on by the merest of threads, and it was really only because of George Romney that the company held together long enough to reach the Promised Land. Romney was a born leader who had cheered on the troops when things got toughest, and he was the one who encouraged the dealer network to try to reach new heights. By the time the 1958 model year was under way there was little doubt that AMC was on the mend. Sales were increasing every month, dealers were hollering for more cars, and despite the fact that the rest of the industry was in a downturn, the Rambler was taking off in the market.

American Motors' 1958 product lineup was strong. The "basic volume" car, as Romney termed it, was the big Rambler on the 108-inch wheelbase. Its lineup consisted of the Rambler Six in a range of four-door sedans, hardtops, and station wagons. Complementing this were the new Rambler Rebel V-8 models offered in the same body types, powered this year by the AMC 250-cubic-inch V-8, now rated at 215 horsepower. The Rebel was no longer a limited production job; instead it was a regular production series that supplanted the former Rambler V-8 line. The Ramblers styling was a facelift this year, with new fenders all around, new hood, new quad headlamps up front, and a modestly reshaped roof. The rest of the vehicle was carryover, but the revamped styling made it appear to be an all-new car. Inside, a new instrument panel included push-button controls for the optional automatic

Top right: This was almost the 1958 Hudson. Originally there was to be an all-new big Hudson for 1958. That program was shelved in favor of designing a new Hudson around the basic Rambler body, with extensive restyling front and rear. Although that idea was eventually cancelled we know what the resulting car would have looked like because this concept drawing by designer Allan Kornmiller has survived.

Left: Put a magnifying glass to the front fender of this handsome sedan and you'll see it says Nash Ambassador. This was the third and final evolution of the 1958 senior car program. In this scenario the senior Nash and Hudson would be built on the basic Rambler body, with minimal restyling. When the decision was made to drop the Nash and Hudson brands this car became the 1958 Ambassador by Rambler. This photo, dated August 20, 1957, shows how late in the year the decision to drop Nash was made.

transmission, which this year was sourced from Borg-Warner. As before, the senior Ramblers were roomy, comfortable automobiles, well-suited for a family of six. Beginning with the 1958 models AMC pioneered a new deep-dip rust-proofing system, submerging all its bodies in a 15,000-gallon vat of special primer paint to ensure that every surface received a full coat of protection.

But there was some sad news for Hudson and Nash enthusiasts—George Romney had reluctantly decided to not have the big cars restyled and instead to drop the Nash and Hudson lines. He called it the most difficult decision he'd ever had to make, but he was convinced that American Motors should, as he put it, "sink or swim with the Rambler." In fact, he was betting the company on that very thing. For 1958 AMC would offer only one big car, and that would be the new Ambassador by Rambler. It was created by using the Rambler main body with the wheelbase extended to 117 inches and adding longer front fenders, along with its own unique grille and trim. The new Ambassador was powered by the big AMC 327-cubic-inch V-8 good for 270 horsepower. Overall the Ambassador was a good deal smaller than the old Hudson Hornet and Nash Ambassador, but it would serve as the spiritual successor to them both. For the most part Nash and Hudson dealers cheered the change; senior line sales had been poor for the past couple years, and they could see that Rambler was the way of the future.

At the other end of the scale was the Metropolitan. Not badged as a Rambler, it was meant to compete against other import makes and in that capacity it did all right, though its sales numbers were always small. This year it got a one-piece rear window.

In January 1958 a fifth series was added to the AMC lineup. This was a so-called new small car called the Rambler American. The American was simply the old 100-inch wheelbase Nash Rambler two-door sedan revised and reintroduced. Minimal new tooling was involved. In fact to create a prototype, company executives searched through its dealers' used car lots for a 1955 Rambler in good shape. Because the front wheelwells had already been opened up, all stylists had to do was open up the rear wheels, install a new mesh-style grille, and remove the old hood scoop. The oval taillamps were made to look different by the simple expedient of turning them upside down and reinstalling them. Tooling for the new American cost just $800,000, chump change in the auto industry, and it meant that AMC now had a low-priced small car that could compete with the imports as well as appeal to a whole new raft of buyers in the lowest price ranges, including people who usually purchased used cars. Pricewise the new American undercut many of the larger imports. Auto writer Tom McCahill tested the American and came away extremely impressed, saying, "There isn't a better buy in the world today." Offered only as a two-door sedan in two trim versions, Deluxe and Super, prices on the American Deluxe began at a bargain basement $1,789, whereas the senior Ramblers started at $2,098 for a Deluxe four-door sedan. Romney had his factories gear up for more production, believing the turnaround he'd been praying for was at hand.

There was a harsh economic recession in 1958, and it hit the automobile market especially hard. Industry retail sales of automobiles during the calendar year dropped by more than 21 percent. In contrast, however, wholesale sales of Ramblers (sales to dealers) during AMC's fiscal year actually rose an amazing 58.7 percent. The story was even better for the calendar year; Rambler retail sales more than doubled compared with the prior year.

All the naysayers who'd been predicting American Motors demise were proven wrong in 1958 because this year, for the first time since its formation, the company reported a net operating profit. It was a good one too, more than $26 million, and because of tax loss carry-forwards from prior years, it was all tax-free. Net sales were $470 million, an increase of 28 percent. Total wholesale sales to dealers during the fiscal year amounted to 189,807 units, a 58.7 percent increase. Working capital grew to $79.9 million. It had been a very good year.

Also good news was the improvement to the dealer network. Hundreds of dealers were flocking to the AMC standard, and the dealer organization now stood at 2,636 Rambler dealers, a vast improvement that would help move even more Ramblers in the future. Fleet sales were up too, 148 percent. As was true in 1957, Rambler resale value was better than the other cars in the low-price market, including Chevrolet, Ford, and Plymouth. Used Ramblers were in very high demand.

Here's a colorful sight—row after row of 1958 Metropolitans awaiting shipment. Note the convertibles have protective coverings on their roofs. In 1958 Metropolitan cars were in short supply as their popularity continued to grow.

Top: Here we see the entire 1958 Rambler lineup represented. In the foreground is the new Rambler American, and in the back row are, left to right, an Ambassador hardtop, a Rebel wagon, and a Rambler Six sedan. It was the most comprehensive Rambler lineup to date.

Bottom: The 1958 Rambler Rebel. This year Rebel became a regular production model and replaced the former Rambler V-8 series. Most stylish of the Rebels was this four-door hardtop model. Look closely at the front door and you can see the emblem marking this as being equipped with air conditioning

There was some bad news on the appliance side; introduction of new appliance models was delayed five months due to strikes at supplier plants, along with difficulties Kelvinator was experiencing with new, more advanced manufacturing equipment. The end result was a 21.4 percent reduction in Kelvinator unit sales.

Experienced market watchers realized that American Motors had closely skirted with bankruptcy in early 1957. But only Romney knew exactly how close it had been. "Frankly," he admitted as things were getting better in mid-1958, "we very nearly got knocked out of the automobile business in the process of succeeding with our audacious decision to challenge the Big Three by outflanking their product position." However, he never publicly revealed that he'd sought to sell the Rambler to Chrysler.

The company eagerly awaited the 1959 model year, and it was well prepared, having begun to increase production capacity in anticipation of another good year. The senior Ramblers received minor styling updates, new rear door skins that smoothed the beltline flowing to the tail fins, new side trim, and a new full-width grille. Ed

Anderson was pleased with the look, saying it was one of best facelifts he'd ever done. The tooling cost was minimal. Ambassador styling changes were also limited to grille and trim updates, along with the new rear doors. Senior Ramblers also got new optional individually adjustable front seats and headrests, an industry first. New this year to the Rambler American line was a two-door station wagon, brought back because of popular demand from folks who had enjoyed the original. Like the American sedan the new wagon was merely an update of the 1955 Rambler, and here again tooling costs were minimal. The little Metropolitan received some welcome updates this year in the form of an exterior trunk lid, vent windows, and larger tires.

Demand for the new Ramblers was excellent. With Rambler on a roll, it was time to take advantage of the momentum. Starting in the fall of 1958, Romney again ordered up higher automobile production. He also continued to crisscross the country preaching his small-car gospel with the zeal of the young missionary he once was. He spoke at civic clubs, business clubs, and various other organizations. "Ladies and Gentlemen," he'd ask rhetorically at a typical meeting, "who wants to have a gas-guzzling dinosaur in their garage?" This very personal campaign won over a great many buyers, and slowly Americans began to grasp the small-car philosophy.

American Motors had a terrific year in 1959 despite competition from the new Studebaker Lark. Wholesales sales of Rambler and Metropolitan cars to its dealers more than doubled during the fiscal year, to 386,414 units. AMC set a new record for sales by an independent maker, shattering the record set by Willys-Overland in 1928. Revenues for 1959 shot up

Above: Almost as pretty as the Rebel hardtop but more practical is this 1958 Rebel wagon. Rambler station wagons were immensely popular with young families and were very profitable for American Motors.

Below: A big part of 1958's success story was the new styling, created by Ed Anderson, seen on the senior Ramblers. Also aiding the sales increase were the addition of the new Rebel and Ambassador series shown here during the new product announcement.

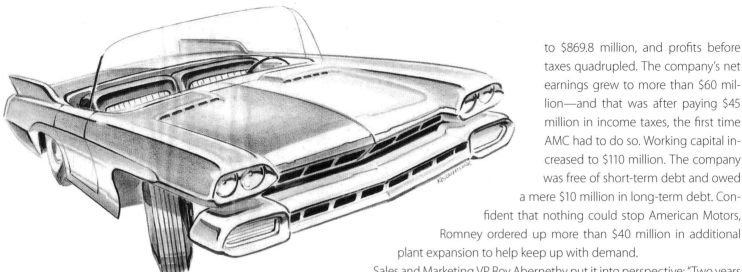

to $869.8 million, and profits before taxes quadrupled. The company's net earnings grew to more than $60 million—and that was after paying $45 million in income taxes, the first time AMC had to do so. Working capital increased to $110 million. The company was free of short-term debt and owed a mere $10 million in long-term debt. Confident that nothing could stop American Motors, Romney ordered up more than $40 million in additional plant expansion to help keep up with demand.

Sales and Marketing VP Roy Abernethy put it into perspective: "Two years ago a dealer could qualify as one of Rambler's Top 100 dealers by selling 100 cars a year. Now the lowest dealer on that list is selling over 500 cars a year and the top-selling dealer is selling at the rate of 3,300 cars a year."

Top: Designer Allan Kornmiller, the man who helped style the 1955 Hudsons, came up with this idea for a late-1950s Rambler convertible. Unfortunately AMC would not offer a soft top in the senior lineup until 1965. Too bad—Kornmiller's design is a beauty.

Bottom: For 1959 the Ambassador received new front-end styling and revised side trim.

During the year a Rambler American took first place in the Mobilgas Economy Run with 25.28 miles per gallon. Second place went to the Rambler Deluxe Six. In June two 1959 Rambler Six four-door sedans established new coast-to-coast economy records of 36.88 miles per gallon for a car equipped with overdrive, and 32.07 miles per gallon for one equipped with an automatic transmission. Amazingly, the overdrive-equipped car used only 84.11 gallons of gas to cross the entire country.

Business results on the appliance side were much improved. Sales were up across the board, and during the year Kelvinator actually sold more refrigerators overseas than in the United States. Its Redisco appliance finance arm saw substantial growth as well. In August assistant automotive styling director Bill Reddig was promoted to director of Kelvinator Styling.

During the first nine months of the 1959 calendar year Rambler stood in third place in sales in 12 states and was sixth nationally, an indication of the potential for success that lay ahead. By the end of 1959 George Romney had become the most famous businessman in the world, the Lee Iacocca or Steve Jobs of his day. Business groups clamored to hear him speak.

But heaven knows there were potential worries. For 1960 AMC would have direct competition from the Big Three when the new Chevy Corvair, Ford Falcon, and Chrysler Valiant went on sale. Surprisingly, Romney wasn't worried. He shrugged off the newcomers, claiming that their increased marketing efforts would focus more attention on the compact market and thus help sell more Ramblers! But the mere fact that GM, Ford, and Chrysler were introducing small cars in the fall of 1959 as 1960 models points to the amazing changes that were happening in the U.S. auto marketplace, and it was almost entirely due to the efforts of George Romney.

In bringing out their small cars, the Big Three were reacting to the growing demand for the Rambler, forced to get into a market segment they really didn't care about. Through his tireless efforts to bring the small-car message to America, Romney almost singlehandedly led America's greatest industry in a new direction. To the public he was known as the apostle of small cars. His grateful dealers presented him with a dinosaur-decorated plaque that read, "To George Romney; critic, lecturer, anthropologist, white hunter of the American dinosaur." Romney said he knew why his company was winning in the marketplace. "We're leaner," he boasted to the press. "We're harder. We're faster."

George Romney had a big goal for 1960—he wanted to produce and sell 500,000 cars. His product line was not greatly altered, but the changes it did have were significant. The senior Ramblers were heavily facelifted, with a handsome new grille, front bumper, and a thinner roofline. The sweptback C-pillars were thinner as well. Rear fenders were restyled and now had much smaller, canted tail fins, and the rear door skins were restyled as well. Side trim was again revised. Banking on the incredible popularity of the Rambler station

The gentleman in the dark suit is AMC styling director Ed Anderson, working on a quarter-scale model of what would become the 1959 Rambler. Anderson was an ex–General Motors styling executive who joined Nash in 1950 as director of styling and was made in charge of all AMC car styling at the time of the merger.

Top: Always pert and perky, the Metropolitan sold especially well during 1959—this would prove to be its best-selling year ever. New improvements this year were vent windows, an external trunk lid, and larger tires. Two-tone paint was standard on all Metropolitans since mid-1956.

Bottom: With smooth lines, nice side trim, and an elegant grille, the 1959 Ramblers' styling refinements produced an exceptional design. This Rebel Custom four-door sedan was a popular offering for buyers interested in Rambler quality and economy in a V-8 model.

wagons, Romney added a five-door, three-seat wagon to the lineup of Rambler Six, Rebel V-8, and Ambassadors. Ambassadors also got a unique compound wraparound windshield for greater visibility, along with a new grille and new rear fenders. To round out his small-car lineup, a four-door sedan on the 100-inch wheelbase was added to the Rambler American line, along with a new trim series, top-line Custom, available on all body types. The OHV six-cylinder engine was now available in the American series. Metropolitans were essentially unchanged.

Exciting things were happening; a Rambler American again won the Mobilgas Economy Run, achieving 28.35 miles per gallon. Hundreds of fleet buyers were flocking to Rambler, placing large orders for taxi cabs, rental car fleets, and service cars for public utilities. Early in the year the company completed an initial contract for production of 250 units of the small Mighty Mite military vehicle and received an order for 1,000 more units.

Romney's main message for 1960 was quality. "The steady elevation of standards of product, selling and service excellence on an efficient basis is the most effective means of retaining customer loyalty and enlarging the scope of our markets here and abroad," he said. Toyota couldn't have said it any better.

The drive for quality came about when Romney realized that he needed to launch the company on another crusade. His earlier quest to save the company had worked. His campaign to make the compact car a viable competitor and bring sales up to a whole new level had also been a success. But to keep moving forward he believed the company needed a new goal to reach. Romney felt his employees, like people everywhere, had to always have a larger goal to work for. He decided to build even further on Rambler's reputation for quality. He would now focus his—and the company's—attention on achieving quality of manufacture that exceeded all other cars, American or foreign, regardless of price. He coined a slogan for it. Rambler for 1960 was "The New Standard of Basic Excellence." Rambler's quality, said Romney, would be "a standard upon which others will be judged for quality construction, materials and craftsmanship." He asked all AMC employees to dedicate themselves to producing the best-built cars on the market.

During the year Roy D. Chapin Jr. asked to be relieved of his duties as executive vice president-automotive and instead be made responsible for fiscal and international activities in both the auto and appliance fields. Chapin was going through a rough period in his personal life and needed some space, and Romney agreed to his request. Bernard Chapman, executive vice president, was given responsibility for all auto and appliance manufacturing, engineering, styling, and procurement, and Roy Abernethy was elected executive vice president in charge of automobile and appliance distribution and marketing. Abernethy also became a director of the corporation.

George Romney had come to believe that the automobile industry was becoming a global business and that to survive long term a company needed to have an overseas partner. In an interview given many years after he left the auto business Romney revealed that around 1960 he sought a merger agreement with both the German automaker Volkswagen and with the UK's British Motors Company (BMC), at that point Britain's largest automaker—and the company building the Metropolitan for AMC. Romney claimed that neither firm was ready for merger at the time, so his proposals went nowhere. It's interesting, though, to speculate how the auto industry would look today if Romney had been successful in his merger goals.

Also around this time Roy D. Chapin Jr. made a formal proposal that American

BRAND NEW RAMBLER AMERICAN 100" WHEELBASE SUPER STATION WAGON (ALSO AVAILABLE IN DELUXE)

America demanded it! Rambler builds it! The new Rambler American with the top economy of all American-built cars, plus more room and comfort than any small European car. The Rambler American combats rising gasoline costs by giving more miles per gallon . . . is the answer to congested traffic conditions because it is easier to park, garage and handle. Now for 1959, the Rambler American presents a brand new station wagon that combines the outstanding economy and maneuverability of a small car with the family room and carrying capacity of a station wagon.

Today's big buy in small cars is the new Rambler American for 1959. See and drive it now at your Rambler dealer's.

Ample Cargo Space for all the luggage and gear needed by a family of five. You'll be amazed how much you can stow away in the cargo deck . . . and still have room for more.

Top: The Rebel Custom station wagon for 1959. The Rebel series for 1959 included this stylish wagon, along with three four-door sedan models, a four-door hardtop sedan, and a station wagon in less expensive Super trim.

Bottom: Joining the Rambler American lineup for 1959 was this American two-door station wagon. AMC brought back this model because of the large number of requests it had received from folks who remembered its forerunner, the Nash Rambler wagon. Like the American two-door, the station wagon was produced mainly from old 1955 tooling.

The Rambler American proved surprisingly popular for 1958 so it returned for 1959 with minor improvements and no real styling changes. The American in Super trim, as shown, was priced at just $1,920 and was a lot of car for the money, offering better quality and value than any of its import competition.

Below: During 1959 American Motors sponsored its own Coast-to-Coast Economy Run to demonstrate Rambler's fuel economy potential. These runs were done under the supervision of NASCAR overseers, who verified the fuel economy claims. The Rambler sedan equipped with an automatic transmission achieved 32.07 miles per gallon, whereas the overdrive-equipped sedan got an incredible 36.88 miles per gallon!

Motors purchase Willys Motors, builder of the famed Jeep line of vehicles. Willys was owned by Kaiser Industries Corporation, which once owned Kaiser-Frazer Corporation. Kaiser Industries president Edgar Kaiser was anxious to unload Willys; the parent company had very little interest in the automobile business, and he was ready to sell. Romney was initially against the idea of buying out Willys, saying he wanted to concentrate on Rambler instead. But out of respect for Chapin he finally agreed to a meeting to discuss it with the Kaiser people. Unfortunately Romney came away from the meeting no more convinced than he had gone into it—the asking price was rather high—and the Willys deal never happened. That was a very large mistake on his part because buying Willys would have given his Rambler dealers a line of trucks to sell and would have greatly increased AMC's overseas presence; at the time Willys had assembly points or sales outlets in virtually every country in the free world. And Willys was consistently profitable because it had little to no competition in its market. A Willys deal probably would have helped AMC obtain some sales of Ramblers to government agencies as well.

For American Motors' 1960 fiscal year Romney was again proven right regarding Rambler's potential. Despite the onslaught of new competition from Chevrolet, Ford, and Chrysler, American Motors' net sales rose to $1,057,716,447, crossing the billion-dollar mark for the first time, while wholesale sales to its dealers totaled a near miraculous 478,249 cars, just missing the half-million-unit goal Romney had set. Working capital dropped a bit, to $96 million, and profits of $48 million were held down only by large expenditures to increase Rambler production; the company had doubled its production capacity over the prior three years at a cost of many millions of dollars. But those expenditures showed up in important ways. In the vital sales-per-dealer rankings Rambler was now third in the industry, an amazing feat for any automotive brand of any size, let alone one that had been written off as a lost cause just four years earlier. The company's appliance finance arm, Redisco Inc., saw a 26 percent increase in business and opened up five new branch offices. For the second year in a row George Romney was named the Associated Press Industry Man of the Year.

The company announced it would resume production of Ramblers in Canada in January 1961. This came about because Executive Vice President Roy D. Chapin Jr. believed that increasing Canadian sales would justify the expense—would in fact be very profitable—and he figured he was just the man to bring off that increase. He begged Romney to purchase a Canadian plant he'd found that would cost next to nothing to acquire. Romney initially refused until Chapin finally declared that if Romney would agree to the deal, he, Chapin, would draw no salary but would instead take a percentage of the profits from the venture—Chapin was that confident of its success. Romney, feeling that anyone who was that passionate about an idea must be right, or at least must be willing to make it happen, agreed to buy the plant and build Ramblers there for the Canadian market. Rambler assembly was also planned for Malta and Australia.

The American Motors lineup for 1961 was especially strong. The mainstream Rambler Six and Rebel V-8 were renamed the Classic 6 and Classic V-8. The Classic series featured new front-end styling that placed the headlamps in the grille area, only now at the outer ends of the grille, giving the cars a much wider appearance. The headlamps themselves were set in thick chrome pods. Letters in an open space beneath the grille spelled out the Rambler name. A new lower hood was also featured, which, in conjunction with the new front fenders, had eyebrow character lines—very stylish. Combined together the new styling elements made for quite a handsome automobile. Inside was a new 'Cushioned Acoustical' molded fiberglass headliner that improved headroom while reducing noise, an improved 'Weather

American Motors's innovative Deep-Dip Rust-proofing system submerged each Rambler body in a vat of rust-inhibiting primer, which helped ensure longer life than that of other cars. This system made sure that each section of the body received the primer, even hard-to-reach areas, and was part of Rambler's quality story.

Top: This is the AMC Styling Studio circa 1960. In the foreground, back to the camera, is designer Bob Nixon. In front of him sits designer Vince Geraci, and the man in the white shirt facing the clay model with his hand to his chin is Anderson's assistant Dick Teague. The other two men are not identified.

Bottom: Here is the Rambler American two-door sedan for 1960. Styling continuity was considered a virtue in the American because it helped keep prices low and value high. It worked; a Deluxe two-door American this year had a base price of just $1,795. The two-tone paint and whitewall tires seen here would have cost the buyer extra.

Eye' heating and ventilating system, and a revised instrument panel. California cars got a new crankcase vent, the first of what would become many improvements to reduce harmful emissions.

Romney was serious about improving the product, so a total of 44 other enhancements were also pushed through, including adding grease fittings to the front suspension lower trunion joint and the shift linkage, recalibrating carburetors for better fuel economy and performance, and an improved directional signal switch. All Ramblers this year got new long-lasting ceramic-armored mufflers and tailpipes for improved durability.

A new die-cast aluminum-block six-cylinder engine was introduced after exhaustive testing. It was the same size and horsepower of the standard cast-iron six, but weighed 80 pounds less, which helped reduce steering effort and improve fuel economy. It was standard on Classic Custom models and optional on the others.

Rambler American for 1961 received the most extensive restyling since its debut. The American's were still based on the 1958–1960 Rambler American basic body, which in turn was based on the 1950–1955 Nash Rambler body, so a major part of the tooling cost was saved by not having to completely redesign the car. Instead, Ed Anderson and his talented crew came up with a reskinning that altered the American's appearance so much that it looked like a totally new and more modern car.

The American's new styling was square and upright, and the frontal appearance had the same sort of eyebrow design as the Classics, so there was now a definite family resemblance between the two. Although the car appeared to be a little larger than the former American, it was in fact 5.2 inches shorter and 3 inches narrower than before. Yet interior space was unchanged, and trunk space was actually improved by 50 percent. *Mechanix Illustrated*'s Tom McCahill tested a new American wagon and liked its quality.

"Built-in obsolescence is not a part of George Romney's way of thinking," he said. "While tooling around the countryside I found myself comparing it with the better imports rather than with its American competitors. It even has the finish and workmanship more commonly associated with the imports." *Car Life* echoed that by stating, "The way the Rambler was put together was not only acceptable but actually admirable. . . . Fit and finish of the body panels was immaculate."

The 1961 Ambassador got some surprising changes this year—a completely new frontal appearance that shared nothing with the Rambler Classic. The look was low and elegant, very European, and ultimately handsome. But it in the end it simply didn't catch the public's fancy and would be used this one year only.

Driver Les Viland, an American Motors engineer and fuel economy expert, swept the 1961 Pure Oil Economy Trials, winning three trophies for best fuel economy. In Class Six, Ramblers managed to finish in 8 of the first 10 spots. In the V-8 category the Ambassador by Rambler won 9 of the first 10 places, including tops in its class. It was a remarkable performance, and the public loved it.

In the meantime George Romney was trying to reach a consensus with the United Auto Workers union on a revolutionary new labor contract. He and union chief Walter Reuther had exchanged many ideas over several months until gradually they began to reach common ground. This resulted in a labor pact that would shock the rest of the industry. By midsummer of 1961 Romney and Reuther had fashioned a ground-breaking agreement that would take into account American Motors' size versus the Big Three, while encouraging workers to be more productive and loyal. With it, American Motors agreed to share its profits with its hourly workers; the idea was that workers would then have a feeling of real self-interest in the success of American

Top: The senior Rambler for 1960 got revised many styling updates, most important of which were the restyled fins, rear doors, and the slimmer C-pillar shown here. Although based on the landmark 1956 Rambler body, periodic updates had kept the big Rambler looking fresh and modern.

Bottom: We're not certain if this Rambler pickup truck, which is identified as a Deliveryman, is a dealer conversion, but it wears a dealer plate and a sticker for a Pontiac, Michigan, Rambler dealer. The photo was in the collection of an AMC executive now deceased; it probably was built by the dealer and shown to the company as an idea car.

Motors and would be more meticulous in craftsmanship and more productive in output. It was a landmark agreement for the times. Reuther termed it, "The most significant and historic collective-bargaining agreement ever signed in the United States."

There was a sharp downturn in the U.S. economy in 1961, and it hit the automobile industry particularly hard. Car sales fell sharply in the first quarter of the calendar year, for Rambler as well as its competitors, and AMC had to spend the rest of the year struggling back. Retail sales of Ramblers during the fiscal year fell 11.5 percent, and Metropolitan sales fell 32.6 percent—an ominous continuation of a drop-off in Met sales that began with the 1960 model year. AMC's revenues fell to $875.7 million. Total Rambler/Metropolitan wholesale sales to dealers came in at 392,971 units. Of that number 384,829 were Ramblers and 8,142 were Metropolitans. Corporate profits fell more than 50 percent to $23 million for the year, a result of lower unit sales, higher tooling costs related to bringing out the 1961 American, more competitive pricing due to

so many new competitors flooding into the compact market, plus the cost of a new, more liberal 12-month/12,000-mile warranty on Rambler cars. On the plus side, working capital increased to $103 million and in August Rambler rose to third place in industry sales on the basis of total registrations for the calendar year—a feat that was unimaginable just three years earlier. Rambler was still growing in the market.

Top: The 400,000th Rambler produced in 1959 was this 1960 model. It was assembled on the second shift on Wednesday, December 30, 1959. This is a completed body awaiting its trip down the final assembly line.

Bottom: One of the newsworthy changes to the 1960 Rambler line was the availability of three-seat, five-door station wagons in the Rambler Six, Rebel V-8, and Ambassador series. In these models the rear wagon door opened up sideways to reveal a small seat good for two adults.

Kelvinator sales started out weak but gradually grew stronger as the year moved forward, and the division reported a slight increase for the year. Overseas, American Motors established a new American Motors Export company in Zug, Switzerland. Overseas sales were up 63 percent for the year, the result of hard work being done by executive vice president Roy D. Chapin Jr.

During 1961 the company began an A-OK Quality Workmanship campaign that resulted in greater employee cooperation in improving Rambler and Kelvinator quality. Rambler production in Canada got under way in January 1961 in a new $3.5 million wholly owned plant in Brampton, Ontario, Canada. Amazingly, the plant operated at a profit in its very first year, fully justifying Chapin's confidence. AMC also invested $3.5 million in an Industrias Kaiser Argentina (IKA) plant partially owned by Kaiser Industries. The investment would provide for production of Ramblers in Argentina for the local market. It was another step in Chapin's plan to continue to grow American Motors overseas sales. A deal was also made with French automaker Renault to assemble Ramblers in Belgium for distribution in Europe. By the end of 1961 Ramblers were being assembled in South Africa, Australia, New Zealand, Malta, the Philippines, and Mexico, and they were being sold in 94 countries around the world.

Left: Styling director Ed Anderson in front of a full-size airbrush painting of a proposed sporty coupe. Although this outlandish-looking car seems out of place in a Rambler styling studio, this design was later made into a quarter-scale clay model and was considered by management for a while before eventually being dropped.

Below: For 1960 the Ambassador by Rambler showed many of the same styling updates as the other big Ramblers, including new canted tail fins, new rear door skin, and revised side trim. The Ambassador's full-width grille gives it a slightly wider and richer look than that the other Ramblers.

AMC's Special Products Division was working on its third order for Mighty Mite military vehicles. The order was for 1,232 units, bringing the total ordered thus far to a paltry 3,482 units. The company continued to wait for a really large order to come along.

But one event in 1961 was quite disturbing. In December styling director Ed Anderson abruptly left the company. American Motors reported to the press that although there was no problem with Anderson's styling work, an "administrative problem" had developed and he had resigned. For his part Anderson told the press he was shocked, and in later years he claimed he'd been fired for asking for a promotion. The real story is that over the course of time George Romney had brought in several outside stylists to get their input on design, and Anderson held a great resentment about that. The situation boiled over during a meeting when Anderson had to sit and listen to presentations from these independent designers, whom he loathed. He suddenly lost his temper and put Romney on the spot, telling him in effect that Romney had to choose between Anderson or the outsiders. Romney had a bad temper at times, and backing him into a corner was never a good idea—and in this case it cost Anderson his job. Romney forced him to resign. Anderson had just signed off on the all-new 1963 senior Rambler models and was hard at work on a new design for the 1964 American. Stylist Dick Teague, whom Anderson had brought in during 1958 to replace Bill Reddig, was elevated to design director, replacing Anderson.

Industry competition was expected to get especially heavy in 1962 when additional new compact models would be introduced by competitors, but Romney was confident his dealers were up to the challenge. Gearing up for the sales battle Romney ordered a price decrease across the Rambler lineup. The Rambler American, tagged at $1,846, continued to be the lowest-priced American car on the market. A confident George Romney also ordered yet another hike in production capacity. He was unwilling to back down from the battle.

The 1962 cars were mainly a further refinement of the basic body shells. The American series received 75 improvements and refinements including a new horizontal-bar grille to replace the somewhat controversial grille seen on the 1961 models, along with

Top: AMC took a step out of the ordinary in 1961 when it gave the Ambassador its own unique front-end styling. Low and very European, the new look failed to catch on with buyers and was discarded at the end of the year.

Bottom left: Ed Anderson and his wife, Helen, relax in the completely restyled 1961 Rambler American, which for the first time offered a full convertible model. This photograph was taken on Anderson's estate outside Detroit.

Bottom right: Ramblers continued to win fuel economy awards in 1961. Here we see AMC engineer and fuel economy expert Les Viland with three trophies he won that year. The cars are a 1961 Ambassador Custom and a 1961 Rambler American.

an increased steering ratio with a low-friction mechanism for easier steering. The American now offered five transmission choices,
including a new E-stick transmission, available with and without
overdrive, which gave the control and economy of manual shift-
ing but eliminated the clutch pedal by using an automatic clutch.
Americans were offered in three series, Deluxe, Custom, and 400.

The 1962 Classic was now offered in just one model range—the
Six—because the V-8 models were dropped. The Classic got a new
grille, revised side trim, a new suspension system that provided a
great improvement in ride quality, plus softer seats with a bit more
rear seat leg room. The B-pillar was narrower this year, giving the
greenhouse a lighter look. Rear styling was all new, with new rear
fenders and door skins that completely eliminated the tail fins for a
rounder, softer look. A new Classic two-door sedan body style, the first in the senior Rambler
series, debuted at the beginning of the model year. Despite being based on a seven-year-
old basic body, the Rambler continued to be a good-looking family car. The Metropolitan
series was unchanged again this year.

There was big news in the Ambassador range. Ambassadors would no longer ride a
stretched wheelbase; instead they would use the same 108-inch wheelbase and body as the
Classic and would share most of their styling, aside from trim differences. Ambassador would
now, in effect, take the place of the former Classic V-8 line and Romney hoped this move
would increase sales of his V-8 products, which were always very much second fiddle to his
six-cylinder Ramblers. In February 1962 a new Rambler Ambassador two-door sedan joined
the lineup, offered in 400 and Custom trim. These rare cars are seldom seen today.

Romney's philosophy of constant product improvement, his desire that Rambler become known as "The New Standard of Basic Excellence," was heartily expressed in some
important product improvements this year. All Ramblers got an advanced tandem brake

Top: Here are some of American Motors products
for 1961: left to right we see a Rambler Classic, an
experimental AMC Muskrat amphibious military
vehicle, a Mighty Mite military vehicle, and a
Metropolitan coupe. These were gathered at
a testing area where the Muskrat was undergoing
some demonstration tests.

Bottom: American Motors CEO George Romney was
a frequent visitor to the styling studios and got to
know all the designers on a first-name basis. In this
photo we see him talking with future vice president
of styling Dick Teague. Teague, a former chief stylist
for Packard, was hired at AMC by Ed Anderson.

Right: American Motor's bread-and-butter product was the senior Rambler, the Classic series available for 1962 in a wide range of six-cylinder models. This year the big Rambler received styling updates to the rear fenders, which eliminated the small canted fins seen on the 1961 cars.

Below: Probably the nicest-looking small station wagon on the market in 1962 was this American 400 series wagon. With four doors, stylish interior trim, and a price tag beginning at just $2,320, it was a good, economical replacement for the typical huge family wagons of the day or the tiny import wagons then available.

master cylinder that provided that even if there was a failure in the front brake system there would still be rear brakes to stop the car or front brakes if there was a failure in the rear brake system. Brake systems with dual master cylinder reservoirs were used on only three other cars at the time: Cadillac, Rolls-Royce, and Jaguar. To include this costly feature on a full range of popular-priced cars was a bold move, indeed, but Romney wanted his Ramblers to be perceived as better than other cars. Why the motoring press didn't make a bigger deal out of the addition of this outstanding safety feature is a mystery. Also instituted was a new 33,000-mile chassis lubrication, rather than the customary 1,000-mile interval, a 4,000-mile oil change schedule to replace the former 2,000-mile schedule and the addition of radiator coolant/antifreeze as standard equipment.

Industry car sales went up in 1962 and American Motors shared in the upswing. The company sold a total of 478,132 Ramblers to its dealers, a 24 percent gain over 1961. Of these sales, 434,486 went to U.S. dealers, and 43,646 went to overseas dealers, including Canada.

The overseas automobile results were especially gratifying. Thanks to the efforts of Roy D. Chapin Jr. and his tiny staff, international sales of Rambler cars were booming. Rambler now accounted for 18 percent of U.S. cars shipped overseas, and total foreign sales were up 136 percent. Rambler was now the best-selling American car in Latin America and was growing in Europe as well. The company ordered an increase in the size of the new Canadian factory, increasing it by two-thirds.

AMC didn't offer a separate breakout of Metropolitan sales because it was in the process of phasing out the once-popular subcompact, and wholesale sales had been almost nil. Rambler's share of the U.S. auto market was 6.7 percent, essentially unchanged. Revenues exceeded the $1 billion mark for the second time in its history and were just shy of the record set in 1960. Net profits to the company were $34.2 million and working capital rose to $116.5 million. AMC's new profit sharing plan paid out more than $12 million to workers, but this worked to reduce corporate income taxes by $6.76 million, and the company saved millions via increased productivity, so it appeared to be a win-win situation.

Discontinuing the imported Metropolitan was not a smart move, although the car was clearly beyond its prime. Import sales were rising, and AMC could have earned a good share of that business if it had fielded a completely new Met, one that offered four- or five-passenger seating. Anderson had been working on a design for a new Met, but why that project never came to fruition is unknown. In later years Roy Chapin Jr. offered his opinion that Romney wanted to concentrate on the American as an import fighter, because AMC would then earn a manufacturing profit as well as a wholesale profit versus the smaller distributor profit it was making on the Met.

Kelvinator had good news. Its unit sales were the best since 1955, and the division had the best share of industry in five years.

One of the best designers on the AMC Styling team was Jim Pappas, who worked on interior design. Here we see one of Pappas's circa 1962 ideas for a restyling of the Rambler American's instrument panel. The symmetrical design is quite striking. Note the glove box door is on top of the dash.

A 1962 Rambler American on the final assembly line. In this shot the engine and transmission unit are being installed in the car from the bottom up, which was the way AMC's assembly process worked.

Redisco had a good year financing appliance sales and had also begun to finance Rambler fleet sales as well.

There was, however, a very dark cloud that appeared early in the 1962 fiscal year. CEO George Romney had begun to listen to people who wanted him to run for governor of the state of Michigan. Former U.S. Vice President Richard Nixon was one of those who encouraged him to run, as was former president Dwight Eisenhower, who went so far as to speculate that Romney would even make a fine presidential candidate in 1964! It's hard to say how long Romney had been interested in public office, but it was a few years at least, and he decided now to sequester himself so he could properly think things over. After days of prayer and fasting he reached a decision that would have a long-term impact on American Motors. On February 10, 1962, he called a press conference to announce that he was throwing his hat into the Michigan gubernatorial race. (At the announcement he was accompanied by his wife, Lenore, and 14-year-old son, Mitt Romney).

On February 12 he asked for and received an unpaid leave of absence from American Motors. Romney wanted to do the right thing, which he believed was quitting and separating himself completely from the company, but he was talked into taking the leave of absence instead by AMC's board of directors. The board naturally had fears about what might happen to AMC without its main driver on board— Romney had come to symbolize American Motors and was a huge part of its success. During the time he was on leave Romney would receive neither salary nor bonus. He was given a new title— vice chairman of AMC. Meanwhile, attorney Richard Cross was brought in to serve as chairman, and sales VP Roy Abernethy was elevated to president. Vice president Roy D. Chapin Jr. later said that the idea was that Cross would keep Romney's seat warm in case the gubernatorial race went against him.

Left: Ever seen this before? This photo, taken in February 1962, shows a neat show car called the Carib. Based on the 1962 Rambler American, this snappy little convertible had a custom interior and specially made nameplates for the rear fenders.

Below: This is an unusual photo. It shows the interior of a circa 1962 factory show car called the Rambler Sportster—see the name on the glove box door. Based on the Rambler American, the Sportster included bucket seats and floor console as shown, as well as Twin-Stick dual shift levers for the manual transmission. But look closely and you can see that there is no clutch pedal and that the car also has a column shifter for an automatic transmission.

What would happen to American Motors in a post-Romney/post-Anderson world was indeed an unknown. The company was planning on a big year in 1963, with completely new lines of cars being introduced. But whatever the financial results were, 1963 would not give them a real hint of American Motors future post-Romney or post-Anderson, because Romney had made all the plans already for the year, and Anderson had directed the styling efforts. In the end 1963 would merely be a harvesting of what these two brilliant men had sown. The nature of the automobile business was that it wouldn't be until 1964 or 1965 before the board of directors would be able to see if Cross and Abernethy had the iron to truly fill Romney's place .

The 1963 model year was one of the most significant in American Motors history because during this year the company introduced completely redesigned Classic and Ambassador cars. The designs had been created by a team led by Ed Anderson before his departure from the company, and they were outstanding.

The objective had been to create a modern design that would look lower, longer, and sleeker, but that would retain its good looks longer than most usual designs. This called for styling that was all-new but a bit on the conservative side. The cars had to be roomier on the inside, no bigger on the outside, and have large trunks as well. European companies had been dealing with similar design parameters for years, so perhaps it's not surprising that the new Ramblers had more than a hint of Euro styling in them. Years later George Romney referred to the 1963 Ramblers as having "almost a Mercedes-Benz look."

The new cars featured clean lines with smooth envelope-style bodies on a lengthened 112-inch wheelbase (four inches longer than the 1962 models), short front overhangs, a

flat roof panel with gently sloping C-pillars, along with large glass areas for a spacious, airy feel. Up front was an unusual, and handsome, V'eed grille that made identification easy even from a long distance. The longish rear fenders provided for a roomy trunk, yet overall length was actually 1 inch less than the 1962 cars. The roofline was 2½ inches lower. Weight was reduced by more than 150 pounds.

New trim series numbers debuted. The basic Classic was the 550 series, the midlevel car was the 660, and the top of the line was the 770. In the Ambassador series there were 880 and 990 models.

The new Ramblers bristled with innovation. A key element of the design was the doors, which featured curved side glass that allowed for larger door openings and greater interior space. The side-glass design provided half an inch greater hip room, and new step-down floors created 3.3 inches more headroom up front, along with 3.25 inches more headroom in the rear. There was controversy within American Motors regarding the curved side-glass. Engineering and cost accountants felt the extra cost of adding this styling feature was prohibitive, whereas Anderson argued that the competition was going to have curved glass windows sometime in the future and because the new body was going to be in use until 1968 or 1969, if Rambler didn't have it now the car would soon look stale and out of date. The extra cost was $2 per car, which doesn't sound like much, but in the auto industry costs are measured in pennies, not dollars. Besides,

Above: The Rambler Ambassador Custom for 1962. This year the Ambassador was built, for the first time, on the same wheelbase as the Classic and supplanted the former Rambler Classic V-8 series. Note the dog-dish hubcaps on this low-line Ambassador.

Right: Here's another show car for 1962—the Rambler Ambassador Vegas station wagon, as seen at the Chicago Auto Show that year. The Vegas featured custom interior trim and an unusual body side treatment. We wonder where this car is today.

$2 per car times half a million Ramblers meant the company would lose $1 million annually in profits if it went to curved side glass. But Ed Anderson's argument had convinced Romney to go ahead with it, and that of course settled the matter.

There was other important new engineering in the 1963 Rambler. As with every Rambler, the new car had a unit-body design, but this year American Motors introduced an advancement that was years ahead of the industry. Called Uniside construction, it replaced the 52 small stampings that ordinarily made up a door-opening frame with a simpler and much stronger design. The entire door opening now consisted of just two pieces, an inner stamping and an outer one that were welded together to make a solid, high-quality framework. This radical new design provided better door fit and helped eliminate dust and water leaks. The bodies also received seven times more galvanized steel than before, and the entire body was dipped in a vat of rust-inhibiting primer right up to the roof. Tire size was reduced to 14 inches this year to help lower the roofline.

Top: For 1963 the Rambler American received a smart new grille, new two-tone option, and a host of product improvements. The power top was standard equipment, unlike many of its competitors, and the American could beat them all in fuel economy.

Bottom: Here we see a car that you're unlikely to see very often—the very rare 1962 Rambler Ambassador two-door sedan. Introduced on February 6, 1962, the two-door Ambassadors sold in small numbers and are rare cars today.

AMC president Roy Abernethy enthusiastically declared that the new cars were "the strongest Ramblers ever built—The safest Ramblers ever built—The quietest Ramblers ever built—The most comfortable Ramblers ever built—The longest-lasting Ramblers ever built—The most service-free Ramblers ever built—The smoothest-riding, easiest-handling Ramblers ever built—The best-performing Ramblers ever built." He also claimed they were the most beautiful Ramblers ever built. He was right on all counts; the 1963 Rambler was simply a standout product. *Motor Trend* magazine considered all the enhancements and improvements in the new Ramblers and awarded its prestigious *Motor Trend* Car of the Year award to the entire 1963 Rambler lineup, feeling it was more important than the Chevy Corvette Stingray and the Buick Riviera, both new for 1963.

Early in calendar year 1963 a new V-8 series was added to the Classics. Powered by a new 287 cid engine pumping out 198 horsepower, the V-8 Classics proved popular. They would eventually replace the Ambassador 880 series.

The irrepressible Tom McCahill of *Mechanix Illustrated* tested a new Classic V-8 at the Daytona Speedway and reported that "this is the best-handling car I have ever driven around the high-speed track. I've driven . . . Mercedes, Triumphs, E-Jags, Imperials and Caddies . . .

Top: This is a landmark car—the 1963 Rambler Classic. The first redesign of the mainstream Rambler since 1956, it included such innovations as Uniside design, Advance Unit-Body Construction, and curved side glass. The entire Rambler lineup won the Motor Trend Car of the Year Award for 1963.

Bottom: The 1963 Rambler Ambassador shared the same body and wheelbase as the Classic series and was distinguished by its fancy interior trim and 327 cid V-8 engine. This elegant Ambassador 990 sedan represents the top of the Rambler lineup that year.

but the Rambler seemed to enjoy it more than any of the others." McCahill also liked the workmanship, saying, "All over the Rambler you find signs of nice workmanship." He called the new Rambler Classic "an excellent, top-value car."

The Metropolitan, alas, was no more. The last few unsold units on dealers' lots were classified as leftover 1962 models—there would be no 1963 model year for the Met.

The Rambler American series returned pretty much as it was before, though with new model names: 220 being the base model, 330 the midlevel trim, and 440 as the top line. A special 440H model was added at the very top, and it appeared in a new body style—a sporty two-door hardtop that was also available in regular 440 trim. All American models got a new grille this year and revised side trim.

Rambler dealers were ecstatic about the new Classic and Ambassador, as well they might be. These were the first all-new cars since 1956, and they were beauties. The dealers entered the 1963 sales arena full of confidence. They realized competition was going to be difficult. Ford had a new Fairlane 500 series to add to the Fairlane series it had unveiled for 1962, and Dodge had a new Dart on a midsize platform, and they would be fierce competitors.

For the fiscal year, 1963 turned out to be the best year AMC had had up to that point from the standpoint of revenues and units sold. Dollar sales climbed 7.2 percent to $1,132,356,298, and profits rose 10.4 percent, despite the extraordinarily high cost of tooling for the all-new Classic/Ambassador cars. Net earnings of $37.8 million were recorded. Working capital rose to $118.8 million. Best news was the wholesale auto numbers; American Motors sold to its dealers 511,038 cars worldwide. Of those, 454,531 were U.S. sales. During the year the final Mighty Mite was built. From January 1960 to January 1963 a total of just 3,922 Mighty Mites were produced for the U.S. Marine Corps.

A cold wind blew in at the end of the calendar year; in December Studebaker Corporation announced it was ending car production in the United States. Studebaker would continue to produce cars on a much more limited basis at its small Canadian plant. It was a lesson in what could happen to a large independent automaker that made too many mistakes. The automobile industry is an unforgiving business.

All in all it was a good year for American Motors, but it should have been better. After all 1963 was an excellent year for the U.S. auto industry, the first time the industry sold more than 8 million vehicles, and in light of that American Motors should have sold more cars than it did. The constantly increasing pressure from competitors was beginning to show; if AMC hadn't had all-new cars in 1963, how much less would sales have been? And 1964 was going to be even harder, with more new entries coming to the compact field. It was at times like this that the company needed a leader like George Romney with the missionary zeal to fire up the troops for yet another battle, but this time AMC wouldn't have Romney. For the next few years American Motors was going to have to follow Roy Abernethy's vision for the future, and it would learn, too late, that his vision was faulty.

Top: New for 1963 in the Rambler American lineup was this sharp two-door hardtop, available in 440 and 440-H trim. Notice how the top has stamped-in bows to give the impression of a convertible—very smart.

Bottom: First shown to AMC executives during a Town Hall meeting held January 22, 1963, the American Motors Forecast I was an interesting concept from talented designer Bob Nixon, who went on to have a fabulous career with the company. Note that this car does not bear Rambler identification.

The 1965 model year saw many changes in the Rambler lineup. One change was that for the first time a convertible model was offered in all three series; American, Classic, and Ambassador. During the year the company produced the 3 millionth modern Rambler.

1964–1967
THINGS GO WRONG

ONE OF THE FIRST CHORES Roy Abernethy undertook when he became president of American Motors was to pull aside John Conde, AMC's longtime assistant director of public relations and tell him plainly, "John, you've got to help me get rid of this 'Romney' image." A stunned Conde, hardly believing what he heard, replied, "Okay, Roy, I will." What else could he say to the boss?

Therein lay the largest problem now facing American Motors; its new president wanted to overhaul the company's image completely rather than refine it and play on its strengths. When Abernethy first took command he started off on the wrong foot by trying to "out-Romney" George Romney, foolishly running an anti-racing print ad that declared that the only race American Motors was interested in was the human race. It brought a shower of jokes and criticisms, mainly saying that the reason why AMC wasn't into racing was its cars were too slow. Now Abernethy wanted to move in an entirely new direction and the problem was he was leaving behind too much of what had worked.

It could be seen in the 1963 advertising in which Abernethy abandoned Romney's message about Rambler's quality leadership and instead emphasized styling and luxury. To be sure, the market was changing, the public was moving to more power and luxury, but it wasn't necessary for AMC to make a sea change in just one year. It's an old axiom that to succeed in the car business you have to stand for something and that message has to be loud and clear so the public understands it. AMC's message was quality and economy,

This is an unusual car. It's a full-size clay mock-up called the Apache, and it represents one facet of the 1964 Rambler American program. What makes it so fascinating is that the Apache appears to be built on a shorter wheelbase than any of the other Rambler American design studies. Could it possibly be a restyling of the 1961–1963 100-inch wheelbase American?

and it could and should have been continued, *along* with a greater emphasis on style and luxury.

And the Ramblers were good-looking this year. The Classic series received a re-styling with a new hood, along with a new grille that filled in the V grille area of 1963, and gave the car a fresh new appearance. A sharp new hardtop body style was added to the model range, offered in six and eight-cylinder versions in 770 and 770-H trim. The rest of the Classic body styles were carryover, but with new exterior trim including attractive new stainless steel rocker panel moldings.

The Ambassador series also received a new grille, along with new exterior trim. The Ambassador also got the new hardtop body style and offered it in two trims—990 and top line 990-H. The sporty 990-H model came with bucket seats and a center console, light group, chrome roof bows, nicer interior trim, and the 270-horsepower 327 cid V-8 as standard equipment.

Dropped from the Ambassador line were two-door sedans, along with the entire 880 series—Abernethy believed that anyone looking for a lower-price Ambassador would buy a 770 series Classic, a bit of logic that's difficult to understand. One opportunity Abernethy missed was a chance to revive the Rebel series. He could have used the Classic body mated to the big 327 cid/270-horsepower engine and offered the combination as a new 880

Also new for 1964 were sharp hardtop models in all three lines. The Classic 770 hardtop was base-priced at $2,397. The Classic shown here is equipped with the optional 287 cid V-8, as testified by the V-8 badge on the front fender.

series Rebel in hardtop and sedan models. This would have neatly replaced the 880 Ambassador while at the same time providing AMC dealers with a high-performance model at a lower cost than an Ambassador 990 and giving the company a sportier image as well. As it was, there was now a significant price gap between the 770 hardtop and the Ambassador 990 hardtop—and AMC had no performance-image car at all. Chalk it up as a lost opportunity, one of many that would come during Abernethy's reign.

Big news for 1964 was the all-new Rambler American series, the first time the small Rambler boasted a completely new design since 1950. The styling job is rightly credited to Dick Teague and his team, though it had a good deal of Anderson's influence in it as well. The American now rode a 106-inch wheelbase, up half a foot from before, but was just 4 inches longer overall and was still the smallest car from an American automaker. Interior room was greatly improved, and the American could now carry six people. Luggage space and under-hood access was greatly improved as well.

But the biggest news about the new American was its styling. Gone was the high-waisted look of the old American and in was a new, lower, sleeker look. The overall styling was similar to the Classic/Ambassador, and that was partly so they would share a familial look and partly because the Ramblers now shared many common parts. The innovative Uniside idea was shared among all sedans and wagons in all three series—Classic, American, and Ambassador—and some of the underbody sheet metal stampings were shared as well. Because of this shared body design the American now had curved-glass doors, the only car in its class to have this premium feature. Naturally, the American was narrower and smaller than its bigger stable mates but Ed Anderson had created a clever design that could spread the cost of tooling over all three series as a cost-saving measure. Romney's planning

The Rambler lineup was exceptional in 1964, with modern Classic and Ambassador designs joined by the all-new American. Here we see some of the company's products on AMC's Wisconsin Proving Grounds test track.

Top left: The Rambler American for 1964. The American was all new this year and quite handsome. Many of the basic body and chassis sheet metal was shared with the Classic/Ambassador series, a clever way AMC was able to reduce tooling costs.

Top right: Increased interior room, clean lines, and modern design were the highlights of the all-new American for 1964. Shown is the top-of-the-line sedan, the 440 model. The American now rode a 106-inch wheelbase, up half a foot from before, but was just 4 inches longer overall and was still the smallest car from an American carmaker.

Right: Here are two of the pretty little ladies who customarily bought Ramblers. Kidding aside, the new American wagon was larger and roomier than before and could haul much more family stuff while achieving the highest fuel economy of any American-made car.

was that the basic body would not change until late in the decade. It was the key element in his strategy of keeping AMC competitive by reigning in tooling costs.

Up front, Americans boasted a new horizontal bar grille that was clean and stylish, along with tunneled headlamps similar to the Chrysler Turbine experimental car that was wowing audiences at car shows everywhere. The stylish roofline and clean body shape added up to perhaps the best-looking compact in its segment.

The American offered a full range of models: two- and four-door sedans, four-door station wagons, two-door hardtops, and a two-door convertible. Basic 220 and 330 models were equipped with a standard L-head engine producing 90 horsepower, and the 125-horsepower OHV six was standard on the 440, optional on the others. The 440-H got a 138-horsepower two-barrel equipped OHV six. As before, a V-8 engine was not available.

The American series also got a new front suspension for a smoother ride, a revised rear suspension, and a wider track for improved handling. All in all, the little American was quite a nice package.

The public loved the new Rambler. Typical was a letter from an enthusiastic American wagon buyer: "I get 25–30 miles per gallon, it is practically maintenance-free, and carries one heck of a load. All in all, you put out a terrific car!" During the year Dick Teague was promoted to vice president in charge of Styling.

A big surprise appeared in January 1964 when American Motors unveiled an experimental sporty fastback coupe called the Tarpon. Unlike anything the company had ever done, it was built on the new Rambler American body and was 180 inches long, with sporty lines and a terrific vermillion red paint job with gold metal flake. Rumors were that the company would get it into production in mid-1965.

On April Fool's Day, 1964, American Motors announced a new model available on a limited-production basis only—the Typhoon. The Typhoon was a specially trimmed Classic two-door hardtop created to spotlight AMC's newest engine, the "Torque Command" 232

Top: The 1965 American convertible was the top-of-the-line American and looked it. Notice that this yellow 440 convertible is equipped with the optional wire wheel covers with knock-off spinners—an infrequent option and highly sought after today.

Bottom: With a base price of just $1,907, the 1965 Rambler American 220 two-door sedan was the lowest-priced car in the Rambler line. But as this photo shows, even the cheapest Rambler was a good-looking automobile.

Top: During 1964 AMC considered producing a sporty car for 1965 built on the American chassis. This prototype, called the Sceptre, was the first effort along those lines. It evolved into the Tarpon show car, though there are several styling differences.

Bottom: In early 1964 AMC unveiled this beautiful Tarpon show car to gauge buyer interest. The car was an immediate hit and led to production plans that eventually changed the car from a compact to an intermediate—a fatal error.

cid inline six-cylinder, a modern engine of the latest design. The 232 mill was the largest displacement six of any U.S. producer and was powerful—145 horsepower and 215 lb-ft of torque. Perhaps the two greatest attributes of the new AMC six were smoothness and durability, courtesy of a new seven main bearing crankshaft. Building a new factory and purchasing tooling for the new engine was expensive, costing some $42 million altogether.

The Typhoon itself was a rather nice product, with bucket seats, center console, special black-center moldings for the body sides and rear, and black finish on the upper, lower, and center grille bars. The Typhoon came only in Solar Yellow paint with a black roof. Typhoon badges graced the rear fenders, along with 232 Six emblems. With a base price of $2,509, only 2,520 were produced.

During the year the company produced the 3 millionth modern Rambler, and the total count of Rambler owners stood at 2.75 million, an ample pool from which to earn repeat sales. The company had about 3,000 dealers in the United States. Because of an expansion project begun in 1963 American Motors could now produce nearly 700,000 cars per year in Kenosha.

With a new American series, and a restyled Classic and Ambassador, 1964 should have been another record year for American Motors; after all, it was for the industry, which reached more than 9 million vehicle sales, more than 8 million of which were passenger cars while the rest were trucks. But instead of sharing in the increase AMC's sales actually fell by about 49,000 in U.S. retail sales, to 379,412 for the calendar year. Wholesale sales to dealers dropped to 455,073 worldwide, still a very good figure but a substantial decline all the same. Overseas Rambler sales were up; it was only in the United States that sales had fallen. AMC revenues totaled $1,009,470,701—topping the billion-dollar mark for the fourth time in AMC history. Working capital fell to $94.6 million. Roy Abernethy stated that the decline in sales volume was due to a reduction in unit sales as well as *a lower proportion of sales of higher-priced models*. This is puzzling because a great deal of effort and advertising dollars had gone in precisely to ensure that sales of the higher-priced models would increase. Obviously, whatever plans and efforts Abernethy had put in place hadn't worked.

In his annual report Abernethy stated, "To some extent buyers continue to identify Rambler primarily with conservative design and economy in a period of increased customer interest in extra options, luxury features, and higher performance. Rambler has been moving with this trend and the lag in identity should be amply corrected by the 1965 Rambler models." This was quite a statement; besides the question of whether Rambler's image needed to be changed that much, there is the very real question as to how Abernethy thought he was going to change perception in just two years. After all, the Rambler image had grown and evolved over a 15-year period, first as a luxury compact in 1950, then as a high-quality alternative to big cars from 1955 to 1962, more recently as a midsize car offering style and economy at an attractive price. To alter its image now as Abernethy wanted would call for a complete reversal, and if he thought he could accomplish that in two years, he was kidding himself. One final point: Abernethy had been sales manager for AMC since 1955, so Rambler's image was the one he had either created or approved.

Rambler American production for 1964 was way up, not surprising with an all-new product, but Classic and Ambassador production (and sales) fell sharply. Classic production was down by about 115,000 units for the model year, and Ambassadors dropped by 19,000. Anybody seeking to figure out why sales of the big Ramblers fell in 1964 need only look at the competition, and in particular the newest entry in the midsize segment—the new Chevrolet Chevelle and Malibu. They were the first Chevrolets designed expressly to compete against

Left: The 1964 Rambler Typhoon was a special version of the Classic, created to introduce AMC's new 232 cid six-cylinder engine. Only 2,520 were built, and all of them were painted Solar Yellow with a black top. The combination of special trim and limited production makes this a highly desirable car today.

Right: AMC president Roy Abernethy was formerly VP in charge of sales, but replaced George Romney when Romney left the company to go into politics. He's shown with the new AMC thin-wall six-cylinder engine outside the Rambler plant.

the Rambler Classic/Ambassador series. Model-year production of the Chevelle/Malibu for 1964 was about 295,000 cars—and Ford Fairlane was about 277,000 cars. To get those numbers they had to take a chunk out of someone else's sales, and in 1964 that was Rambler. Despite its freshened styling the Rambler was struggling to compete against the sheer size and power of the Chevrolet dealer organization. It should be mentioned, too, that the Chevelle and Malibu were pretty decent cars, handsomely styled, well-priced, and riding a longer wheelbase than were the Classic and Ambassador. Here was a case where Rambler's quality message should have been used to highlight a big difference between the two cars.

Another huge reason for the drop in Rambler sales is that George Romney—AMC's guiding light—was long gone, comfortably ensconced now as governor of Michigan. Romney's ability to fire up the Rambler dealer network and the assembly line workers was legendary, and although Abernethy was a very competent sales manager, he was no George Romney. Besides not having the speaking skills that Romney mustered, Abernethy lacked the drive, the sheer, all-burning passion that Romney had put into the job. And now American Motors was beginning to feel his loss.

Top: From the American Motors Styling Studio archives comes this photo showing a full-size clay model of a proposed front end restyling for the 1965–66 Classic/Ambassador. This particular design shows a simple yet elegant egg crate grille, quad headlamps, and twin wind splits on the hood.

Center: From the same time period as the previous photo, this is a look at two possible designs for the rear of the Rambler American. Notice the other Rambler clay in the background.

Bottom right: One of the glamour models for Classic in 1965 was this 770-H hardtop. In 1965 the Classic was completely restyled to make it look larger and roomier in the hope it could better compete with the hot-selling Chevy Malibu and Chevelle.

Above: One show car making the rounds of the auto show circuit during 1965 was this attractive Rambler American convertible dubbed the Carousel. Featured were an impressive custom interior and unique alloy wheels. The Carousel nameplate is on the rear fender.

Left: AMC engineer and fuel economy expert Les Viland. Engineering and tuning carburetors for maximum efficiency were two of his special talents. Viland won many trophies in various fuel economy events, including the Mobilegas Economy Run.

Top: The new Classic convertible for 1965 was sporty and stylish, as this 770 model illustrates. Only 4,953 were built that year as American Motors continued to struggle against falling sales.

Bottom: A unique idea for a station wagon roofline was displayed in this concept car, called the Rambler St. Moritz. Built on the Rambler Classic body, it featured side windows that flowed up into the roof. These windows were heavily tinted to help control solar gain within the cabin.

In April 1964 Ford Motor Company introduced yet another competitor for Rambler—the Mustang hardtop. Similar in size to AMC's Tarpon concept car, the youthful and sporty compact Mustang quickly became the hottest car on the market and began eating into sales of all compact cars, including the American. The pony car market would become one of the most important in the industry, and AMC would be out of it for three critical years, a mistake that can be directly attributed to Roy Abernethy.

Elsewhere in 1964 AMC was investing in a new $7 million engine plant in Mexico, to be jointly operated by AMC, its Mexican partners, and partner Kaiser Jeep. A small assembly plant was also being set up in Chile to build Ramblers and Renaults.

The appliance business was good in 1964, with Kelvinator unit sales the highest since 1956. The company celebrated its 50th year in business. Overseas results were also better, reaching a new record. New appliance licensees were added in Iran and Brazil. Redisco's finance volume was up as well.

Negotiations for a new three-year contract with the UAW were concluded after a brief strike. The new contract was a modification of the landmark 1961 profit-sharing agreement. Profit sharing was discontinued this year, supplanted by an added week of vacation pay for hourly workers, which could go to two extra weeks during a good year. Although it was a change the union voted for, this was the beginning of the end to the harmonious working relationship that George Romney had fostered with the union.

For 1965 Roy Abernethy decided that the answer to AMC's problems was to increase the size of his senior Ramblers, positioning each into a separate market category. The American would remain in the compact segment, where it was expected to continue doing well, whereas the Classic for 1965 was made into a larger car, planted firmly in the intermediate-size market, where it belonged. Though still riding the 112-inch wheelbase and utilizing the same basic body, the Classic was completely restyled to make it look larger and roomier. New rear fenders were 5 inches longer on sedans, 3 inches longer on wagons. Front ends had more presence and looked much more expensive. The Rambler's lines were squarer, more elegant than before. It was an extremely well-done restyling job.

Ambassador was larger as well, and now rode on its own 116-inch wheelbase. Rear styling was similar to the Classic, but frontal styling now was completely different. Whereas Classic had horizontal quad headlamps, Ambassador had stacked quad lamps similar to the Ford Galaxie 500. The overall look was crisper, sharper, and very attractive. The 880 series was revived in an effort to increase Ambassador sales.

However, this spreading out of the Rambler models went against the program Romney had put in place in 1962, and because the Ramblers now had so many body and chassis differences from each other, the company's tooling cost began to skyrocket.

The Rambler American saw little change this year, though it did get a new grille and new taillamps. The American offered top value, without question, but its use of a standard L-head six on 220 and 330 models was very much out of date. Even Studebaker, which was still hanging on in Canada, had stopped using L-head engines years before.

Mechanical changes were numerous. Standard engine on the Classic 550 was a new and much more modern 199 cid inline six, a smaller version of the 232 Torque Command Six. The 232 mill was standard on the 660, the 770, and even the 770H model. Optional on all Classic's was a 155-horsepower version of the 232, along with the carryover 287 cid V-8 and new this year, an optional 327-cubic-inch, 270-horsepower V-8, formerly reserved for the Ambassador. This was a needed improvement because the hot Chevy Malibu SS series was really taking off in the market this year and buyers were looking for more power. It's at this time that Abernethy's mistake in not reviving the Rebel as a performance model was most keenly felt. In a back-pedal move, Ambassadors now came with the 155-horsepower six as standard equipment, a change that was hard to understand in a market that was crying for more horsepower. After all, when Ambassador was a smaller car it had come only with the firm's biggest V-8. Now that it was a big car, the company was putting a six

Top: For 1966 Rambler American was given this handsome restyling, making it appear larger and more substantial. Front-end sheet metal was all-new, 3 inches longer. The rear end was a bit longer as well. Americans now came with the 128-horsepower, 199-cubic-inch six as standard equipment.

Bottom: In February 1965 AMC introduced its new sporty car, the Marlin. The Marlin was a bigger version of the Tarpon concept and was built on the Classic chassis rather than the American's. This move took it out of the pony car segment and practically insured that the car would never sell in decent volume. Only 10,327 Marlins were produced for 1965.

in it. It was a sign that Abernethy was beginning to grasp at straws looking for solutions to his sales problems.

The Ramblers had a few other bits of obsolete technology that were hurting the company's quality image. Old-fashioned vacuum windshield wipers, which virtually all other brands had dropped years before, were still standard equipment on every Rambler, including the luxury Ambassador. Modern electric wipers were optional now, but most people didn't realize the difference and settled for the balky standard wipers, to their eventual regret. In addition, AMC's standard three-speed manual transmission lacked synchromesh on first gear, so downshifts to first usually resulted in a loud clashing of gears. Either of these two old-tech items could have been replaced by modern technology for only a few dollars, but AMC held on to them as if they were somehow golden. And it hurt their image.

Although the new styling of the 1965 models was nice to see and probably necessary as well, because the Big Three compacts and intermediates were stealing Rambler's market, the extent of the changes and the attempt to go head to head with the Big Three was costing little AMC many millions of dollars. This in turn was raising its cost basis, making it harder to turn a profit. American Motors breakeven point rose with each million spent and the only way to make a profit was to increase unit sales as well. It also went against the planning done by Romney and Anderson, who'd wanted to introduce

Top: The Rambler Classic for 1966. American Motors continued to see its car sales drop in 1966. This year net sales fell to $870 million, and a loss of $12 million was recorded—AMC's first loss since 1957. In June 1966 Michigan businessman Robert B. Evans, who owned 200,000 shares of AMC stock, was named chairman of the board in the hope he could engineer a turnaround.

Bottom: The 1966 Ambassador line entered the year with little exterior change but many new features and improvements. Public response to the up-level models was encouraging.

gradual changes to the senior styling, much as they has done with the 1956–1962 models. Regardless, Roy Abernethy confidently predicted increased Rambler volume for 1965.

In February 1965 the company introduced another new model. Called the Marlin, it was styled like the Tarpon show car but with an important difference. Where the Tarpon was a compact pony car, the Marlin was a midsize fastback.

The Marlin goes down as the greatest missed opportunity in AMC's entire history. At the time of its gestation as the Tarpon, Ford had yet to introduce its Mustang, and AMC could have tooled up the compact Tarpon in six months or less, introducing it as a 1965 model along with the rest of its 1965 lineup, thereby lagging Mustang by only five months. Instead, Roy Abernethy personally vetoed the idea of basing the Tarpon/Marlin on the compact Rambler, arguing that it should be on the intermediate Classic platform so that it would hold six passengers, and offer a V-8 engine—which the American couldn't do at the time. By the time the Marlin was redesigned on the midsize Classic body and introduced to the public half of the model year was gone and the compact Ford Mustang—based on the Falcon compact—was selling like hotcakes, easily the most exciting car on the market. More than a million Mustangs would be sold in the first two years. The Marlin, in comparison, was a dismal failure, selling fewer than 11,000 units for 1965. It was a perfect example of what happens when an old man tries to decide what a young man's car should look like.

There was nothing wrong with the Marlin's styling—the Tarpon had been the hit of the auto show when it was presented in 1964, and the crowds were wild about it. But the Marlin was simply too big. Buyers were looking for compact pony cars, not midsize models. Plymouth had introduced the Barracuda, with size and styling very similar to the Tarpon, and it sold very well, though not at the rate Mustang did. Dodge later introduced the midsize Charger, with styling similar to the Marlin, and it too proved to be a disappointment. Compact was where the pony car market was, and Abernethy's Marlin missed it entirely.

One other problem also hurt the Marlin—after Vince Geraci finished restyling the car on the Classic body Abernethy dictated that the roof be raised by 3 inches, spoiling the low profile and adding another nail in the Marlin's coffin.

If AMC had built the Marlin on the American chassis, there is no doubt that it would have sold many times more cars than it did and helped AMC gain an image as a young-thinking

Above: The Ambassador for 1966. Hardtops got the new crisp-line roof, and a luxurious new DPL hardtop, as seen in the photo here, debuted. *Motor Trend* tested a new Ambassador DPL and raved about its interior, suggesting other luxury cars would do well to imitate it.

Left: Dated September 9, 1966, this photo shows a proposal for a very elegantly styled AMC Ambassador. Note the hidden headlamps, a feature never used in any production AMC car. It's a shame some of these designs never made it to production.

Top: Midway through the 1966 model year AMC began to offer its new 290 cid V-8 in the Rambler American. To introduce it, a run of special Rogue hardtops was produced, each painted gold with a black top. The V-8 was available in all models of the American.

Left: In June the company unveiled a special automobile showing dubbed Project IV, consisting of four idea cars for the public to consider. The concept cars included this stylish AMX, a short wheelbase fastback sporty coupe. Public response to the AMX was so enthusiastic that chairman Robert Evans pushed to get it into production. The production car debuted in showrooms two years later.

organization. The lack of a V-8 engine was not as big a deal as Abernethy thought—Ford was selling tens of thousands of six-cylinder Mustangs. And anyway, the problem would have been resolved after the 1966 models debuted, when the revised American could offer a V-8. As it was Marlin would suffer through three disappointing years, not selling enough units to pay for its tooling, and preventing AMC from fielding a more competitive car until 1968.

Ambassador production soared for 1965, but American and Classic both fell, and for the year American Motors sold fewer cars than in 1964, despite Abernethy's assurances that there would be an increase. Worldwide wholesale sales for the fiscal year were 412,736 cars versus the 455,073 sold in 1964. In view of the money spent to restyle both Classic and

Ambassador along with introducing the Marlin, this was an exceptionally poor showing. Add in the fact that 1965 was the best year in the U.S. auto industry up to that time and it becomes a tragedy.

It showed up in the annual report. Total corporate sales fell to $990,618,709, and net earnings plummeted to just $5.2 million. A portion of the lower sales results, along with a good share of the lost profits, was caused by a strike by the United Auto Workers in the fourth quarter that affected both the U.S. and Canadian plants. The U.S. plants went down for three crucial weeks, the Canadian plants six weeks. Along with losing perhaps 25,000–30,000 units of production, the strike hampered the launch of the 1966 products and was a very expensive and foolhardy move by the UAW. Striking AMC when it was already heading downward was a mistake, pure and simple, but union/management relations had cooled considerably since Abernethy took over and a greedy, shortsighted union was now out for anything they could get.

Working capital, which in 1963 totaled $118.8 million, had fallen to $94 million in 1964 and now at the end of 1965 it stood at $84 million. Although AMC was still a large, solid company it was clearly heading in the wrong direction.

The appliance picture was mixed. During the year Kelvinator introduced a line of designer appliances that really caught the public's eye. Called the 'Kelvinator Originals," they were refrigerators, ranges, and dishwashers with different styling themes that had names like Year of the Dragon, Delft, Hacienda, and Federal. A favorite was Carriage Lamp, which decorated the refrigerator with gold handles and carriage lamp appliqués. Designed under the direction of Bill Reddig, the high-line Originals generated lots of positive buzz. But overall appliance sales were down for 1965. Redisco, however, reported another good year.

Overseas sales of Ramblers, including the total already mentioned, set a new record, 74,560 cars. Canadian sales would have set a record if not for the strike.

Roy Abernethy said the outlook for 1966 was good. After all, he argued, the company had spent nearly $158 million dollars in the prior three years on capital improvements and tooling. And that was the shame of it all. Spending money like it was going out of style, Abernethy still hadn't been able to duplicate the success his predecessor had accomplished on a shoestring. However, the company looked for an increase for 1966.

The 1966 AMC/Rambler lineup had a curious mix of changes and sameness. The American series came in for the greatest changes, with styling that greatly improved its appearance. Front-end sheet metal was all new and 3 inches longer, giving the American a richer, more balanced appearance. Rear styling was new as well and about ¾ of an inch longer. Still, at 181 inches overall the smallest Rambler continued to be the shortest car built in America. AMC finally dropped the old fashioned L-head engine—years late—so American now came

The AMX II, similar in size to the AMX, was a related concept but with more traditional styling. Although it's a very attractive automobile, potential buyers preferred the original AMX.

Top left: The Cavalier, a four-door compact sedan, introduced the idea of interchangeable body parts, wherein the right front fender interchanged with the left rear and the left front fender was the same as the right rear. An earlier version was made that looked more like a Rambler American. Styling elements from the Cavalier were later used on the 1970 AMC Hornet.

Bottom left: The Vixen was a coupe version of the Cavalier. Public response to the Vixen's styling was not enthusiastic, as it had too many controversial styling touches, including the long doors, rear side window vents, and unusual rear styling.

Right: The AMC Vixen's rear styling included what was known as the sugar scoop, a deeply recessed rear window and a blackout rear deck. The rear panel styling influenced the later AMC Hornet.

with the 128-horsepower 199-cubic-inch six. It was a big improvement; in January 1966 at the Daytona Speedway a Rambler American managed to win both the acceleration tests *and* the fuel economy crown in Class Six. The American lineup was trimmed this year by the elimination of the 330 series cars. Now the American was offered in base 220 and high-line 440 trim, along with a new top of the line model called the Rogue hardtop that effectively replaced the former 440-H.

The Classic returned with minor restyling. Station wagons got new, more stylish rooflines and all models received a new grille and taillights. The Classic hardtops got a crisp new roofline as well, a really attractive piece of restyling. Like the American, the Classic line was pruned by the dropping of the mid-level 660 series. Also like the American, the Classic line received a new top-line model, the Rebel hardtop, which replaced the 770-H.

The story was the same with the Ambassador. Minor styling updates were accomplished, hardtops got the new crisp-line roof, and a luxurious new top of the line DPL hardtop debuted. *Motor Trend* tested a new Ambassador DPL and raved about its interior trim, suggesting that other luxury cars would do well to imitate it.

The Marlin got a new grille and new interior materials and now had a bench front seat as standard. Marlin received a large price cut in an effort to improve its dreadful sales.

All American Motors cars now received a safety package of features to improve vehicular safety. Items included a padded instrument panel and sun visors, front and rear seat belts, an outside rear view mirror, backup lights, windshield washers, and higher-strength windshield glass.

Top: This never-before-seen mock-up shows a concept car called the Rebel II, planned for a 1967 introduction. Note the badge on the rear fender. It's built on the Rambler American's 106-inch wheelbase but is larger and much more stylish. It's a shame this one didn't get put into production.

Bottom: Here's a side view of a proposed new Ambassador for 1967 introduction. Note the Chrysler-like styling of the rear doors and fenders, the massive look of the entire vehicle. The sign above it says that the overall length of the car is 207 inches, width is 75 inches, and wheelbase is 118 inches.

This year Abernethy decided to separate his two upper line models from his lower lines so the Ambassador and Marlin no longer carried the Rambler name. They were now designated Ambassador by American Motors and Marlin by American Motors.

The many changes in model lineups and names reflect the confusion that had settled in on Roy Abernethy. On the one hand, he desired to move American Motors more up-scale—not a bad thing by any means. But he did it by dropping the Rambler name—a prime asset—from two lines of cars while leaving it on two others, creating confusion and accomplishing little. Surprisingly, for a man determined to upgrade the Rambler image, Abernethy also dropped the mid-range American 330 and Classic 660 series—which at one time were the bread and butter models—while leaving in place the stripped 220 and 550 cars—completely refuting his own philosophy of improving the Rambler image. If dealers were confused, imagine how the public felt.

The hoped-for sales improvement didn't come, and AMC had to halt production for the first two weeks of January 1966 because there was a 93-day supply of cars on hand, versus an industry average of 45 days. Then in February 1966 the company was forced to shut down production for 10 days to balance inventories.

In March 1966 Studebaker finally bowed to the inevitable and exited the auto business. It had never really recovered from the devastating losses of 1954–1958, and its sales had sunk to an uneconomic level. Its death was fair warning of what could happen to an automaker that failed to watch its costs or grow its volume. American Motors was now the last independent automaker in the United States, aside from a handful of specialty firms.

In April 1966 the company announced a new 290 cid Typhoon V-8 engine, which replaced the old 287 mill. The new 290 was a modern thin-wall block design and would now be available in all models of the

Top: In December 1967 American Motors and Gulton Industries announced a new joint venture to explore the possibility of producing an electric car. To build interest in the idea AMC stylists created the Amitron show car, a diminutive commuter car with futuristic styling. The Amitron never progressed beyond the plastic push mobile seen here. This car still exists.

Bottom: AMC chairman Roy D. Chapin Jr. with the 1967 Rambler American. In February 1967 Chapin cut Rambler American prices by $234 to a new low price of $1,839—making it the lowest-priced American car by far and just $200 more than a VW Beetle. Chapin also moved to drastically cut costs throughout the company.

Rambler American series, the first time the smallest Rambler had offered a V-8. The first 1,700 engines were installed in specially trimmed Rogue hardtops.

But AMC continued to sink. In June Michigan businessman Robert B. Evans, who had bought some 200,000 shares of AMC stock, was named chairman of the board. His appointment showed how panicky the board had become. Evans had no automotive background whatsoever, and his shares gave him ownership of perhaps 1 percent of the company, but the board reached out to him because he had a reputation for success and getting things done. He succeeded Richard Cross at the helm, though Cross stayed on as a director.

Also in June the company unveiled a show it called Project IV, consisting of four idea cars for the public to consider. The concept cars included the AMX, a short wheelbase fastback sporty coupe; the AMX II, a similar-sized car with more traditional styling; the Cavalier, a four-door compact sedan that tested the idea of interchangeable body parts; and the Vixen, a coupe version of the Cavalier. Public response was enthusiastic, especially for the AMX.

Robert Evans began pushing for production of one or more of the Project IV cars, needed, he felt, to inject some youthfulness and excitement in the lineup. He also arranged for Roy D. Chapin Jr., his longtime friend, to be promoted to executive vice president and general automotive manager, taking the general manager job away from Roy Abernethy.

Evans told *Forbes* magazine that he had faith in the existing AMC management. He emphasized what he felt were the most important needs for AMC. "First," he said, "we must have a fuller line of standard cars that are at least as good as those of the Big Three and hopefully better. Next we must have a so-called personality car . . . to appeal to all segments of the market. . . . So we must now build cars that will attract and excite youth, such as the AMX, which will be in the line next year." He also suggested that AMC would enter the subcompact market within two years.

American Motors didn't seem like a safe bet for car shoppers in 1966. The company was losing money, sales were poor, and rumors circulated that it might fail entirely. All this caused a great loss of confidence by the public. A big part of it was because American Motors' image was fuzzy now, part Rambler and part luxury AMC, and it didn't convey a solid, understandable message the average consumer could understand. This could, of course, be corrected over a period of years providing enough money was available to push through a new image, but AMC was fast running out of both money and time.

Left: A popular product was the Rambler American station wagon, seen here in top-line 440 trim. The little Rambler was roomy enough for a family of six and all their luggage and had the best fuel economy of any American car. All Rambler American models got a new, more stylish instrument panel in 1967.

Right: The Rambler Rebel was all new for 1967 and very handsome, as this 770-series sedan shows. Rebels were completely redesigned this year and were wider and longer than before.

Top: During 1967 American Motors Engineering built a special Rebel to be used for high-performance carburetor testing and for developing racing parts for sale to the public. Powered by a 390 cid V-8, it could run in the 11-second bracket. This car heavily influenced the later 1970 Rebel Machine. The car was later sold and is still in existence.

Bottom: The new Rebel SST hardtop for 1967 was a very exciting car. With sleek new styling and powerful engines, it offered buyers an attractive, sporty package with traditional Rambler quality as well.

One could see it in the financial results for the year. Net sales fell to $870 million, and a loss of $12 million was recorded—AMC's first loss since 1957. Working capital fell to $52.7 million. Retail sales in America fell to 271,466 versus 338,176 the year before, and wholesale sales to dealers worldwide were 345,886—a drop of more than 65,000 units. On the appliance side, though, both Redisco and Kelvinator reported sales increases.

AMC fought back for 1967 with all-new big cars, improvements for the American, and a new five-year/50,000 mile warranty on the drivetrain.

The redesigned senior models were an expensive gamble by Abernethy, one he was sure would finally turn things around. Completely new inside and out, and featuring a wide range of engines including a new 343 cid V-8, the big AMC cars were beautiful to behold, fully competitive with anything from the Big Three. The Ambassador now rode a longer

118-inch wheelbase, its sleek, sculptured lines stretched out 202.5 inches bumper to bumper, and it was 4 inches wider as well. The Marlin was built on the Ambassador chassis this year, so it was bigger than before, more handsome, and considered part of the Ambassador lineup. Abernethy thought that perhaps a larger Marlin would sell better; once again he would be proved wrong.

The Classic line was renamed Rebel. The new Rebel lineup shared its basic body with the Ambassador but rode a 114-inch wheelbase and had its own unique front end styling. The new car was a vast

improvement over the Classic, a stylish family car with options to make it a very sporty machine. Rebel shared a new four-link rear suspension with Ambassador/Marlin.

The American got a stylish new two-tone paint option and added a convertible model to the top-line Rogue series, and all models got a new, more stylish instrument panel.

The senior new cars won wide acclaim from auto writers, with *Mechanix Illustrated*'s Tom McCahill flatly stating, "There isn't a better intermediate-size car sold in the United States than the 1967 Rambler Rebel." Although praise was high, the public still held back, afraid perhaps of buying a possible orphan.

The sad truth was that despite the new cars and many new features, the 1967 model year got off to a rocky start sales-wise and the company was languishing. By January 9, 1967, the board of directors had had enough. With Robert Evans holding court the board summarily forced Roy Abernethy into retirement. Replacing him as president was William V. Luneburg, a gruff, profane ex-Ford executive who had been with AMC a few years and had a tough, no-nonsense attitude. Evans himself stepped down, and in his place the board elected Roy D. Chapin Jr. as chairman.

Chapin was a known quantity. His father had been one of the founders of the Hudson Motorcar Company, and he himself had worked there prior to the merger with Nash. Since then he had been quietly working his way up the ranks of executives, being shown little favoritism despite his standing as one of the company's larger stockholders. Chapin had done an outstanding job building up AMC in overseas markets, and he had definite ideas about what needed fixing in the domestic market. He had a quiet, confident air, good connections in the finance community, and a plan to bring AMC back to prosperity.

A look at the financial numbers for 1967 shows why the board took the drastic action it did. Dollar volume had dropped again, to $778 million, and wholesale auto sales fell to 291,090 worldwide. The resulting loss was incredible—$75 million, though that included a number of paper losses, like write-offs of tax benefits deferred in prior years, revaluation of foreign investments, and other write downs. Working capital dwindled to a mere $35 million. To help pay bills the profitable Redisco finance subsidiary was sold for some $31 million.

The Abernethy years had been a disaster, and now they were over, with Chapin and Luneburg called in to clean up the mess and try to get American Motors on the road to recovery.

Top: In 1967 the Marlin was moved to the Ambassador platform and was completely restyled. The bigger, sleeker Marlin, though attractively styled, failed to catch on in the marketplace, and only 2,545 were produced. This was the final year for the Marlin.

Bottom: Also in 1967 an AMC-affiliated company, IKA-Renault of Argentina, began building a new version of the Rambler American called the Torino. Minor restyling was done by Pininfarina. The Torino went on to have a brilliant racing career and was well beloved by Argentineans.

The two top executives at American Motors in 1968 were President William V. Luneburg (left) and Chairman Roy D. Chapin Jr. (right). With them are two symbols of a resurging AMC—the Ambassador SST and the Javelin coupe. The house appears to be Chapin's own residence.

1968–1969
CHAPIN AT THE WHEEL

THE YEAR 1967 STANDS AS THE LOW POINT in American Motors history, a time when the company could easily have gone out of business. At one point there was even a danger that AMC would not be able to make its payroll two weeks hence. At a long, difficult meeting with the company's bankers, trying to beg for funding, a frustrated Bill Luneburg reached in his pocket, pulled out a ring of keys, and threw them on the table, telling the bankers, "Here's the keys to the factory—who wants 'em?" The stunned bankers by no means wanted to end up owning a busted car company, and they finally agreed to loan AMC the money to keep it afloat. It had been a close thing.

Long before the 1968 model year began Roy D. Chapin Jr. and Bill Luneburg were hard at work trying to save American Motors. To the press Chapin declared that the new management team was going to "Run, not walk." In February 1967 Chapin announced a new policy. The Rambler American's styling was no longer going to change on a yearly basis. Instead it would stay the same, and the money thus saved on tooling would go to make it a better value. He then cut Rambler American prices by $234 to a new low price of $1,839—making it the lowest-priced American car by far, just $200 more than the dowdy, ancient VW Beetle. Sales rose strongly and stayed strong. Luneburg and Chapin moved to cut costs drastically throughout the company. They also began making presentations to various influential financial and news groups, trying to change public opinion by pointing out the inherent strength of the corporation and its efforts to produce a

Right: The 1968 AMC Ambassador was in the news because it now came with air conditioning as standard equipment on all models. Only a handful of luxury makes had standard air conditioning , making the Ambassador stand out in the crowded full-size market.

Above: This is the mid-range Rebel 770 for 1968. Note the new door handles and the attractive new grille. The 770 hardtop seen in the background was also available in SST trim.

Left: The biggest news for AMC this year was the all-new Javelin pony car, which replaced the ill-fated Marlin in the lineup. Javelin offered clean lines, more standard equipment, and a lower price than Camaro or Mustang.

comeback in the market. In June 1967 AMC, at the urging of Bill McNealey, signed on with the hottest young advertising agency in the country, Wells, Rich, Greene, headed by the lovely and extremely talented Mary Wells. The agency and Wells would be a big part of AMC's future success.

AMC had completely missed the pony car market, and Chapin was determined to correct this mistake as quickly as possible. He and Evans had already okayed the development of a competitor, and it was ready for introduction as a 1968 model. Called the

Javelin, it was designed to provide a sportier car for the money than Mustang or Camaro while offering styling that was fresh and exciting. A sleek, handsome fastback built on a 109-inch wheelbase, it effectively replaced the luckless Marlin in the company's lineup. The new Javelin proved to be a moderate hit, attracting many new shoppers who had never visited an AMC dealership before, though selling fewer than 60,000 units for the year. However, its influence on AMC's image was even more important than its modest sales results. Roy D. Chapin Jr. later recalled that when his dealers first saw the Javelin some of them came up to him with tears in their eyes because they were so grateful finally to see a ray of hope from the foundering company. In December 1967 AMC announced that the newly formed Javelin Racing Team would campaign the Javelin in Trans-Am racing.

The American returned for 1968 with prices beginning at $1,946 for the basic two-door sedan. The lineup was trimmed this year to two- and four-door sedans in base trim,

Top: American Motors got into Trans-Am racing in 1968. In this photo we see driver George Follmer hopping into his Javelin racer in a Le Mans–style start, in which drivers have to race to their cars before starting off. This photo was taken during Javelin's first time at the track, in Sebring, Florida.

Bottom: In 1967 and 1968 AMC fielded a special Rebel dragster named the Grant Rebel. Shown here is the 1968 version, the Grant Rebel SST, driven by Charlie Adams. This car was very competitive, running in the mid-8-second range. After 1968 AMC concentrated most of its performance efforts on Trans-Am racing.

Top: Mid-1968 brought the introduction of one of the greatest American cars of all time: the awesome AMX. A true two-seater GT, it was the only American sports car on the market other than the Corvette.

Center: The AMX was built on a shortened Javelin chassis and came with many performance features as standard equipment. A V-8 engine, four-speed transmission, dual exhaust, tachometer, and bucket seats were all standard.

Bottom: Beginning in 1968 Javelins were assembled in Germany by the noted coachbuilder Karmann GmbH. Here we see them on the final inspection line at Karmann's plant.

Another photo of the first AMC Trans-Am race, in Sebring, Florida. This is the number 25 Javelin, driven by George Follmer.

four-door sedans and wagons in 440 trim, and a hardtop in Rogue trim. The Rogue convertible was dropped from the line. Little was new on the American this year. One change was that it was now the only model in the Rambler series, because the Rebel was spun off on its own just as the Marlin and Ambassador had been. All senior cars this year received fancy new recessed door handles, as did the Javelin. *Popular Science* road-tested a new Rebel 770 and came away very impressed, noting that the "Rebel had more interior space than the other intermediates [and] has a lot of good features to offer that you don't find in other intermediates." The Rebel offered two ragtops this year, a stripped 550 priced at $2,736 and an SST at $2,999. Neither model sold very well, as convertibles in general were fading in popularity.

The convertible model was dropped from the Ambassador lineup. But Ambassador had big news this year—air conditioning was now standard equipment on all models. Sales had been going nowhere, and marketing chief Bill McNealy was searching for a way to make Ambassador stand out in a crowded market. He found the answer with the standard air conditioning idea, and sales of the Ambassador began to rebound strongly. It was a brilliant marketing move.

In February AMC unveiled yet another new car—the awesome AMX. Built on a shortened Javelin chassis, the new AMX was the only American two-seat sports car on the market

aside from the standby Corvette. It came very well-equipped, with a standard 290 cid V-8 engine, four-barrel carburetor, four-speed manual transmission, dual exhausts, wide-profile tires, tachometer, and reclining bucket seats. It was a true Gran Touring machine and offered as options the 343 V-8 and a new engine, the potent AMX 390-cubic-inch V-8, the biggest engine AMC had ever produced, good for 315 horsepower. AMX's styling was impeccable, being sensuous and formidable-looking at the same time, and its performance was incredible. Roy D. Chapin Jr. was especially proud of the new sports car, feeling it embodied all the renewed strength and dynamism of American Motors. AMX became the preeminent symbol of AMC's new vitality.

Good things began to happen at American Motors. During the year the racing husband-and-wife team of Craig and Lee Breedlove set 106 national and international speed records with the new AMX. Under the direction of new performance chief Carl Chakmakian Javelin began to compete successfully in the Trans-Am

Above: A collection of AMC's hottest cars was brought to Los Angeles airport in late 1968 for the 1969 dealer introduction of the newest AMC cars. Standing with them is Carl Chakmakian, an AMC engineer. Chakmakian is the man who got AMC into racing.

Right: One of the more successful drag racers was New Yorker Jesse Sneider, who campaigned a Rambler Rogue for Richmond Rambler, beginning in 1967.

series, and AMC cars were getting into drag racing as well. A new spirit was taking hold at American Motors.

In March 1968 AMC officials met with the Shah of Iran to dedicate a new facility in Teheran to manufacture new Rambler Americans for the local market. It was the first American car to be manufactured in Iran—prior to this Ramblers had only been assembled there. Then in October 1968 came an announcement that Javelins would be built by German coachbuilder Karmann at a plant in Rheine, West Germany, for the European market.

As a preview of future styling themes American Motors unveiled a new concept car called the AMX GT. It was something to see, with its 97-inch wheelbase and a hatchback body style that predicted the shape of a future AMC subcompact.

Roy D. Chapin Jr. was confident he was on the right track, but he still needed to improve his balance sheet. To accomplish this he arranged in July to sell assets of the Kelvinator appliance division to White Consolidated Industries. Kelvinator by this point was losing money and needed more capital and attention than AMC could provide, so it made sense to sell it and concentrate on the company's core automotive division. Having sold Redisco finance earlier, it was best to unload Kelvinator now.

So fiscal 1968 ended up being a complete turnaround from what Chapin himself called "the dark days of 1967." Net sales for the automotive division grew to $761 million, an increase of more than $109 million, and a profit of $11.7 million was reported. Working capital more than doubled to $77.9 million. Chapin noted, "We now have the resources to take advantage of opportunities as they are developed." He had some big ones in mind, but was keeping his thoughts to himself.

For 1969 Chapin budgeted for 300,000 U.S. car sales and continued to improve and perfect his product line. The American returned, now dubbed simply the Rambler

Top: Along with the Big Bad colors, AMC introduced new appearance options for the 1969 Javelin, including the hood scoops and rear spoiler shown here. Although the shading makes this car appear to be dark orange, it is actually Big Bad Orange—note the painted front bumper.

Bottom: Shown here is a 1969 AMX, with the special factory Big Bad Blue color. Longtime AMC enthusiast Gordy Chilson is at the wheel.

Right: In 1969 employees of American Motors started their own racing team called T.E.A.M., which stood for Technical Employees of American Motors. They raced very successfully. Shown are, left to right, Jim Alexander, who headed up the effort, and Ike Knupp, who was the driver. The third man is unidentified.

Below: Prepared for AMC by Hurst Performance, the SC/Rambler, sometimes called the Scrambler Rambler, was an amazing muscle car. Equipped with the AMX V-8 engine and four-speed transmission, it was a terror on wheels and is one of the hottest AMC collector cars today.

because there was no longer a separate Rambler brand, only a model. The Ramblers were still quite popular, with sales increasing ever since the 1967 price cut.

The Rebel line returned with a new grille, new deck lid, and new taillamps, and it also featured a wider track. Inside was an all-new instrument panel. Model names were changed. Rebel now offered a two-door hardtop, four-door sedan, and station wagon models in base or SST trim.

For 1969 Ambassador saw the most change. Its wheelbase was increased to 122 inches, and it received all-new front and rear styling that was quite elegant—the hood even had cusps, as the luxury Packard once did. The idea was for the Ambassador to have a longer wheelbase than Chevy, Ford, and Plymouth had, making it more competitive. The base line Ambassador series was now limited to a single four-door sedan. Wells, Rich, Greene came up with a clever slogan too: "It will remind you of the days when money really bought something."

Javelin returned for its second year with a new grille and numerous small engineering and styling updates. AMX likewise featured engineering refinements and some additional choices in racing stripes.

AMC also introduced some special products. Early in 1969 the company unveiled three new mod colors for the Javelin and AMX that were wild—Big Bad Blue, Big Bad Green, and Big Bad Orange. And in a surprise move AMC also fielded a new performance car—the

Top: Still attractive after six years in the market, the Rambler hardtop is seen here in blue paint with a black vinyl roof. It's equipped with a V-8 engine—note the engine emblem on the front fender.

Bottom: During 1968 AMC showed this concept car to the public. Called the AMX-GT, it predicted the styling of the 1970 Gremlin, which the company's designers were working on. This car was a non-running mock-up, a push mobile, as Dick Teague termed it.

Above: You didn't have to order any performance options to get the Big Bad Orange paint, as seen here with a six-cylinder-equipped 1969 Javelin.

Top right: In 1969 movie actor James Garner owned a racing team known as American International Racers. He took a fleet of specially prepared Ramblers to Mexico to race in the Baja 500 that year.

Bottom right: The SC/Rambler was an important image builder for American Motors, and its outlandish paint schemes made sure the car was noticed going down the street. Here we see R. William McNealy and George Hurst admiring an SC/Rambler at the racetrack.

Brooks Stevens Associates
INDUSTRIAL DESIGN

awesome SC/Rambler, with performance modifications done by Hurst Performance. Based on the Rambler American, the red, white, and blue-painted SC/Rambler was powered by the AMX 390 engine and came with dual exhaust, four-speed gearbox and performance suspension as standard equipment. With limited production and a price tag of just $2,998 the SC/Rambler quickly sold out, and additional units were produced with a different paint scheme.

On June 30, 1969, the company produced its last Rambler in the United States. From 1950 to 1969 more than 4 million Ramblers has been built, and now the Rambler name was being allowed to die out, though it remained in use in some overseas markets. The sad truth was that the Rambler image and proud name had taken a beating under Roy Abernethy, and now it stood for, at best, a low-bucks economy car, at worse, a cheap ride for losers. Chapin felt it was time to make a break with the past.

Midway through the model year AMC introduced a new corporate symbol, called the A Mark. Made of red and white triangles and a blue rectangle, this classy identification would continue to the end of its time as an automaker. Along with the new logo came a program to strengthen and upgrade the company's dealer network with new designs for dealership facilities.

Top: Brooks Stevens proposed this advanced safety vehicle for American Motors in 1968. The idea was that the rounded front end would allow the cars to slip past another car rather than colliding. Note the limousine-style doors.

Center: Talented designer Bob Nixon proposed this gorgeous Sports wagon for the Javelin line. Too bad it wasn't produced. It's sharp-looking and would have been unique in the market.

Bottom left: During 1969 AMC began to investigate the idea of putting an American mid-engine car into production. This full-size clay, called the AMX, was one of several designs that were tried.

When its fiscal year closed on September 30, 1969, American Motors could claim a small victory: its automotive operations had yielded a small increase in profit. That was about all that was good news however, because sales had fallen to $737,448,700 and the company's net profit fell to $4.9 million. Worldwide wholesale sales of cars fell to 309,740 units, a drop of more than 13,000 vehicles. On the plus side, net working capital rose to nearly $98 million.

Roy D. Chapin Jr. had some ideas about what to do with that money, and they were big. On October 20, 1969, AMC and Kaiser Industries reached an agreement in principle for the purchase by American Motors of all the stock of Kaiser Jeep Corporation. It took some time to figure out the exact price, and the deal was subject to approval by AMC's shareholders, but all the same it was essentially a done deal and it was huge. Kaiser Jeep sales in 1968 totaled $476.9 million, and the company had about 1,600 dealers in the United States and many more overseas. Jeeps were sold in more than a hundred countries worldwide. Though small by the standards of the U.S. automotive industry, Jeep was still a half-billion dollar corporation, and Chapin saw great potential in it. After all, he had been trying to get AMC to buy Jeep since 1960. Chapin got it at a bargain price: $70,213,597.

As the year drew to a close the company began introducing its new cars. Chapin made a vow to introduce a new car every six months until 1972, and it would begin with the 1970 small car that was to replace the beloved Rambler. A new decade was about to dawn and with it would come many changes to American Motors—some good and some unfortunate.

Above: This clay, dubbed AMX/2, was designed by Bob Nixon. Note the differences in the roofline and side windows compared with the prior design.

Right: This model, dubbed the AMX/3, was preferred by design chief Dick Teague and, not surprisingly, was the one chosen for production.

Top: The 1969 AMC Rebel hardtop was a stylish machine and well-suited for a family of six. This year Rebels had a wider track, new grille, and new taillamps.

Center left: This design drawing, dated October 29, 1969, shows an idea for a next generation Javelin or AMX. Note the 401 badge on the front fender.

Bottom left: The Ambassador SST hardtop for 1969. The big Ambassador got even bigger this year, with its wheelbase stretched to 122 inches.

6

1970–1974
A NEW GENERATION

IN MANY WAYS 1970 CAN BE SEEN AS the birth of a new American Motors. The company now was committed to replacing or updating its entire automobile lineup, and it would begin this year. The Rambler was already gone, and its replacement, called the Hornet, was being introduced in late September 1969 as a 1970 model. AMC had also shed its nonautomotive divisions to concentrate strictly on the automotive field, and it also added two transportation companies, Jeep Corporation and its spinoff, General Products Division, to its corporate roster. General Products Division (there had been a similar unit at Kaiser-Jeep) was structured by AMC to handle all of Jeep's military and governmental vehicle sales and production. Under Roy D. Chapin Jr. Jeep Corporation would concentrate on retail business, while General Products handled the rest. The General Products charter included an objective to grow its business and also enter into new transportation fields.

Besides Jeep AMC also bought Holmes Foundry Ltd., the company that cast its engine blocks. Another company purchased in 1970 was Windsor Plastics, a manufacturer of injection-molded parts. American Motors had earlier purchased Canadian Fabricated Products, the company that produced interior trim for its cars, and plastics maker Evart Products.

But the 1970 fiscal year, beginning October 1, 1969, didn't start off very well. The Kenosha union struck the AMC plant for five weeks during October and November—just as the company was trying to launch the new Hornet. Chapin noted that "The strike involved work standards rather than economic

Jeep Corporation became a part of American Motors at the beginning of the 1970 fiscal year. Shown here are three limited-edition Jeep CJ-5 Renegade IIs, along with an enthusiastic fan. This year the Jeep Renegade II came with alloy wheels rather than the wide steel wheels seen on the Renegade I.

Above: Here we see an early idea for the upcoming new compact Hornet. The overall lines are very similar to the actual production car, especially the flared wheel openings. The grille shows some resemblance to the 1973–1977 grille themes used in production.

Below: The Hornet for 1970 replaced the aging Rambler and was another image-changer for AMC. Here a model dressed in a Hornet-like dress shows off the new Hornet. Note the redline tires and 304 V-8 emblem. In time, AMC would spin off the Gremlin and Sportabout from the basic Hornet body.

issues and its duration was unwarranted and unfortunate." The company lost five weeks of production when it needed it most, and the strike served to stall the momentum of the launch of a critical new product. Once again the union had chosen to strike at the worst time. It would greatly affect the company's bottom line that year.

The 1970 lineup of cars was very exciting. The new Hornet compact was worlds apart from the old Rambler, with real styling that mimicked the long-hood, short-deck look of pony cars, though with much more room, a better ride, and generous trunk space. One particular standout feature was the flared fender wells, which gave the Hornet a wide aggressive stance and much more presence than did the slab-sided competition. Hornet was a compact developed with AMC's "Philosophy of Difference" in mind. One way Hornet greatly differed from competitors such as Ford Maverick was that Hornet offered a wide array of options so that buyers could have their automobile plain, sporty, fancy, or anything in between. In other words, being a small car no longer meant it had to be a cheap car. In addition, Hornet offered a choice of three six-cylinder engines and a new 304 cid V-8. Two- and four-door models came in two trim levels—base and SST. With prices that began at a mere $1,994, Hornet was clearly a winner.

Javelin and AMX both returned with some minor styling updates. Both got new grilles and longer, pointed hoods. AMX now came with the new 360 cid V-8 as standard equipment. Exciting news was the availability of a limited edition red, white, and blue-painted replica of the Trans-Am Javelin, complete with a 390 cid V-8, Ram-Air hood, and front and rear spoilers. A special Mark Donohue Javelin, with a rear spoiler supposedly designed by the race driver himself, was also available. Just 2,501 were sold that year.

Rebel came in for some unusual restyling efforts. This year the AMC intermediate got all-new styling on the rear half of the car: new quarter panels, roof, and deck lid. Up front the changes were minor—mainly an attractive new grille. Because Ambassador shared the same basic body as the Rebel, it too shared in the new rear styling and also got a fine new grille. A special high-performance Rebel, called the Rebel Machine, also debuted. It featured

Left: The AMX sports car had several appearance changes for 1970, including a pointed hood and new grille. This was to be the last year for the classic two-seat AMX, as it would be replaced in 1971 by a version of the four-seat Javelin.

Below: Seen here at Michigan International Speedway is legendary race car driver Mark Donohue and his No. 6 Trans-Am Javelin. Over time, the Javelin established an impressive racing record.

Top: The 1970 AMC Rebel got new rear styling this year. Changes included the reverse-slope C-pillar, a longtime AMC style mark, plus new rear fenders and back panel. The Rebel was an excellent value, offering more room than competitive intermediates as well as more trunk space.

Bottom: The one-year-only Rebel Machine was a muscle car in the truest sense, equipped with a special 390cid V-8 engine, four-speed transmission, styled wheels, dual exhaust, and a host of other goodies. It could be ordered in the red, white, and blue paint scheme shown or in any regular AMC color.

a red, white, and blue paint scheme that was impossible to ignore, and it was powered by a special 390 cid V-8 and came loaded with performance goodies. Other colors were made available as well.

The Jeep purchase agreement was finalized on December 2, 1969, approved by the stockholders in February 1970, and made effective backdated to October 1, 1969—the beginning of AMC's fiscal year. American Motors now had a line of trucks and sport utility vehicles it hadn't had before and with it more growth potential than even Chapin realized. Because the 1970 Jeeps were already in production when the company was purchased there was little to nothing AMC could do product-wise that year. But plans were being laid for the future. In the meantime, a sporty CJ-5 model called the Renegade I debuted on a very limited basis. It quickly sold out.

On April Fool's Day 1970, American Motors announced another new car, one that would go on to become one of the most beloved AMC cars ever—the Gremlin. The new 1970½ Gremlin was America's first subcompact car and the first true import fighter. That it came from American Motors seemed appropriate because, after all, AMC was America's gutsy small car pioneer. In retrospect, it was actually extraordinary that the country's smallest automaker managed to beat GM, Ford and Chrysler to market in a new segment with what was sure to be a volume seller.

The Gremlin was one of the cleverest automotive designs of all time. Essentially Dick Teague and his team based both the Hornet and Gremlin on one basic body and had his designers—chiefly Bob Nixon and Vince Geraci—design it so that the 108-inch wheelbase Hornet could be cut down to a 96-inch wheelbase Gremlin. From the doors forward the two cars were nearly identical; the only significant change to create the Gremlin was to shorten the wheelbase and design a new back end. It yielded a four-passenger subcompact with striking good looks. Chapin and Teague et al. decided that the Gremlin's unusual styling was exactly what was needed. They wanted a design that would be controversial and that would be talked about, and they got it. The buying public loved the Gremlin, and new customers flocked to AMC dealerships by the thousands. There was one fly in the ointment, however; the company was way too conservative with its sales projections and didn't build nearly enough Gremlins to meet initial demand.

One very positive aspect of the Gremlin program was that it was bringing in a significant number of younger buyers and owners of other makes into dealer showrooms, and that was mostly plus business for the company.

A great change was taking place at American Motors. However, throughout 1970 the company was actively involved in merging together two great industrial enterprises—AMC and Jeep—and it was a very costly and time-consuming process. Just how expensive it was could be seen in the annual report to the stockholders, in which Roy D. Chapin Jr. revealed that the corporation took a loss for the year and that it was a big one; $56.2 million on sales of $1,089,787 crossing the billion dollar mark for the first time in years. Worldwide wholesale sales of passenger cars came in at 307,362 units, a slight drop from the prior year. Of that total, domestic wholesale car sales were 253,919 units, far short of the 300,000 domestic sales

Chapin had planned for. Worldwide Jeep sales of 93,171, which included government-destined vehicles from the General Products Division, fell about 6,000 units as well. AMC's working capital dropped to $76.2 million.

The reasons were clear enough. One large factor in the loss was the strike by the union at the beginning of the fiscal year, a loss of five weeks of production at a very critical point. But assimilating Jeep into AMC was the greatest cause of the loss. Still, a somber Roy Chapin Jr. emphasized that "Jeep can be and will be a major profit contributor to American Motors." By the end of fiscal 1970 Jeep as a whole was operating profitably in the company's fourth quarter.

For 1971 Chapin again budgeted for 300,000 domestic car sales plus a sizable increase in Jeep and overseas car sales. A new product group was created both to develop the Jeep vehicle lineup so it would be more in line with customer desires and to create new Jeep models. The man who earlier created the Ford GT 40, Roy Lunn, was put in charge of Jeep Engineering.

The year 1971 would go into the books as the busiest new product introduction schedule ever in AMC's history. The Gremlin returned with little change, but with better

Top: Mid-year in the 1970 model run, American Motors created a sensation when it introduced the first American subcompact car, the Gremlin. It hit the market six months ahead of GM and Ford and was an immediate hit.

Center: AMC's Gremlin offered two models initially: a two-seater priced at $1,879 and a four-seater priced at $1,959. The four-seat Gremlin came with a fold-down rear seat and hatchback rear window. The two-seat model had a fixed back window and no rear seat.

Bottom: The Ambassador for 1970 received the same styling changes as the Rebel—new roofline, new rear fenders, and new back panel. During this year AMC bought Holmes Foundry Limited, the Canadian company that cast its engine blocks.

Here is a proposal for a new AMX circa 1971. The stylist who drew this beautiful car is unknown, but the rear end design is particularly attractive.

In 1971, the AMX became the Javelin-AMX, still a separate model from the Javelin. This year a special Mark Donohue Javelin-AMX was offered with a spoiler supposedly designed by Donohue himself.

Although it was built on the Gremlin's 96-inch wheelbase, the car shown here was called the Hornet GT. It was a running prototype that featured different styling on each side. The side shown here has a conventional subcompact look, with full rear windows much like the later Chevy Chevette. Note the Hornet front fenders and unique grille.

The other side of the Hornet GT has more of a Grand Tourer look. The slope of the rear window and the shape of the rear side windows make this version particularly attractive. It's too bad this car wasn't produced as an upscale offering.

availability along with a sporty new option package called the X that was very appealing. Hornet returned as well, and it had two exciting new models this year—the SC/360 and the Sportabout.

The SC/360 was a compact muscle car designed to go fast and fly under the insurance companies' radar—not get hit with the ruinous performance car insurance surcharges that were killing the whole muscle car business. It was a Hornet two-door sedan with a 360 cid two-barrel V-8 under the hood, along with the usual performance goodies—stick shift, wide tires, and slot-style wheels. Optional was a more powerful four-barrel version of the 360 engine.

The new Sportabout was a compact station wagon with a twist: it had a fastback rear to give it sportier styling. Teague and his team were looking for a more European look, and they succeeded. No other domestic producer had anything like the Sportabout, and it was an instant hit. Sportabout was a premium model, available only in SST trim, and, because it commanded a much higher price than the sedans, it was immensely profitable for the company.

Javelin was all-new this year, styled in Chuck Mashigan's studio. It was a very bold design, with a sloping hood, deeply recessed grille, and bulging front fenders and rear quarter panels reminiscent of one of high-performance European exotic cars.

The classic AMX two-seater was gone. In a bid to reduce complexity in the factories and also save on tooling costs Bill Luneburg ordered that beginning in 1971 the AMX had to be built on the Javelin body. So AMX was renamed Javelin-AMX—it was still a separate model, not an option package as some people think—and it was fitted with enough styling changes to make it all work. Javelin-AMX got its own distinctive grille and stripes, along with a standard 360 cid V-8.

There was also a new midsize car, though it wasn't quite as new as it seemed. This year AMC designers restyled the Rebel's front end and lengthened the wheelbase, which, combined with the new rear styling done in 1970, yielded a car that looked all-new. Along with the new styling came the decision to rename it the Matador (an old Dodge name) and introduce it as an all-new car. The Matador wasn't simply a facelifted automobile, however; for 1971 AMC's new midsize car would have no base model, no stripped-down price leader. There would be a single Matador trim level, and it was rich—full carpeting, nice upholstery, and everything first class. "To make the other intermediates look stingy," said the company. The Matador lineup included a two-door hardtop, four-door sedan, and a station wagon. There was no longer a separate Machine model, but buyers could purchase its near equivalent by ordering a Matador hardtop with the optional Machine Go package, which could be had with either a 360 cid four-barrel V-8 or the new 401 cid V-8, good for 330 horsepower. Today, Matador Machines are extremely rare and very desirable.

In the Ambassador line the base four-door sedan model was dropped and a plush new top-line Brougham series debuted, available in hardtop, sedan, and wagon models.

In March 1971 AMC reorganized the General Products Division and renamed it AM General Corporation, with the talented Cruse Moss as president. Prior to joining AMC Moss had been a Kaiser Jeep executive. He went right to work on growing the new company, completing an agreement with Canadian bus maker Flyer Industries under which AM General would build and sell, under its own brand name, versions of the Canadian buses.

At Jeep engineers continued working to cut costs on each vehicle line while also improving quality and performance. To accomplish this they began to incorporate as many standard AMC parts and components into the Jeeps as possible, improving heating, defrosting, starting, etc. On senior Jeeps—Wagoneer and Gladiator trucks—Engineering worked to substitute AMC's V-8 engines for the GM V-8's that had been used. (The big Jeeps had already been using AMC sixes.) Over time Roy Lunn and his staff would completely reengineer the senior Jeep chassis, greatly improving it. Work was also preceding on a redesign of the Jeep Universal (CJ-5 and CJ-6) models so that AMC engines could

Top: During 1973, AMC's subsidiary AM General Corporation sold hundreds of its new transit buses. The Washington, D.C., Metropolitan Transit Authority placed an order for 620 buses, one of several large orders won by AM General.

Bottom: The 1971 Jeep Wagoneer offered three engines of American Motors design and manufacture: the 258cid V-6, the 304cid V-8, and the 245-hp 360cid V-8. The new, more powerful engines were introduced with no increase in price. Note the stylish Jeep script on the front fender.

replace the outdated four-cylinder and six-cylinder engines that were currently in use. Recognizing the amazing sales potential of special models, Jeep introduced three more limited production vehicles: the Jeep CJ-5 Renegade II, the Jeepster Commando SC-1, and the very desirable Hurst Jeepster. All of these packages consisted merely of appearance items; little to no performance parts were included. All three were powered by the Jeep V-6 engine.

It was during the 1971 model year that American Motors unveiled an advertising slogan for its passenger cars that was probably the best in their history. Its source was the marketing whizzes at ad agency Wells, Rich, Greene, and it asked a simple yet profound question: "If you had to compete with GM, Ford and Chrysler, what would you do?" That rhetorical query instantly made clear that AMC was a small company competing with the big boys, giving AMC the image of a gutsy underdog, fighting the good fight for America's consumers. After all, Americans love an unlikely competitor, the little guy who against all odds manages to beat the big guy. The new catchphrase also made people sit up and read the ad copy, which explained

Above: Jeep sales began to improve in 1971, but they were still very low and Jeep captured only 17 percent of the four-wheel-drive market. Dress-up options on this CJ-5 include chrome front bumper, wheel discs, hood side stripes, and whitewall tires.

Right: American Motors' advertising agency came up with a terrific slogan for 1971: "If you had to compete with GM, Ford and Chrysler, what would you do?"

exactly what AMC was doing, that is, bringing out the first American subcompact, the Gremlin, bringing out the only compact sports wagon on the market, making the Javelin so aggressive looking that it might scare off a few people, etc. It was a big hit.

Although American Motors was on the right road, it wasn't very far along it, and 1971 ended up being far less than the company's management had hoped for. Wholesale unit sales of cars in the United States came in at 251,142, a slight decrease and extremely disappointing in light of all the new products that had been introduced. Domestic Jeep sales, which now included only Jeep-brand vehicles sold for retail, not AM General's military and postal vehicles, were 35,455 units, about a 23 percent increase. Overseas volume for both Jeep and AMC was 58,000 units, a 9 percent increase. Working capital rose to $90 million. Meanwhile, AM General recorded sales of $261 million and had a healthy backlog of business valued at $340 million. The division no longer reported unit sales, only dollar volume.

Profit-wise, things were looking up. AMC reported a profit of $10.1 million for 1971, which was a $66 million turnaround from the prior year loss, though not a very large profit margin on a dollar volume of $1.2 billion. Chapin made no prediction of what level of unit sales he expected in 1972, but he did state that "our number one objective is to increase penetration in the passenger car market."

Model year 1972 didn't see any new cars introduced. After such a hefty product launch in 1971 the company needed to take a breather and put its house in order. It was time to focus on marketing too. In response to growing consumer complaints about the poor quality of U.S.-built cars, AMC decided to take bold steps to address those concerns. Under the direction of Group vice president-product Gerry Meyers, a thorough review was done of AMC cars and the decision was made to cut the number of models from 21

Top: AMC stylists were constantly looking for ways to make the Gremlin attractive to more buyers. One suggestion was this Gremlin D/L woody, with wood-grain side panels to give it a mini–station wagon look. This design was drawn by Eric Kugler. Note the slide-out bin in the rear.

Bottom: One of the most popular packages was the Gremlin X, which gave the little Gremlin a very sporty look. The appearance packages were very profitable for AMC For 1972, a fold-back sunroof was also available.

Right: Beginning in December of 1972, AMC dealers could order the Hornet Sportabout with the special "cane" exterior trim shown here for delivery in January of 1973. The cane-look could be ordered as a separate option or to substitute for the wood-grain side panels in the D/L package. When ordered separately, the cost was $94.50.

Center: The Javelin for 1973 sported a sharp new grille. During the calendar year, AMC dealers retailed 26,311 Javelin and Javelin AMX cars, a slight increase from 1972. For the year, the company retailed a total of 395,831 cars.

Bottom: Beginning in February 1972, Javelin SST models could be ordered with a special Cardin interior. The wild interior featured stripes on the door panels, seats, and headliner and was designed by Pierre Cardin and Vince Geraci of AMC Styling. A stylish fender badge was included.

to 15 to reduce complexity in the manufacturing plants. Dropped were the cheapest models; the two-passenger Gremlin, base model Hornets, base Javelin, and the base DPL model in the Ambassador line. The company was getting away from the stripped-down market and moving slightly upscale.

There was also a concerted effort to make the cars better. Quality standards were tightened up and the engineering department went through each model line to correct any weak spots and to increase durability and reliability. In all, more than a hundred engineering changes were made to the 1972 cars (along with a significant number to Jeep vehicles). One of these was long overdue: electric windshield wipers and washers were made standard equipment across the board, finally replacing the long-obsolete vacuum wipers and pump washers. Why AMC had stubbornly held on so long to such anachronisms is both unknown and unfathomable. The company also began using Chrysler-built automatic transmissions rather than the Borg-Warner units they'd been using for many years. The Chrysler transmissions were durable and needed less maintenance. A full synchromesh three-speed manual transmission was finally available too, though as an extra cost option.

To back up all these improvements and project an image as a consumerist company American Motors debuted a new warranty that eliminated all the legal mumbo jumbo and hidden restrictions and spelled out the new terms in plain language that anyone could understand: "When you buy a new 1972 car from an American Motors dealer, American Motors Corporation guarantees to you that, except for tires, it will pay for the repair or replacement of any part it supplies that is defective in material or workmanship." It was by far the strongest warranty on the market. The coverage was good for 12 months or 12,000 miles and reassured people that at least one car company was on their side. This new program was an immediate hit with consumers and was one of the factors involved in the sales increase that AMC would experience this year.

Advertising agency Wells, Rich, Greene did a bang-up job rolling out the new Buyer Protection Plan and on the regular advertising as well. One theme that especially resonated with people was an ad quoting one auto writer who had stated that "[t]he best built cars out of Detroit this year may come from Wisconsin. That's where American Motors makes 'em."

Top: Matador sales turned up sharply in 1973 as American Motors enjoyed one of the best years in its history. This Matador hardtop was a stylish family car able to hold six people and their luggage.

Left: *Car and Driver* magazine called the new Hornet Hatchback "the styling coup of 1973." It could be ordered with the sporty X package, as seen here, and offered optional denim-look interior trim.

So it was something of a shock when Roy Chapin Jr. fired the agency partway through the 1972 model year. He felt they weren't giving AMC enough attention. The ad agency picked to replace Wells, Rich, Greene was Cunningham and Walsh, a more traditional agency.

The auto industry this year was gravitating to using net horsepower ratings on engines rather than the standard gross horsepower ratings that had been in use for so long, so all AMC engines now had lower horsepower numbers. However, because emission standards were still fairly lenient the cars' power felt about the same, despite the lower power ratings.

The 1972 Gremlin had many mechanical improvements this year but the big news was the availability of a V-8 engine, something buyers had been asking for. Naturally, the 304 cid V-8 fit easily under the hood and transformed what was already the quickest economy car on the market into a real hotrod—one magazine called it a "poor man's Corvette." A sunroof was also now available.

The Hornet line returned for 1972 with a new sunroof option but minus the SC/360 model, which was discontinued after it sold only 784 units. But in its place was a new X sport package available on two-door sedans and Sportabout wagons, which could be ordered with either of the sixes, the 304 V-8, or new this year, the 360 cid two-barrel V-8 good for 175 net horsepower. The 360 V-8-equipped Hornets were real muscle cars, capable of surprising performance. A Rallye package was also available on Hornet two-doors.

In addition to the sporty X package the Sportabout also offered a D/L package that injected a bit of luxury into the wagon, and a Gucci package that provided an interior designed by fashion designer Dr. Aldo Gucci. The Gucci interior consisted of upholstery with Gucci's trademark green, ivory, and red stripes, matching door panels, and fender badges. This was the beginning of a series of Designer Interiors that American Motors would pioneer.

Javelin got a stylish new grille, a very handsome one, plus new optional stripes. Also introduced for Javelin were 10 new exterior colors. But the really big news on Javelin was

Left: Jeep CJ-5 for 1973. Jeep was proving to be a very profitable line of vehicles. Although American Motors had increased the production rate several times since 1970, the company still had trouble keeping up with demand.

Right: The Gremlin was a particularly successful product for AMC and brought in many buyers who were new to the company. During the 1973 calendar year, AMC dealers retailed 133,146 Gremlins.

the availability of a new interior designed by French fashion designer Pierre Cardin. It was a wild interior with stripes that ran across the seats and also the headliner. This year a special Trans-Am Victory package was offered on specially equipped Javelins to celebrate AMC winning Trans-Am for the second year in a row.

There was little change on the 1972 Matador line, aside from a new grille and minor trim differences. Sadly, the Machine Go package was discontinued. The Ambassador was the almost same story—all that was new were a new grille, standard bumper guards, and some molding changes.

Jeep products, on the other hand, experienced many changes for 1972. The CJ-5 and CJ-6 models, formerly known as the Jeep Universal, were redesigned with a longer wheelbase and longer front-end to be able to fit new engines under the hood. The entire body was retooled for easier assembly and higher quality. The former Jeep four and V-6 engines were dropped, with the stalwart AMC 232 cid six now standard equipment. Optional were a 258 cid six or a 304 V-8, the first time a V-8 had been offered in a CJ vehicle. AMC did something unusual when it redesigned the CJ series; it made the vehicles look the same as before. Gerry Meyers realized that the basic Jeep had a look and an appeal that were impossible to improve on, so he kept the little Jeep the same while making

it better. The Renegade model returned to the lineup, equipped now with the new V-8 engine. Unlike the earlier models the new Renegade didn't bear a Roman numeral—just the Renegade name.

Jeep Commando (the Jeepster name was no longer used) got a complete redesign of the front end, an unusual look that was completely different from the rest of the Jeep line. The styling is believed to have been done by Jim Angers, former Kaiser Jeep stylist. The Commando now rode a longer wheelbase and offered the same engine choices as the CJ. This year Commando offered a limited production SC-2 model Wagoneer and Jeep trucks came in for some mechanical improvements.

The automobile market was up in 1972, as it was in 1971, but this year AMC shared in the gains, with domestic passenger car sales coming in at 303,303 units, finally crossing that 300,000 unit mark that Chapin had been trying for years to reach. Jeep sold 46,000 units in the United States, said to be an all-time record and up 25 percent from the prior year. Unit

Top: Sales of the Gremlin were still very good in 1974, with retail sales of 104,871 units during the calendar year. Gremlin this year received a new body-color grille that gave the little economy champ a richer look.

Bottom: Realizing that they would eventually need to restyle the Gremlin AMC, management had its design staff work on different proposals. In 1974 one of these proposals was built to test public reaction. Called the Gremlin XP, its triangular rear side windows gave the Gremlin much-improved rear vision.

Top: In 1974 the Renegade sports package for the Jeep CJ-5 was made a regular production option, available all year long. The optional package was a large factor in the steadily increasing popularity of the Jeep.

Bottom: The Hornet Hatchback returned for 1974 with few changes. Despite its good looks and moderate price, the hatchback never achieved the popularity of, nor sold as well as, the more expensive Hornet Sportabout.

sales overseas were up slightly at a total of 59,251 cars and Jeep vehicles, so in all AMC sold more than 400,000 vehicles.

The 1972 annual report showed what those increased sales meant to AMC. Dollar volume reached a record $1.4 billion, almost double 1969's numbers. Net earnings from operations totaled $16,457,000, a significant gain on its own, but because of tax-loss carry-forwards the total net profit for the year was $30,157,000—the best since 1964. Working capital rocketed to $148 million. The company now had 1,951 passenger car dealers and about 1,500 Jeep dealers, with 540 dealers selling both lines.

At AM General dollar volume fell about $30 million, but the company was preparing to enter the transit bus field and the outlook for the future was good.

American Motors entered the 1973 model year brimming with confidence— and why not? It had a strong product lineup and plenty of momentum. Demand for the Gremlin was growing by leaps and bounds, and a new Levi's interior trim was available. It gave buyers the look and feel of denim upholstery and trim but was actually a spun nylon fabric, necessary to meet fire safety and wear standards. The Hornet was catching on and this year got new front-end styling and also had a new model to show—the Hornet Hatchback. The hatchback featured fastback styling that was very attractive, and gave the Hornet a look almost as sporty as a pony car. The car offered great utility as well, with a fold-down rear seat and lift-up rear hatch. Bucket seats were available and so was a sporty X package. And both Gremlin and Hornet got a new three-speed synchromesh transmission as standard equipment, finally doing away with the old nonsynchromesh first gear.

Javelin got a new recessed grille this year, and both Javelin and Javelin AMX received a smooth-roof design. Matador and Ambassador likewise got new grilles, new interior colors plus new trim combinations.

Also for 1973 the Ambassador line was trimmed to just a single series—Brougham—in two-door hardtop, four-door sedan, and station wagon models.

Jeep sales were on fire, and the company kept it stoked with an array of product improvements. Foremost was an intensified approach to quality. As production kept being increased at Jeep some shortcuts and quality lapses had occurred and this year AMC added more inspectors to help improve the way the vehicles were built.

Jeep trucks got new double-wall pickup boxes, a new tailgate, and improved clutch linkage. Jeep CJ also saw many enhancements and regular availability of the Renegade model, which was offered beginning in January 1973.

The senior line Jeeps, Wagoneer and Truck, debuted a revolutionary new four-wheel-drive system called Quadra-Trac. With Quadra-Trac the four-wheel-drive shift lever and free-wheeling front hubs were eliminated. The system offered full-time four-wheel drive, which could be used on any type of surface, including hard, dry pavement where other four-wheel drives had to be disengaged to prevent axle damage. It was a groundbreaking

The big AMC product news for 1974 was the all-new Matador coupe. Built on a 114-inch wheelbase, the stylish coupe could be ordered with an optional X sport appearance package, which could be backed up by optional V-8 engines up to a 401cid with four-barrel carburetor. Matador retail sales climbed almost 50 percent in 1974.

The Matador four-door sedan and station wagon models were mostly carry-over for 1974, though they did get an extended hood and an unusual-looking new grille. AMC dealers retailed more than 77,000 Matadors for the year.

improvement because it eliminated the last complaint about four-wheel drive, that is, having to deal with shift levers and hubs and having to shift in and out of four-wheel drive. Everything was now automatic and traction was superb. Jeep advertising boasted, "Someday every four-wheel drive vehicle may have a system like it. Jeep has it now." Today most SUV's do indeed offer a fulltime system, and so do many cars. In January 1973 AMC acquired Mercury Plastics Company of Mt. Clemens, Michigan, adding it to their growing plastics group. During the year the company also purchased a plant in northern Wisconsin and formed Coleman Products Company to produce wiring harnesses for AMC vehicles. It was another step in Roy Chapin Jr.'s program to produce in-house more of the parts that went into his cars and Jeeps.

During the year the company's new transit bus, built by AM General, was brought to market and scored an order for 620 buses for the Washington D.C. Metropolitan Transit Authority. The company also worked on orders for postal vehicles. The division's total backlog of orders stood at $210 million.

The U.S. auto industry enjoyed another good year in 1973, with sales up almost 10 percent over 1972. But AMC managed to outpace the industry, reporting retail sales for the calendar year that were about 30 percent higher. In the annual report AMC reported U.S. passenger car sales of 380,000 units from September 1 to October 31. The report didn't specify if that was retail sales or wholesale, but later statements make it appear that the 380,000 were retail sales. That was the highest level in nine years. Jeep vehicle sales came in at 67,000 units in the United States, a huge increase from 1972. Unit sales of passenger cars and Jeep vehicles in Canada and overseas markets were 67,374, up roughly 14 percent. In total AMC sold more than 514,000 vehicles in fiscal 1973 (not counting AM General), which was more than 100,000 units more than 1972. It was also the highest total unit sales in AMC history to that point.

The company recorded an operating profit of $44.5 million, the best since 1960 and, even better, a net profit (after adding in tax loss carry-forwards) of $85,976,000 for 1973, nearly three times the 1972 number and a new record. Working capital climbed to $178,952,000.

Demand for AMC cars was so great that the company decided that rather than shut down for two weeks for model changeover as they normally would, this year they would have a running model change, in which the assembly line keeps pumping out cars, with the 1974 model changes phased in as the line kept moving.

The surprising success after so many years of struggle certainly must have felt good to AMC's management, but unfortunately it created a false sense of security within them. There were problems staring American Motors in the face and there were more on the way. In October 1973 OPEC (the Organization of Petroleum Exporting Countries) decided to impose an oil embargo on the United States in punishment for America's support of Israel. It created a crisis in gasoline supply. The effects hit the auto industry hard. In addition, the U.S. economy was being hurt by an on-going bear market that saw declines in the stock market that lasted from the beginning of 1973 to the end of 1974. In two years the U.S. economy would slow from 7.2 percent real GDP growth to a 2.1 percent contraction, while inflation (by CPI) jumped from 3.4 percent in 1972 to 12.3 percent in 1974. The result could be guessed at. Retail automobile sales began to drop toward the end of 1973, though initially it hit only the Big Three makes, whereas AMC sales continued to climb. As AMC entered the 1974 model year management felt confident that sales would continue to rise there because, they felt, AMC had the right products (small cars) for the market. The target Chapin and Luneburg set for U.S. unit car sales in 1974 was well over 400,000 cars.

Another problem at AMC was that the company was not increasing Jeep production fast enough. In 1973 Jeep had a 17 percent share of the four-wheel-drive market, down from more than 20 percent it held in the late 1960s, and it was clear that Jeep could gain a much larger share if it would only produce more vehicles. But management consistently underestimated the wildly growing four-wheel-drive market so although it was selling more Jeeps every year and making huge profits on them, the raw truth is that AMC could have done even better.

Perhaps the most damaging effect of AMC's most recent success was that it encouraged company product planners to abandon AMC's time-honored strategy of using one or two basic bodies to produce several different models and using those

Top: For its final year of production the Ambassador line was cut to just two models, the Brougham four-door sedan and Brougham station wagon. Both received styling changes that included a longer hood and new grille. In its final year 16,428 Ambassadors were retailed.

Bottom: The 1974 Javelin AMX came with bumper guards, front disc brakes, and a sport steering wheel as standard equipment. This year the standard engine was a 304cid V-8, in recognition of soaring fuel prices and car insurance surcharges.

Top: The big product news at Jeep for 1974 was the introduction of the new Cherokee. Though based on the Wagoneer body, the Cherokee appealed to a younger audience. In this photo, wearing red, white, and blue headdresses, we see AMC president Bill Luneburg (left) and chairman Roy D. Chapin Jr. (right). Before using the Cherokee name, company leaders consulted with the Cherokee people.

Bottom: AMC and Jeep dealers were given the opportunity in 1974 to order a specially equipped Jeep J-10 pickup for use as a parts and service vehicle. Included on the limited edition truck was the exclusive red, white, and blue paint scheme seen here, along with the cargo cap with AMC logo.

bodies for several years. At the time, the Hornet, Gremlin, and Sportabout shared one basic body and Matador and Ambassador shared another. It had been this way since 1970 for Hornet and Gremlin, and 1967 for Rebel/Matador/Ambassador. The shared-body idea was a strategy set down by George Romney back in AMC's earlier days to reduce tooling costs dramatically, thereby offsetting some of the Big Three's volume advantage. It began with the 1956 Rambler and was perfected in the 1963–1964 products. As the company found to its everlasting sorrow, when Roy Abernethy got away from that strategy and instead tried to match the Big Three car for car the company soon spent itself into financial trouble—the "dark days of 1967." Now, as could be seen in the annual report, the company product planners had two new cars planned, one for 1974, the other for 1975; neither would share a body with any other product and because of that capital expenses for the next two years were going to exceed $100 million annually. That was an incredible amount of money for a small automaker like AMC, but so long as the company kept earning big profits it would be able to handle the costs. However, if sales began to slide and profits dropped, it could put AMC into serious financial troubles. It was an old fact about the auto industry: when things were good you could make a lot of money in it, but when things were bad the losses could be enormous simply because the nature of the industry is that it deals in very large numbers. To an outsider it appeared that AMC management was getting a bit reckless with money.

The incredible demand for Hornet and Gremlin also caused some potential new products to be cancelled or delayed. One of them was a sporty hatchback coupe on a 96-inch wheelbase called the Hornet GT. Another was a small pickup truck built on a Hornet two-door chassis, called the Cowboy. Even a Gremlin pickup had been proposed—a rendering of it survives.

American Motors had an all-new Matador coupe to sell in 1974. It was an attractive intermediate-size coupe with tunneled headlamps, a sloping grille, and a fastback rear—apparently product planners felt that although large fastback coupes had never sold very well in America, this one would. At the time, buyers were in love with inter-mediate-size coupes, which were among the hottest selling cars on the market. But what really got buyers' juices flowing were the formal rooflines, padded vinyl half-top, and opera windows seen on most of the competition. Ford had them, Chevy had them, Plymouth had them, Buick, Olds and Chrysler had them, Dodge had them, and so did Mercury. They all had them because that was what was selling. The Matador coupe, however, didn't offer a formal roof-line, padded top or opera windows. So the Matador was different from the others right from the start

Top: At the start of the 1974 model year, Gremlin sales were very strong and the assembly line struggled to meet the demand. In this photo we see completed Gremlin bodies coming down the line.

Left: AMC's subsidiary company AM General, already the world's largest manufacturer of tactical vehicles, was a major producer of postal vehicles as well. Besides the ubiquitous Jeep Dispatcher DJ-5, the company also produced this ½-ton delivery van for the U.S. Postal Service.

The new Matador rode a shorter 114-inch wheelbase and was available in coupe style only; regular coupe, Brougham coupe, and a very sporty Matador X coupe. Prices began at just less than $3,000, so they were well-priced. Matador offered engines that ranged from the base 232 cid six up to the mighty 401 cid V-8. The option list was long and comprehensive. One very impressive new option was the Oleg Cassini interior trim, designed by the great fashion designer who once counted Jackie Kennedy among his clients. With the Cassini package, the cloth upholstery, door panel inserts, headliner, and sun visors came in jet black accented by copper floor carpeting and copper details on the seats, grille, and elsewhere. The Matador sedan and station wagon were carryover models, with relatively minor changes. They got a new grille and all-new instrument panel.

The Ambassador line returned with just two models—Brougham sedan and Brougham station wagon, both sporting attractive new grilles. The Ambassador two-door hardtop was dropped. It had shared its body with the Matador hardtop, which was now replaced by the Matador coupe. Apparently AMC never considered the possibility of creating an Ambassador coupe on the Matador coupe body. That's too bad, because by producing an Ambassador coupe with a formal roofline they would have had something with great sales potential, a personal luxury midsize car. American Motors had been whittling down the Ambassador lineup year by year, sales had suffered as a result, and this was to be its last year. A new formal coupe model would certainly have revitalized Ambassador. Put it down as another missed opportunity.

Top: AM General Corporation also supplied Canada with right-hand-drive delivery vehicles, including this DJ-5C Dispatcher, which wears the colors of the Canadian Postal Service.

Bottom: After AM General formed a joint agreement with battery-maker Gould Incorporated, the two companies worked to develop and produce an electric-powered delivery vehicle for the U.S. Postal Service. The Postal Service awarded the company a $2 million contract for 350 battery-electric DJ-5E Dispatcher vehicles.

For 1974 Gremlin got some minor restyling: a new grille, new lower back panel and quarter panels that, despite being restyled, looked about the same as before. There was a new Rallye-Pac option available for the Gremlin X, which included full instrumentation, tachometer, Levi's interior trim, a front sway bar, and a leather-wrapped steering wheel. The 1974 Hornet lineup saw little change, as did the Javelin and Javelin-AMX. The latter now had disc brakes as standard equipment.

Jeep had big news for 1974. The slow-selling Commando was replaced by a new model called the Cherokee, which had much better sales potential. The market for large, comfy SUVs was exploding, and Jeep now had a solid entry to compete against Chevy Blazer and Ford Bronco. Tooling costs were minimal because the new Cherokee was essentially a two-door Jeep Wagoneer with sporty trim. It was available in a stripped-down model or in sporty Cherokee S trim, which soon became the volume model. Like the other big Jeeps the Cherokee could be ordered with the revolutionary Quadra-Trac

system. Although AMC management couldn't know it, in time the new Cherokee would become one of the company's most iconic vehicles and among its strongest profit-makers.

The CJ-5 model had many improvements and this year, for the first time, the Renegade package was available as a regular production option all year long. The company still had a ways to go in civilizing the CJ; it didn't offer a radio, automatic transmission, or air conditioning. The Jeep Wagoneer, on the other hand, now came standard with Quadra-Trac and automatic transmission.

The first quarter of 1974 went well, with record dollar volume, a decent profit, and retail domestic car sales of 100,000, the best in nine years. Demand for the Gremlin and Hornet was outpacing production, so the company was making the necessary changes throughout its system to produce more electrical wiring, plastics, interior trim, engines, etc. so they could then raise car production. Roy Chapin Jr. said he could sell more than 418,000 cars in the United States if he could only get the components. Six-cylinder engines were in short supply, and the company was investigating putting the old Jeep V-6 back in production to supply Jeep initially but also to install in AMC cars at some future date. The company was also seriously considering building another big assembly plant to supplement the Kenosha and Brampton, Ontario, plants. Where they would construct it was unsaid, but it would be designed to build 250,000 cars per year. During the year AMC acquired a second plant to manufacture wiring harnesses in Iron River, Michigan. The company also acquired a new million-square-foot stamping plant in South Charleston, West Virginia, with enough capacity to serve most of the company's needs for the foreseeable future. All this, of course, cost money and took a bit of time, but in the meanwhile management

An interesting concept car first shown in 1974 was this sleek Gremlin G-II. The G-II mated Hornet front fenders with a Gremlin body that was modified by giving it a fastback roof and full lift-back hatch. The G-II design eventually evolved into the AMC Spirit Liftback.

planned to sell more than 600,000 cars and Jeeps in the current year. A second shift was phased in at Kenosha as AMC's total North America work force rose to 32,300.

In November 1973 the company announced a new special edition Matador D/L package. It was a good-looking design, with a new padded vinyl roof featuring opera windows, plus a long list of extras like a 360 V-8, power steering and brakes, spoke style wheels, and more. Why the company didn't make it a regular production model is a mystery.

The company announced in February that it would pay a 10-cent semiannual dividend on its stock. What was significant about this was that it was the first dividend AMC had paid out since 1965.

In March 1974 Evart Plastics announced it was completing a $5 million expansion program to raise its output by one-third, creating 200 new jobs in the process.

During the year AMC also signed agreements with a Korean company to form a new company called Shinjin Jeep Company to build Jeeps in Korea and with another company to

Another interesting concept car from 1974 was the Voyageur, which featured Hornet front fenders, a unique grille, cane work side panels and rear panel, and a slide-out "Grem-Bin" designed to make loading easier. This vehicle survives today.

assemble Jeeps in the Philippines. Company officials were trying to make a deal for Jeep assembly in Australia as well.

American Motors Corporation entered a new market in 1974 with the purchase of Wheel Horse Products of South Bend, Indiana, a leading maker of gasoline-powered lawn and garden tractors. Wheel Horse soon expanded its business by acquiring General Electric's outdoor power equipment operation, which offered a line of battery-powered lawn and garden tractors.

During the year Buick, in need of a fuel-efficient engine for its cars, approached AMC about buying the old Kaiser V6 engine line, which originally had been designed and built by Buick. Having decided to increase production of its own engines, AMC was happy to sell it to them.

By the third quarter of the 1974 fiscal year AMC sales were still strong but profits were starting to decline. The cause was primarily that the company's costs were skyrocketing because of the rampant inflation then extant, along with a general shortage of raw materials that was driving up prices. Although the company increased the price of its cars during the year it was not enough to offset the higher costs. Profit margins were being squeezed.

All year long saw a great deal of turmoil in the auto industry, as sales at the Big Three plummeted, and those companies began to lay off thousands of workers. AMC, on the other hand, was adding employees as it ramped up production. For once the company was making good money but, human nature being what it is, the union soon decided that its members needed much more than AMC was giving them. In the fourth quarter, September, right at the end of the company's fiscal year and during its buildup for the 1975 new car introduction the union once again called a strike, which hit both the Kenosha and Brampton plants. Although it was eventually settled, it once again killed the momentum of the new car rollout, cost the company $13 million in lost profits, and turned an expected fourth quarter profit into a loss. The greed and shortsightedness of the militant local union in Kenosha was a sorry fact, and apparently they hadn't learned anything from the demise of Studebaker, a car company that was killed by similar union tactics.

Looked at on an entire year basis, 1974 was good. Record sales of more than $2 billion were reported. Domestic passenger car retail unit sales came in at 385,000, 5,000 more than the prior year but below the 400,000-plus that Chapin had hoped for—blame the union for that. Wholesale sales were 379,000 units. Jeep sales in the United States were strong at 72,000 units. International sales totaled a whopping 95,794 cars and Jeeps, and the overseas dealers were hollering for more. Sales in Canada set a new record for both cars and Jeeps. So in total the company had produced 552,000 vehicles, another record, not the 600,000 they'd hoped for but a very good number regardless. Net profits were $27,546,000, quite a drop from the prior year but AMC had already used up the last of its tax-loss carry-forwards so it

had to pay more than $14 million in taxes. Working capital fell to $157 million. Market share in passenger cars was 4.7 percent, up nearly a point. The company's plastics group had sales of almost $60 million.

Chapin claimed that under more ordinary circumstances the company would have made record profits to go along with the record sales. He talked about several things that held down earnings, such as rising expenses and the strike. But the company also took a big hit in the pocketbook by a $9 million loss recorded at AM General, the second year in a row that division had lost money. The cause both times was the effort to get AM General in the bus-building business. Startup and ongoing costs were much higher than anticipated.

In the 1974 annual report Roy D. Chapin Jr. mentioned that the company would introduce an all-new small car in March 1975 called the Pacer. It was going to a different sort of car, he said, and it was meant to be the first of a range of all-new small cars that the company was developing. Pacer, said Chapin, "will demonstrate how we intend to pursue our philosophy of difference in the years ahead. . . . It is bold, different, and unique in concept." The Pacer was certainly going to be all that. It was also destined to be the last all-new AMC car that the company would introduce.

Top: Another styling study, this one not shown to the public, was the "Hellcat," a mock-up of a possible sporty car to replace the Javelin and AMX later in the decade. Note the "Hellcat" script on the door and "401" badge on the front fender.

Bottom: This Amigo concept was an early proposal for what became the 1975 Pacer. The basic body looks similar to the production car except that the doors are almost normal size—not the huge, heavy doors used on the Pacer. In addition, the front end is much smaller.

Predating the Matador coupe project was this full-sized mock up of a possible Ambassador two-door hardtop. Note how the grille resembles the production 1974 Matador. The photo is dated 1970.

1975–1977
THE GAME CHANGES

FOR THE 1975 MODEL YEAR the assembly line at American Motors once again was doing a rolling changeover to the new models, again so that they wouldn't need to halt the assembly line and thereby lose some car production.

Fuel economy was on everyone's mind, and AMC, lacking a four-cylinder engine, tried hard to improve the gas mileage of its sixes. The average fuel economy of AMC cars was up 17 percent this year, and in tests the company found that the Gremlin equipped with the 258 cid six ranked highest of all AMC cars in fuel economy. It makes one wonder why they didn't make the big six standard equipment, which would have made customers a lot happier. Statistics showed that 89 percent of Gremlin buyers were new to AMC, an astounding conquest rate.

AMC's U.S. dealer network was in fine shape. Profits were way up, and there were 179 dealers who sold more than 500 cars a year, compared with just 50 five years earlier. The average sales rate per dealer (the number of cars retailed by the dealers) had doubled over the prior four years, and AMC dealers once again ranked third in the industry in sales per dealer, a remarkable feat and clear evidence of the value of an AMC franchise.

Roy D. Chapin Jr. said that for 1975 the emphasis would be on basic quality and value rather than exterior change, despite the fact that Gremlin and Hornet were well overdue for a restyling—the duo had been given only minor appearance changes in the six years since their introduction. Production of more than 400,000 AMC cars was scheduled for the year.

Top: This is another full-size mock-up, this time of a proposed 1975 Ambassador four-door sedan. This photo is dated 1970, which means it was probably meant to go into production in either 1972 or 1973.

Bottom: The legendary race driver Mark Donohue of Newtown Square, Pennsylvania, drove this Penske-prepared Matador coupe in NASCAR racing. The engine was a 366-cubic-inch version of the AMC 360 V-8 and was prepared by Traco Engineering.

Gremlin and Hornet returned for 1975 with little new to attract buyers. At the time the 1975 cars were being planned the duo had been selling like mad, so the decision was made to not do any styling changes this year. The Gremlin and Hornet were good solid cars, but there was no getting away from the fact that they were beginning to look stale. Unfortunately, during 1975 the auto industry was going through a severe sales slump, and both Gremlin and Hornet would have benefited greatly with some new styling and new features. They also would have benefited from a four-speed transmission, which essentially all of AMC's competitors had. AMC didn't offer one even as an option, a serious mistake; young people wanted "four-on-the-floor." Toyota was beginning to offer five-speed transmissions, so AMC was really falling behind, equipment-wise.

The same was true of the aging Matador sedan and wagon. They received minimal changes for 1975. The coupe likewise got only minor changes, but the coupe at least was still fresh and exciting so it shouldn't have mattered. For some reason management cut the number of Matador coupe models to just one, as the X and Brougham became option packages instead of distinct models. The Matador line now constituted the largest cars built by AMC—the stalwart Ambassador was dropped, as were the Javelin and Javelin-AMX. The big 401 cid V-8 was dropped as well from the passenger car, in light of increasingly tough emissions and fuel economy mandates. It was still available on the senior Jeeps.

The cars were well-priced, though inflation had taken its toll. The Gremlin was now $2,798 base price, up nearly 50 percent from its 1970 price. Hornet started at $3,074 for a two-door sedan. Matador prices began at $3,446.

Like the AMC passenger cars the Jeep line for 1975 was carryover, with only minor appearance and mechanical enhancements.

Left: Another formidable contender in performance circles was Wally Booth, an outstanding driver who raced this Hornet Hatchback and also campaigned a Gremlin. Booth's Hornet carried a 355 cid destroked version of the AMC 360 V-8.

Below: This is an early proposal by Norbert Ostrowsi for the car that became the Pacer. Although very attractive, this idea was not used because the company was searching for a more radical design.

Bottom: For 1975 AMC debuted a special Touring option for the Hornet station wagon, which added soft-touch vinyl upholstery, painted wheel covers, and special trim. Hornet wagons generally accounted for about 40 percent of Hornet sales.

Hornet Hatchback with "X" Package

Hornet 4-Door Sedan with "D/L" Package

Hornet Sportabout with "Touring" Package

Matador "X" Coupe

Matador "Brougham" Sedan

Matador "Brougham" Wagon

Three popular Hornet models for 1975 were the Hatchback, four-door sedan, and station wagon. Sales volume-wise American Motors had an off year in 1975, with unit sales of cars down nearly 90,000 units. The company posted a loss of $27.5 million that year.

With the demise of the Ambassador the Matador lineup became the largest cars offered by AMC in 1975. The senior line offered a coupe, four-door sedan, and station wagon model.

As with the Gremlin, Hornet, and Matador, management assumed the Jeep CJ, Cherokee, trucks, and Wagoneer would continue to sell well without any noticeable styling changes. There were, however, mechanical improvements; CJs got a new frame, new wiring harness and a Levi's trim option. Standard equipment was upgraded to include the passenger front seat; prior to this it had been an extra-cost option. The truck line had a new Pioneer trim package. Early in the year Jeep introduced a new Cherokee Chief package on a new wide-wheel version of the two-door Cherokee body. Cherokee Chief was a very sporty vehicle with wider axles, white spoke wheels, fender flares, and fat tires. It was an immediate success and would in time become the most popular Cherokee model.

Sales at AMC dealers were still strong as the 1975 model year opened in September 1974 although a weak economy and high inflation had put a damper on retail sales at nearly every other automaker. The industry slump that began during the third quarter of 1973 was continuing into 1975. Since 1973 industry sales had dropped by more than 3.5 million units, the sharpest drop-off since the Depression. But American Motors had been swimming against the tide, racking up great sales in 1973 and 1974. However, AMC did suffer an operating loss of $10.4 million (before taxes and credits) for the first quarter. The net loss was $5.58 million. Part of the problem was continually rising material costs plus higher costs for labor. Another big part of the problem was that the union struck—again—in the most critical quarter of the year.

Sales soon began to droop, in line with the industry. But help was on the way. Beginning February 28, 1975, AMC dealers could start retailing the all-new small car that had been in development since 1971—the Pacer.

The Pacer was a different sort of small car, and nothing like it had ever been offered anywhere. It was virtually a symbol of management's "Philosophy of Difference." When AMC management created that philosophy they had spoken about its potential rewards—and also expressed a willingness to assume the risks of innovation. With the Pacer they would have both.

Essentially, the Pacer was a large small car. It rode a 100-inch wheelbase, same as the original 1950 Rambler, and measured a mere 171.5 inches long, about 2 inches longer than the subcompact Gremlin. But the Pacer was roomier than all other compacts and subcompacts because class-leading interior space had been one of the design criteria behind it, and because the Pacer was wider than any other small car. The result yielded an interior that was as roomy as many intermediate cars.

The Pacer's styling was impressive, breaking away from conventional shapes and proportions. Created by teams headed by Chuck Mashigan and Bob Nixon, the Pacer as they designed it was a fleet, athletic-looking small car. Mockups were shown to small groups to test reactions to the unusual styling and the result was very positive—the Pacer got rave reviews. But

Top: Base price of the Gremlin for 1975 was $2,798, over $900 more than the original base two-seater had cost, and the car didn't look all that much different, though many improvements had been made through the years. The X sport package was a popular option.

Bottom: Jeep CJ-5 for 1975. Jeep sales had been growing by leaps and bounds ever since AMC bought that company. Worldwide Jeep sales were up again in 1975, though they declined slightly in the United States.

the Pacer came to market considerably bulked up after company lawyers insisted that, because future crash and safety standards were at that point unknown, the Pacer must have additional structural steel to make it able to pass any imaginable standard that might come. That decision made the Pacer one of the safest cars on the road, but when combined with the excessive width it also made it quite heavy. Although it was about the size of a Gremlin and was powered by the same engine, the Pacer was about 350 pounds heavier. This didn't seem to be a problem initially, but it would become one in time.

Originally, the Pacer was to have been powered by a General Motors–supplied Wankel rotary engine; the engine of the future, everyone called it after Mazda introduced its rotary models a few years earlier. Gerry Meyers had made a deal with GM president Ed Cole for sufficient engines for the high production that was planned for Pacer. The car would have been much lighter with the rotary, but the deal fell through when GM decided, at virtually the last moment, not to go through with its rotary engine program, citing fuel economy concerns with the new engine. The Pacer, meanwhile, was nearly ready for production. A stunned Gerry Meyers did the only thing he could do at that point—he ordered his engineers to

Here we see four celebrated AMC racers: left to right, Mark Donohue, Shirley Shahan, Roger Penske, and H. L. Shahan.

MARK DONAHUE   SHIRLEY SHAHAN   ROGER PENSKE   H.L. SHAHAN

shoehorn the AMC six under the Pacer's low hood. In the end they had to let the back two cylinders protrude into the passenger compartment, though interior designers did a good job restyling the instrument panel so that it wasn't so obvious. But the new engine added weight, which meant springs, shocks, and many other components had to be made stronger, which added more weight. A heavier transmission had to be fitted along with a heavier rear axle. By the time the lawyers' demand for a stronger body was fulfilled the Pacer weighed more than 3,000 pounds stripped. Air conditioning and automatic transmission and other options added a good deal more weight, taxing the little six engine's ability to deliver good gas mileage and performance.

Since the Pacer was not going to be the rotary-engine car of the future but rather an overweight compact, AMC decided to focus on its roominess, calling it the "first wide small car." The company came up with ways to emphasize Pacer's interior space, including holding a 6-foot-long submarine sandwich in the back seat.

Although the Pacer was being introduced at a bad time, smack in the middle of a tough recession, Roy D. Chapin Jr. set a sales goal of 80,000 units in the first year: "I think this car can pull us out of the slump

ahead of the industry." He felt that the Pacer would draw people into showrooms and help increase sales of his other cars as well. The new car was launched with preview showings, called "Pacer to People" meetings, in major cities across the country. It found instant acceptance everywhere it was shown. People liked the Pacer's overall size, its roomy interior, and its generous use of glass; in fact the Pacer had more glass area than any other car on the market save the biggest Cadillac. And they loved its styling, seeing it as fresh and exciting. It was designed to correct all the things that people disliked about small cars by having an outstanding ride, good handling, exceptional visibility, and plenty of interior space for people and packages.

But the Pacer had its own body/chassis, not shared with any other AMC product, and that is a very costly approach to the car business. The Matador coupe had one body, the sedan and wagon another, and the Hornet and Gremlin still another, so the Pacer was the fourth separate body shell in a four-name lineup of cars. AMC had made itself successful by building cars on shared bodies; it cut tooling costs by a large percentage. Now it was going in the opposite direction, just as it had in 1965. The company had a lot of money riding on the Pacer's success.

Top: One idea looked into during the early 1970s was the possibility of adding a small sporty pickup truck to the line. It would have entered production around 1974–1975 if approved. This design sketch illustrates what a Gremlin pickup could look like.

Bottom: This is the Pacer as it was originally conceived; tighter, fleeter, and much lighter. This was called the Dallas car, so-named because it was first shown in Dallas, Texas, to a selected group of ordinary people to judge how its radical design would be accepted by the public. The response was overwhelmingly positive, encouraging AMC to go ahead with the project.

The new car hit the market like a whirlwind. Thousands upon thousands of people flocked to showrooms to see the futuristic Pacer. And it sold like nickel cigars. It seemed as though everybody in America wanted one. The car was clearly a hit. Within just a few weeks Chapin raised his estimate of sales to 95,000 and boosted Pacer production by 32 percent. By May AMC was grabbing 8.5 percent of the small car market.

At a base of $3,299 the Pacer was priced higher than the larger Hornet and was pitched as a premium small car—just as it should have been. However, the base car was not well-equipped at all. It came with an old-fashioned bench front seat, three-speed manual transmission with a column shifter, skinny bias ply tires, and cheap door trim. AMC should have upgraded the car to meet its price point.

The press loved the new Pacer. It was on the cover of *Car and Driver*, *Small Cars*, and *Motor Trend* magazines and was the subject of literally hundreds of articles around the globe. One headline read, "Suddenly its 1980!"

But because it had its own body, bringing the Pacer to market cost the company $60 million in tooling cost, its largest product investment ever. That expense, along with inflation-driven rising costs and other problems, caused AMC to report a big loss in the second quarter, some $47.3 million this time, bringing the six month loss to $57.8 million. Besides the tooling costs, Jeep sales were down for the first six months, and although the Pacer was on fire, the other AMC cars were not selling well at all. Total passenger cars sales were poor, which was dragging down the bottom line. However, Roy D. Chapin Jr. expected the second half of the year to be profitable.

By the third quarter of 1975 AMC was back to earning profits, and sales of the Pacer were so hot it was making company executives giddy—they hadn't had so successful a car since the Rambler's best days. The company had a flood of orders and the dealers were reporting the heaviest floor traffic in a decade. The Pacer had become the most successful first year car ever introduced by AMC. Chapin told the shareholders he was boosting production

Above: This is the rear view of the Dallas car. Note the plain, straight bumper and rear taillamps that appear to be decals.

Right: Here we see the four great designers who were most responsible for the Pacer program: left to right is Chuck Mashigan, Vince Geraci, Dick Teague, and Bob Nixon.

again and that by September the annual production rate on the Pacer would be nearly 184,000 cars!

Although the company was now operating profitably, it wasn't earning enough to wipe out the losses piled up in the first six months, so AMC ended up reporting a loss for the 1975 fiscal year. The operating loss was $35.5 million on dollar volume of $1,893,138,000, but tax credits reduced this to a net loss of $27.5 million for the year—equal to the prior year's net profit. Working capital fell to $129 million. A large part of the blame goes to poor car sales; dealers retailed 296,000 AMC cars in the United States, down from 385,000 the year before. In contrast, Jeep wholesale sales fell only 500 units, to 69,300. Wholesale car sales were 319,107 compared with 379,107 the year before. Because wholesale sales were down 60,000 units but retail sales were down 91,000 units, that meant that dealer inventories were higher than before. Chapin was hoping that Pacer sales would carry the company through the coming year, as sales of the other cars were very weak.

Despite the loss there was some good news. Sales of cars and Jeeps outside the United States were a record 106,366, though about 40,000 of that total represented sales in Canada, which AMC usually didn't include in international sales totals. Altogether the company sold 495,282 vehicles, a pretty good volume. During the year the 500,000th Gremlin was produced, along with the 400,000th Jeep built by AMC. AM General, buoyed by a massive 113 percent increase in sales, managed to earn a tiny profit of $188,000 on dollar volume of $339.3 million. And it was finally getting the bus business in order—it produced its 1,000th bus early in the year and its 2,000th that October. A new second-generation bus design would go into production in 1976. AMC's plastic's group operated profitably for the year, as did its Wheel Horse division. Also in 1975 the company signed up 90 new AMC dealers and 195 new Jeep dealers.

Interesting news was that AMC reached an agreement to purchase from Volkswagen's Audi division the design and tooling for a new four-cylinder engine. Initially AMC would

Top: The AMC Pacer was the most successful first-year car in AMC history, but its sales trajectory was like a rocket launch—straight up and then straight down. The overwhelming popularity of the car in the first six months leaves many to wonder why it peaked early and then went into a steady falloff in sales.

Bottom: Another possibility for sale in the mid-1970s was a pickup based on the Hornet. In 1971 AMC stylists created this fiberglass mock-up of a possible Hornet pickup dubbed the Cowboy. The project manager was Jim Alexander and two prototypes were actually built, one with a six-cylinder engine, the other with a 360 V-8. The V-8 truck still survives. The grille design shown here was not used.

import built-up engines for installation in some of its cars, but would transition to assembling and later, manufacturing the engines at a new plant in Richmond, Indiana it would purchase.

When the 1976 model year opened it was clear to even a casual observer that AMC was pinning most of its hopes on the Pacer. The Gremlin—now in its seventh year on the market— got very little in the way of appearance changes except for a new grille, and the lack of change was more than a shame. The refusal to restyle the Gremlin was costing AMC many sales because the design was old. Any owner of a 1970 or 1971 Gremlin who wanted to buy a new one could see that it was essentially the same car; it just cost a lot more. Ditto the Hornet; it received only minor interior and exterior trim changes. The Matador coupe got a new grille along with a Barcelona appearance package to replace the former Cassini model.

For 1976 Gremlin offered two models—a stripped base model and a better-trimmed Custom. The base model was priced at a bargain basement $2,889, the Custom was only a bit extra at $2,998.

Top: During 1975 AMC subsidiary AM General was building the M-151 MUTT. Shown here is a MUTT equipped with a TOW missile. By this time AM General was the world's largest producer of tactical military trucks.

Bottom: In 1975 AM General got into the motor home chassis market with a clever product it had developed. Called the Pow-R-Pak, it consisted of two modules, a front module with engine, transmission, and drive wheels, and a rear module containing dual wheels. All a motor home builder had to do to complete the chassis was add frame rails—and thus could build a variety of wheelbases.

There still was no four-speed option for the Gremlin or Hornet, though the Pacer got one as an option beginning in April 1976. This transmission, along with a new two-barrel version of the 258 cid six that was added earlier, was meant to address complaints the company was hearing about the new car's lack of power and poor fuel economy.

Even Pacer had little that was new. Beside the new transmission the Pacer got modifications to its distributor and carburetor to improve power and gas mileage, plus a new 2.53:1 economy axle. A new Rally package offered additional gauges, a tachometer, and upgraded interior trim, and nine new body colors were available in addition to six colors that were carryover. And that was it.

Toward the end of 1975 Pacer sales began to slow down. By now there were a lot of Pacers on the road, and many of the buyers were complaining about sluggishness and poor gas mileage . Prospective buyers were turned off by articles that focused on these two weaknesses. And dealers were experiencing a good deal of pushback regarding the styling. By December 1975 AMC had to cancel a week's worth of 1976 Pacer production so that sales could catch up to inventories. As the trade magazine *Ward Auto World* noted to Chapin, "You've been building 4,000 Pacers a week since September but selling 2,000." Dealers' lots were filling up with unsold Pacers.

Jeep had big product news this year— a new CJ-7 model on a longer wheelbase.

What was different about the CJ-7 versus the long-wheelbase CJ-6 that had been available for nearly 20 years (and which remained in production for export sales only) is that the CJ-7 was designed to be a sport utility vehicle, not a workhorse mini-truck. It used the same engines as the CJ-5 but offered an optional automatic transmission, a first for a CJ vehicle. Quadra-Trac four-wheel drive came with the automatic gearbox, so buyers now had a CJ that anyone could drive. The CJ-7 rode a 93.5-inch wheelbase, 10 inches longer than the CJ-5, and had much better interior space for passengers and their luggage and a much better ride. Equally important, the CJ-7 offered an optional one-piece removable plastic hardtop for superior weather protection. Product planner Jim Alexander saw the new Jeep as a replacement for the old Commando. The Jeep truck now offered a fancy Honcho package

Top: There was not much change in the Matador for 1976, but it remained a good, solid family car for people who didn't demand the latest in styling. Although the company had once considered replacing this car with a newer product, by 1976 there was no money to do any major change.

Bottom: The Gremlin X for 1976 wasn't very different from the 1975 model and was overdue for some face-lifting or restyling. This year Gremlin offered a stripped base model and a well-equipped Custom. The base model was priced at $2,889, the Custom at $2,998. There still was no four-speed option for the Gremlin.

We don't know why Ed McMahon is standing next to this Pacer, but it's a pretty good photo so we thought we'd include it. Pacer sales for 1976 were trending downward.

that really dressed it up. The other Jeep models were mostly carryover, though they got new frames and many refinements and improvements.

Roy D. Chapin Jr. said in August 1975, when details of the 1976 car models were announced, that he expected AMC to enjoy a 33 percent increase in sales for 1976: "We think 1976 should be a good year for us." However, it didn't turn out that way.

Trouble was brewing. Although the U.S. auto industry sales rate was up substantially in 1976, AMC was not sharing in it. At the six-month mark AMC sales had been ahead of the prior year and the company was running profitably. Then in the third quarter car sales nosedived, down more than 25,000 units, and the company reported a loss for the quarter.

The losses continued for the rest of both the fiscal and calendar year. By the end of calendar year 1976 industry car sales would be up by nearly one and a half million cars, whereas AMC's would be down by nearly 75,000. Every AMC passenger car model was affected, including the Pacer. Part of the problem was that AMC's dealer network was starting to shrink; by year-end the company was down to 1,713 passenger car dealers. The number of Jeep dealers rose to 1,608 and of those 1,049 sold passenger cars as well. If AMC had been able to

Left: An AMC Pacer was campaigned during 1975 by drivers Amos Johnson and Dennis Shaw of Team Highball, Inc. Johnson and Shaw had already won the 1975 IMSA series. The Pacer was powered by the 232 cid AMC six.

Below: In late 1975, as sales of the 1976 Pacer were slowing down, AMC launched a special $3,599 Pacer Sundowner edition, which included Custom interior, rear wiper and washer, styled road wheels, remote control mirror, and a roof rack—all at no charge.

convince every Jeep dealer to also sell AMC cars the company would have been in much better shape; but it couldn't force them.

In July 1976 the company established what it called the Office of the President consisting of three men: William V. Luneburg, president and chief operating officer, R. William McNealy Jr. as vice chairman (he'd held that position since November 1975), and Gerald C. Meyers, executive vice president. It was the beginning of a program to groom successors for the time when Luneburg and Chapin would retire. The idea was that Bill McNealy would become chairman and Gerry Meyers would be president.

For 1976 AMC dealers in the United States and Canada retailed a total of 292,087 cars. AMC didn't break out how many were sold in the United States and how many in Canada, probably because the size of the drop in sales in the United States would have scared investors and stock analysts.

During 1976 Jeep sales set another record in the United States, with 95,719 sold at retail during the fiscal year. Jeep's share of the four-wheel-drive market was now 16 percent, though it had 40 percent of the sport utility market. Where it was especially weak was in truck sales. Jeep was practically a nonentity in the truck market, with a meager 3 percent share.

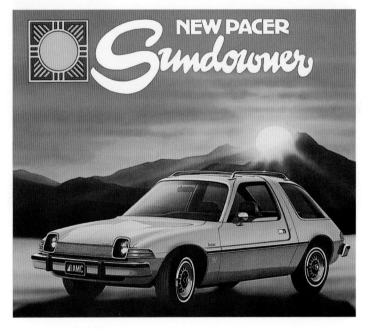

NEW PACER *Sundowner*

Although Jeep sales were hot all throughout the year they could not offset the massive losses from the car division, and AMC reported a net loss of $46.3 million for fiscal 1976. It was a sharp disappointment for Chapin, who had predicted a turnaround this year, but it wasn't quite as bad as it looked: $30 million of the loss was in nonrecurring items such as the large expense of restructuring auto operations to reduce its breakeven point, a $5 million write-down of the equity in its Mexican operation, and a $15 million write-off of deferred income

AMC president William V. Luneburg (standing) and chairman of the board Roy D. Chapin Jr. circa 1976. Although the two men were not panicked about the continuing sales downturn that year, they must have been concerned. Chapin had predicted a sales increase for the year, but that didn't happen, as sales continued their downward slide.

tax benefits. Total dollar volume was up a bit, to $2.3 billion, but ominously, the company's working capital fell to just $59.7 million, one-third of what it was three years earlier.

AM General had a record year in 1976 with $402 million in sales and a pretax profit of $18.9 million, mainly due to increased transit bus deliveries and a growing overseas business.

International sales fell to 55,010 cars and Jeeps outside the United States and Canada—that was more than 10,000 fewer vehicles than the prior year. Mexico continued as AMC's largest overseas passenger car business, where Vehiculos Automores Mexicano (VAM), AMC's long-time Mexico affiliate, held 10 percent of the overall car market and 20 percent of the market for U.S.-designed cars.

Altogether AMC sold 439,524 vehicles for the 1976 fiscal year. All of AMC's other businesses were going strongly: Wheel Horse and the plastics division. Cars were the only thing holding AMC back from making profits.

For 1977 there was a little bit of new product news. The Gremlin finally got a facelift by way of new, shorter front fenders, a new hood, and a new grille. Gremlin was now 4 inches shorter in length than before and better-looking too. At the rear the lift-over height was much lower, providing for a larger rear window and easier loading and unloading of luggage and packages. It was a good restyling of the Gremlin, but it was at least two years late and should have been more extensive. After all, from the side Gremlin didn't look all that different from before.

Gremlin now had three models available: the base car, which carried a six-cylinder engine and three-speed transmission, a Custom model with six-cylinder engine, and a new Custom 2-liter (introduced in February 1977) equipped with AMC's Audi-designed four-cylinder engine. The four-cylinder Custom weighed 250 pounds less than the six, which helped improve gas mileage and made having a four-banger in the Gremlin a viable idea. The 2-liter Custom came with a four-speed transmission, which was also offered as an extra cost option on the six-cylinder Custom. This feature was another item that was long overdue—Gremlin and Hornet should have offered a four-speed in 1972, if not earlier. Gremlin's level of standard equipment was increased this year, finally, and now included full carpeting, front disc brakes, carpeted cargo area, and a cigarette lighter, among other things. The V-8 engine was dropped.

The Pacer got a new model added: a new station wagon body style. During development it had been referred to as the Paceabout. It was built on the basic Pacer body/chassis so the cost of tooling was not bad—especially because the company sourced the dies from Japan to keep costs down—and it was an exceptionally good-looking wagon. Interest in it was very strong. AMC officials expected the new wagon to account for more than half of Pacer's sales for 1977.

The Hornet line of cars also got a new model, the Hornet AMX. This was a Hornet hatchback with sporty features added, including a front air dam, fender flares, roof targa band, dual flat black mirrors, bucket seats, tachometer, floor console, and DR78x14 radial tires with styled road wheels. The standard AMX powertrain was the 258 cid 2-barrel six mated to a four-speed transmission. The 304 V-8 was optional. There was little new in the rest of the Hornet line, though standard equipment levels were raised. The four-speed was finally available on the Hornet, but only on the hatchback model and the AMX. If you wanted a four-speed in a two-door sedan you were out of luck.

The Matador sedan and wagon saw only minimal changes, but the coupe offered a gaudier Barcelona II package to replace the former Barcelona, which had offered more discrete luxury.

Jeep for 1977 had its strongest lineup ever: CJs plain or with the Renegade package, a new Golden Eagle model, the hot-selling Cherokee Chief, a new wide-wheel two-door base model, and a new four-door Cherokee. There was also the stylish and highly desired Wagoneer, and the truck line, which offered Pioneer and Honcho dress-up packages.

Top: When the market for conventional transit buses dried up AM General began to build these bendable buses designed by bus maker M.A.N. of Germany. The bendable feature made the bus easier to maneuver in city traffic.

Bottom left: Despite the long-overdue redesigned front and a price cut, Gremlin sales continued to fall in 1977. It was a shame but without a redesign of the side panels the Gremlin just didn't look new enough.

Bottom right: The 1977 AMC Hornet offered room, a decent ride, and top quality, but unfortunately it was beginning to look out of date compared with the more modern cars from domestic and foreign competitors.

Left: The Matador Barcelona II was a rather gaudy-looking attempt to attract attention to the company's fading midsize lineup. And it proved surprisingly popular.

Right: Longtime AMC/Jeep designer Chuck Mashigan, shown in his personal Jeep CJ-7 Golden Eagle. Mashigan was a talented designer who is probably best known for creating the original two-seat AMX for 1968.

Gremlin sales were stalled, and in the first quarter Chapin put through a $253 price reduction, making the new base price $2,995. Pacers were given a $253 rebate.

AMC managed to squeeze out a tiny profit in the first quarter of 1977—$1.2 million, $600,000 of which was due to currency fluctuations, on total sales of $559 million. AMC car sales sank to 48,788 in that quarter.

Industry sales were good in 1977 but just as in 1976 the increase was mainly in larger cars. However, even among small cars AMC was being outpaced. But AMC was determined to stay the course. Ronald Gilchrist, general marketing manager, told the industry trade paper *Automotive News* that "The market in '76 turned upside down on us but we're positive about '77. The question is not *if* the small car market will return but *when*." AMC planned to focus much of its sales efforts in 1977 on the Buyer Protection Plan. "It is being rejuvenated inside as the most important thing we have to sell," said Gilchrist.

But sales continued to fall, AMC was bleeding red ink and management at last realized it had to restructure the company to bring its passenger car breakeven point down even further. By February Chapin had whittled it down to fewer than 250,000 cars annually—it had been more than 300,000. But in that same February cars were selling at an annualized rate of 180,000 units—and the company was posting huge losses in its car operation that the huge profits generated by Jeep couldn't offset entirely. To reduce overhead and gain some quick cash AMC agreed to sell its brand new South Charleston stamping plant to Volkswagen Manufacturing Corporation of America.

In the second quarter sales were still not good. In March Marketing Group VP Eugene Amoroso left the company—he resigned, according to the press announcement, but most people believed he was given the boot in the wake of the company's two-year sales slump. Dale Dawkins, who joined AMC in 1971, was named his replacement.

Rumors were going around that AMC was going to be taken over by another company. Other rumors making the rounds said that AMC was looking into assembling cars for Honda as a way to utilize excess production capacity in Kenosha. On March 1, 1977, AMC observed its 75th anniversary. With roots dating back to the 1902 Rambler, it was one of the oldest car companies in America.

Midyear Chapin knew something had to be done to change the public's opinion of AMC. To do that he needed to change the opinion of journalists and stock analysts across the country, so he once more had his Styling Department put together a showing of special concept cars to illustrate the company's capabilities in small-car design. The traveling show was called Concept '80, and for it the stylists came up with six vehicles. Concept One was a replacement for the Gremlin, a true lightweight subcompact with great styling based on a series of clay models that were being developed in the design studios. Concept Two was similar in size but had styling reminiscent of the Pacer. Concept Gran Touring was a sharp, premium small car with sporty overtones. Concept AM Van was a small van on a short wheelbase and was a crowd favorite. Concept Jeep II was a redesigned small CJ-type vehicle and Concept Electron was simply the old Amitron show car with a new coat of paint. The showings, in several major cities across the country, helped shore up AMC's image.

In May 1977 Bill Luneburg retired, and Gerry Meyers was elected president of the company. Despite the seeming conclusiveness of his election, it still remained to be seen who would get the top spot when Chapin retired, though the heir apparent was Bill McNealy. Meyers was taking over a firm on the brink. Newspapers and magazines were filled with stories about AMC's problems, which of course depressed car sales even further. One anonymous mid-level AMC executive was quoted as saying, "I think we'll be out of the car business in a year—our sales are lousy."

The Gremlin finally got some attention from company product planners in 1977 when it received a mild facelift, a new four-cylinder engine, and a price cut to $2,995. There were three Gremlin models this year, a base six, a four-cylinder Custom, and a six-cylinder Custom.

Gerry Meyers was angry about the current situation but optimistic about the future: "By all rights we should sell a quarter of a million cars per year. It's just ridiculous that we're not."

But the truth was the sales picture was bad and getting worse month by month. The market simply wasn't coming back for AMC. Pacer sales utterly collapsed and for the 1977 calendar year would come in at fewer than 45,000—and this was a vehicle tooled up for 184,000 units. Matador sales continued to fall, and Gremlin was weak also. The only car line that was holding up was the Hornet. For the fiscal year AMC passenger car sales fell to 226,640 units in the United States and Canada (AMC didn't want to show how badly sales had fallen in the United States so it again reported combined U.S. and Canadian sales). Overseas car and Jeep sales totaled 50,300, down a bit from 1976.

But 1977 ended up being a profitable year for AMC. It earned a meager $8.2 million profit on dollar volume of $2.2 billion—hardly anything to cheer about. Jeep was the reason for the net profits. Working capital rose to $98 million. At this point the company was losing something on the order of $100 million annually on cars but earning $90–$100 million on Jeep. Jeep vehicle retail sales in the United States and Canada came to 117,077 units, well above the forecast. In total AMC sold 394,017 vehicles for 1977.

AM General was profitable this year and that, combined with the $2.7 million earned by the other operations, was enough to nudge the company into black ink. At any other firm management would probably have bowed to the inevitable and moved to discontinue its

Top: The new-for-1977 Hornet AMX was an attempt to recapture some of the excitement from the 1960s muscle-car era.

Bottom: One of the vehicles in the Concept 80 show that American Motors was touting that year was this Concept Electron, which was merely the earlier Amitron with a fresh paint job.

Left: The company had high hopes for its unique Concept Jeep II vehicle, which was a full-size Concept Jeep that toured as part of the Concept 80 show. However, the small Jeep got very negative reaction from traditional Jeep buyers.

Below: AMC may have considered face-lifting the Hornet for 1978, as this Hornet with 1977 Gremlin front end shows. This unauthorized photo was taken at an AMC storage yard.

passenger car lines, but the men in charge of AMC had spent their lives in the car business; they were wholly committed to staying in it and would be able to as long as the car operations didn't lose any more than it was now. They could do this so long as Jeep sales continued to rise. But if Jeep sales fell. . . .

AM General had an excellent year, earning $13.5 million on $377 million of business. And the company won the bidding to provide the U.S. Army with a new line of M-915 series heavy trucks. The $253 million contract for 5,507 units had options that could double the order.

As usual, the plastics group and Wheel Horse were solidly profitable.

Considering AMC's stale product line and lack of money, the outlook for 1978 appeared bleak. But American Motors stylists had a new car waiting in the wings, and it would surprise everyone. The new Concord D/L was a stylish car developed on the cheap and required almost no new tooling. The Concord would be the company's first offering in the luxury compact market, and it would give AMC a measure of success along with enough hope to keep on going.

Biggest Army truck contract ever to AM General.

The United States Army has contracted to buy 5,507 M915 Series heavy trucks (with an option for 5,507 more) from AM General Corporation, Wayne, Michigan. This is the largest U.S. Army truck contract ever issued.

Except for certain military features, the M915 Series Truck is a configuration of commercially proven components—such as Hendrickson Suspensions.

The Army's objective is to minimize logistics support problems by using as many common components as possible in each of the six models. The series consists of three types of chassis; 6x4 for on-highway; 6x6 and 8x6 for on/off highway. The on-highway trucks are equipped with Hendrickson RTE-380 Suspensions, and the off-highway units with RT-450's.

Hendrickson Suspensions were chosen to match the rugged performance requirements of the contract, and for their dependability and proven low maintenance cost over the long haul . . . on or off the highway!

In 1977 AM General won the biggest truck contract it had ever received up to that time, an order for 5,507 M915 series heavy-duty trucks—with an option for 5,507 additional trucks. The base contract was valued at $253 million.

1978–1982

THE FRENCH CONNECTION

A GREAT DEAL OF CHANGE WAS IN THE WIND. Things were happening.

Just after the 1978 new car announcement that October 1977 Roy D. Chapin Jr. relinquished his role as CEO and in a surprise move turned those responsibilities over to Gerry Meyers rather than Bill McNealy. Chapin was staying on as chairman—it would reassure the banks and the stockholders—but the mantle of power was now in Meyers's hands.

A recently discovered company memo from October 1977 by a high-ranking AMC executive indicates that Chapin did something else unusual. The memo states that Chapin discussed with Allstate Insurance chairman Archie Boe a way for Allstate to acquire American Motors. It could be done, the memo says, for $150 million, which would be mostly in Sears stock (Allstate was a subsidiary of Sears-Roebuck at the time). Under this plan the passenger car business would survive, though downsized to lower its breakeven point. How far this discussion went is not known at this time.

There was a new Jeep plant coming to the Middle East. For some time AMC had been on the Arab blacklist because it did business with Israel. But despite that, in November 1977 AMC announced a new joint venture to build Jeeps in Egypt. Apparently the lure of having a Jeep factory was great enough to make the pragmatic Egyptians forget about the boycott, at least so far as AMC was concerned. A new 200,000-square-foot building was being erected and would give the new venture capacity to build 10,000–12,000 Jeeps annually. Called Arab-American Vehicles Company, it was 49 percent owned by

The Concord for 1981. Like other automakers, AMC sales were down this year because of a severe recession, high unemployment, and high interest rates. Many thousands of buyers decided to put off buying a car this year.

AMC, with a consortium of Arab countries holding the other 51 percent. This firm survives to the present.

But even bigger events were twirling about in November. Although Chapin had referred to Bill McNealy as his successor as recently as that August, the board of directors decided they wanted to consider other possibilities. Ex–General Motors vice president John Z. DeLorean had earlier approached Chapin with the idea of merging his own DeLorean Motor Company into AMC, with DeLorean himself becoming chairman and CEO of the combined operation. As a former top-level GM executive, DeLorean's reputation was sterling; the events that would cause his downfall were still far into the future. Chapin assigned one his trusted lieutenants to look into DeLorean's car company and found that at that point it consisted mainly of just a prototype and some office space. The board turned down DeLorean. But the whole episode caused them to begin to think of other possibilities for the top job. They were no longer certain that Chapin's succession plan was the correct way to go.

The board was split over whether to choose Bill McNealy or Gerry Meyers to be the new chairman after Chapin retired. In the end it was decided that the two men should

Top: The dramatic red paint scheme on the Concept AM Van show car is highlighted by yellow and orange stripes. Note the porthole window, a very 1970-ish styling touch. Leaving the body sides plain would create a utilitarian van that could have been sold to small businesses, whereas the gussied up van would appeal to thousands of young buyers.

Center: The Concept Grand Touring was the old Hornet GT prototype with a new paint job, a new interior, and an added vinyl landau top. This concept was one of the public's favorites and probably should have been put into production, but AMC didn't want to risk scarce development dollars.

Bottom: Another view of the Concept Grand Touring shows off its elegant grille and interior. One of the key design elements of the car is the special wire wheels. Note, too, the painted bumpers. The Grand Touring concept car used the Hornet Sportabout rear hatch.

Left: The new AMC Concord D/L for 1978 was an exceptionally nice package and proved that AMC could create an upscale compact car good enough to compete with anyone. The two-door D/L shown was the most popular model that year.

Below: The Pacer received its first restyling in 1978, and it was done mostly to create enough space under the hood for a new optional 304 cid V-8 engine. It was hoped the facelift would also make the Pacer look a little more conventional.

present to the board their plans for the future of American Motors. November 18, 1977, was set as the day for reviewing their ideas. It was going to be a shootout.

When that fateful day came both men were prepared. Bill McNealy went in with a plan that began with a basic but profound analysis. "AMC's problems are simple," he said. "We lose so much money in the passenger car business it hides our other profitable business." Jeep, he noted, was earning $100 million per year, but cars were losing about the same amount. And Jeep was in danger of being badly, possibly fatally, wounded by future SUV gas mileage rules, none of which were then known. McNealy felt it was time to begin developing new Jeeps to meet a gas-short future. "We must decide whether to spend our limited capital to protect a threatened Jeep (Engineering believes we can produce a whole new generation of lightweight Jeeps for $100 million) or put $55 million into the new four-cylinder engine [for cars] plus $100–$400 million for new bodies to protect the endangered and unprofitable passenger car business. The conclusion is not debatable." McNealy wanted to take full advantage of Jeep's incredible earning power by downsizing passenger car operations while also making distribution deals with Peugeot and at least one other import make, likely Volvo, Peugeot, or one of the smaller Japanese companies. He wanted to utilize one of AMC's greatest assets—its dealer network—"[M]aking AMC dealers the supermarket of good cars," he said. Then, after the import car deals became a reality the company could write down the rest of its auto operations and cease building its own cars. As part of his plan he suggested having Lehman Brothers find a large successful company that could take advantage of purchase accounting to buy AMC and utilize its losses to offset taxes on future earnings.

It was a well-thought-out plan and a good idea, all things being equal. But permanently exiting the passenger car business was anathema to most of the directors and officers of the corporation. They'd spent their lives in the auto industry and simply couldn't face a future that didn't include cars. McNealy's plan left them uncomfortable.

For his part, Gerry Meyers presented a plan to tackle what he saw as the twin problems facing AMC: greater demand for Jeeps than the company had the production capacity to meet and too little demand for cars, and hence too much passenger car capacity. His idea to fix both was to convert the Brampton, Ontario, car plant to build Jeep CJs (McNealy had also suggested this), which would reduce passenger car overhead and costs while providing an extra 50,000 units of Jeep production. He also advocated turning the Milwaukee body plant into a parts plant and consolidating all passenger car production into Kenosha, which would greatly reduce costs. On a longer-term basis he also wanted to increase Toledo's output and add senior Jeeps to Kenosha's assembly lines. All this would greatly increase profits while reducing overhead. It, too, was a great plan, all things being equal.

Left: AMC designers struggled to come up with new stripe patterns to freshen the Gremlin's looks. For 1978 the Gremlin got the new striping shown here, and it was very attractive. Note that this particular Gremlin X has the 2.0-liter engine and Levi's interior trim, as the side decals proclaim.

Right: The 1978 Gremlin GT. A limited-production model produced in the final year of Gremlin production, the GT was powered by the six-cylinder engine and included wheel flares, painted bumpers, spoke style wheels, and a host of other goodies. These rare vehicles are highly collectible today.

Left: For 1979 the Gremlin became the Spirit sedan, with larger side windows, new interior trim, and a sharp new grille. The Spirit sedan retained the Gremlin name in Mexico.

Below: AMC stylists regularly created designs for new cars that could be built on existing body shells. In this one we see a very attractive sport coupe built on the Concord two-door sedan body.

Like McNealy, Meyers advocated an alliance with a foreign automaker, but he wanted it to be a manufacturing as well as distribution agreement. He wanted to utilize the other party's technology to build a line of advanced, highly fuel-efficient front-wheel-drive cars in Kenosha.

Either plan would eventually doom both the Pacer and the Matador because neither plan called for investment in those cars, and both acknowledged that having four separate body plants was much too costly an approach for a small maker like AMC. It was a backdoor recognition of the failure of basing the automotive lineup on too many separate body shells. By doing so the new car programs of 1974 and 1975 had drastically increased automotive overhead and drained the corporate coffers, leaving nothing left for badly needed new products or overdue updates. This is what led to the bad situation they were in. The men at the top had gambled all of AMC's money on two cars—the Matador coupe and the Pacer—and they had lost, endangering the corporation itself.

One fatal flaw in both plans was the assumption that Jeep sales were going to continue increasing every year. It was easy to believe they would; after all, they had been increasing for seven years. What could make them stop now?

In the end the board of directors chose Gerry Meyers's plan. It was now fixed that he would become the new chairman when Roy D. Chapin Jr. retired, which was still in the future. Bill McNealy, angry at being denied the position that had been promised him earlier, resigned from American Motors effective November 18, 1977. His leaving was one of the more unfortunate events to happen at AMC, for losing McNealy was to lose a very talented executive.

Now it was time for American Motors to get back to the business at hand. At least for 1978 there was a car that appeared all-new, even if it was only a heavily disguised luxury spinoff of the Hornet. Offered in two- and four-door sedans, a two-door hatchback, and four-door station wagon, the new Concord was a nice product by itself although in base

Top: New Spirits and Concords in the marshalling yards waiting to be put aboard new car haulers so they can be trucked to dealers.

Bottom: One of the greatest restyling jobs ever was the transformation of the Gremlin into the Spirit Liftback, shown here. The Spirit Liftback was completely restyled from the doors back and got a new grille, but the basic car was retained. The new Spirit was sportier and much more attractive than was the old Gremlin, though it never sold as well as Gremlin did in its heyday.

form it was not all that much different from the Hornet. What made it special was an inexpensive luxury group called the D/L package. AMC had used the D/L name several times in the past but this year the company was going all-out to make the D/L a volume package. The Concord D/L package included a vinyl half top with opera windows on the two-door or a vinyl landau top on the four-door sedan. Inside were gorgeous individual reclining seats, wood-grain overlays for the instrument panel, a quartz digital clock that was very impressive, thick carpeting, sound insulation, and much more. Concord's suspension was upgraded, and the car rode very smoothly and quietly—and handling was quite good too.

Key to Concord's new look were the shorter front fenders from the Gremlin, a very stylish die-cast grille and modification to the rear styling. These combined with the vinyl top and plush interior to give one the impression of an all-new car.

Interestingly, Ford had introduced a luxury compact in 1975, the same year as the Pacer launched. Called the Granada, the compact Ford was an immediate—and lasting—hit. In its 1975–1980 model run (the same as Pacer's) more than 2 million were sold. Ironically, one of the vehicle types considered by AMC executives before they decided to build the Pacer was a luxury compact—which would have come out in 1975 and probably have been a roaring success like the Granada. Unfortunately by choosing to do the Pacer instead AMC was doomed.

Top: Concord got new front-end styling for 1979, giving it a richer look. Quad rectangular headlamps were considered very modern and stylish at the time, and the new look was well received. Note the hood ornament, another important styling touch in the 1970s.

Bottom: One idea for an expanded passenger car lineup was to create two new series of cars from the basic Hornet body. The top two cars are a luxury compact, likely the Concord, whereas the bottom two cars are less-expensive two- and four-door family sedans. Why was this idea abandoned? It probably would have yielded higher sales volume.

The Pacer, whose sales were sinking lower day by day, was gussied up for 1978 with a host of former optional equipment now standard, including the D/L package, electric clock, painted wheel covers, and custom steering wheel among them. The Pacer also got new front-end styling with a raised hood and unusual grille. The raised hood was to provide space for a new optional 304 cid V-8 engine, introduced to address complaints about a lack of power.

The AMX returned, this time using the Concord's front fenders and without the Hornet prefix, and it was a very handsome machine. The Gremlin returned with only minor changes, including a new instrument panel, but this year offered new striping on the Gremlin X package and a special Gremlin GT model that offered painted bumpers, large wheel flares, spoke-style wheels, a wide side stripe, and more. It was the sportiest-looking Gremlin ever—and too bad it didn't offer a V-8 option. In other product news, this year the Barcelona package was available on the Matador sedan as well as the coupe.

Jeep trucks this year offered a new '10-4' appearance package, which consisted

mainly of stripes and a decal. The Golden Eagle and Honcho packages were carried over from the prior year.

CJs got a host of improvements such as standard front disc brakes, ashtray, cigar lighter, passenger assist handle, and H78 tires. The heater was redesigned. The Cherokee and Wagoneer also got some new standard features and minor appearance changes. Early in the 1978 model year Jeep introduced a new model called the Wagoneer Limited, loaded with luxury features, including leather upholstery and a large price tag. The response was overwhelming, and the company soon found itself unable to keep up with demand.

In November 1977 an exultant Gerry Meyers told a reporter, "I stand for the passenger car business," and said that the company would field "five new offerings in the next seven or eight months." The Gremlin GT was one of them, as was the Concord Touring Wagon, an update of the old Hornet Touring wagon. He said a planned small station wagon program was still on track.

February 1978 brought rumors that AMC was in negotiations with French automaker Peugeot to form some sort of partnership. AMC executives denied the rumors.

March 1978 was a busy month. Executive vice president Ian Anderson, the number-three man at AMC, quit to go to Volkswagen. Like McNealy, he was unhappy at being passed over for the top slot. Also that month the company unveiled a special show car called the Crown Pacer. It was an attempt to gauge reaction to several styling features meant to make the Pacer look more conventional, such as smaller rear side windows, colored bumpers, an upright grille, and hidden headlamps. Late in the month the company announced that it was converting its passenger car assembly plant in Brampton, Ontario, to Jeep CJ production. That move helped greatly to reduce automobile overhead while boosting badly

Top: AMC CEO Gerald Meyers shakes hands with Renault executive Bernard Hanon after concluding the initial deal for AMC to distribute Renault cars in the United States and Canada (except Quebec). Hanon was a veteran Renault man and was instrumental in pushing for the AMC/Renault alliance.

Bottom: Early in development the car that became the Eagle was called the Pathfinder. Here we see a never-before published photo of a Pathfinder station wagon. The Eagle was conceived and developed by Roy Lunn.

needed Jeep production, but it caused rumors to the effect that AMC was preparing to exit the car business—which hurt sales.

Actually, business was turning around. At the end of March AMC was able to announce a quarterly profit of $2.7 million, the sixth consecutive quarter of profitability. But the profits were all a result of increased Jeep sales; passenger cars overall were still on a downturn, though the Concord was selling very well. AMC signed on a new ad agency—Grey Advertising, a New York–based firm.

In April AMC dropped a bombshell—the rumors were true after all; it was negotiating with a French automaker—Renault—to establish a marketing and manufacturing agreement between the two firms. This was Gerry Meyers's plan; he wanted to become the importer of Renault cars to sell through the AMC network, which would help keep dealers profitable while giving AMC extra income. But longer term he wanted to be able to tap Renault's small-car expertise and components so that he could bring out a line of completely redesigned AMC cars with high fuel efficiency and front-wheel drive. Meyers envisioned his factories turning out hundreds of thousands of Renault- and AMC-badged cars within just a few years.

It was a good deal for both sides. In the stroke of a pen AMC was gaining access to some of the best fuel-economy and front-wheel-drive technology available from a financially solid company. For Renault it was an easy decision to go with AMC. The Renault dealer network consisted of 440 mostly small dealers who retailed about 13,000 cars in the United States during 1977. If Renault ever hoped to become a bigger player in the American market it needed a larger and more experienced network—one like AMC's. Insiders figured that affiliating with AMC would boost Renault's U.S. sales above 50,000 per year.

The deal hadn't come easily. Earlier in the year, after visiting several European makers with no luck, Meyers started negotiating with Peugeot of France. They reached an agreement that called for distribution of Peugeot cars—no manufacturing, no technology sharing, no Jeep distribution, just AMC selling French-built Peugeots in America. It was not the all-encompassing deal Meyers had hoped for but it was a deal. He went to New York to sign the agreement that had been worked out with Peugeot when, only hours away from signing, a Renault executive called him and asked, "Are we too late?" Meyers replied that he just about was, but what did he have in mind? The Renault man explained that they were looking for a close alliance with AMC, one to include manufacturing in America as well as distribution and that they would share their technology with AMC. That changed Meyers's mind. In truth, he had been a little uncomfortable with the Peugeot deal. He later recalled to the Peugeot people, "AMC just didn't smell right. They didn't want anything to do with us aside from having us sell their cars. The Renault offer was much better."

Here's another shot of a Pathfinder, this one a two-door sedan. In the end the Eagle name was considered more appropriate for the new car.

Right: AMC stylists were extremely talented and able to remake the Gremlin into the Spirit sedan. But had management approved, even more could have been done. This photo shows a sport version of the Spirit sedan with wheel flares, wire/spoke wheels, and a Concord-type grille.

Below: The new for 1980 AMC Eagle series of four-wheel-drive automobiles was offered in three body styles; two- and four-door sedans and a four-door station wagon. Apparently no thought was given to converting the Concord Hatchback to an Eagle, though it probably would have proved popular.

AMC Concord D/L two-door models got a new landau roof this year, along with revised opera windows. Concord was improved in details nearly every year of production and for a time was a highly competitive entry in the luxury compact market.

Although the Concord sold very well throughout the year the rest of the car lines continued to sink. Luckily, Jeep was still hot and for the 1978 fiscal year AMC was able to report a net profit of $36.6 million on sales of $2.58 billion. Working capital was a healthly $152 million. Jeep sales in the United States and Canada soared to 152,396 units, whereas passenger cars fell slightly to 193,803 units. Overseas AMC cars actually rose a bit—they were very popular in Mexico—to 20,734, and overseas Jeep sales were 28,271, a slight decline. In all the company sold 395,204 vehicles, not counting AM General.

AM General had an off year, posting a loss of $5.2 million. The problem was that the bus market had completely dried up, and because of that AM General decided to exit the unprofitable business. The cost of closing out the transit bus part of the business was high. The company would remain in the bus business in a small way selling specialty units : articulated buses and electric trolley buses. AMC's nonautomotive subsidiaries posted record sales for 1978.

Roy D. Chapin Jr. retired from AMC effective September 30, 1978, and turned the chairmanship over to Gerry Meyers. The company now needed a new president, as the board didn't want Meyers to hold all three major titles—president, chairman, and CEO. The board soon named former Ford executive and Singer vice president W. Paul Tippett to be the new president of AMC.

By year-end Gerry Meyers had completed filling the ranks of his executives, hiring ex-Chevrolet executive James Tolley as vice president–public relations and Wilson Sick as finance VP. Other top executives included AMC veterans Cruse Moss, head of AM General, and Larry Hyde, Group vice president, cars and Jeep vehicles.

For 1979 American Motors had two new cars to show. The Spirit Sedan was a very attractive update of the Gremlin body shell, with large side windows, a sharp new grille and bumpers, quad rectangular head lamps, and a much nicer bucket seat interior; if only AMC had done this in 1975 or 1976, what a difference it would have made. But the real surprise was the Spirit Liftback, also Gremlin-based but wearing a revision of the styling seen on the earlier Gremlin G-II concept car. It too got nicer interior trim, with bucket seats standard. The Spirits were available in three trim levels: Base, which was roughly equivalent to the Gremlin

Right: The Spirit D/L sedan for 1980. The Spirit sedan was sold primarily as a value for the money car, as the styling was a little dated by 1980. The big side windows opened up the back seat area to sunlight and made it feel less claustrophobic.

Below: The Spirit for 1980. As we can see here, this particular Spirit is equipped with the optional GT package. This was available on both Base and D/L model Spirits and was a good seller mainly because it offered a lot of car for the money and, with the six-cylinder engine, good performance as well.

Custom, D/L, which substantially upgraded interior trimmings and exterior moldings, and the Limited, which came with a slew of extras as standard equipment and boasted leather seating surfaces. The Spirit Liftback also offered a cool GT package with black-out moldings and a sporty flavor that proved very popular. Spirit was a continuation of the strategy Meyers had of upgrading AMC cars so they could command a higher price (and thus higher profit) than the low-buck Hornet and Gremlin. The 1978 Concord sales mix had been 80 percent D/L models.

Spirit models offered as standard the 2-liter four-cylinder, with three optional engines: the 232 cid six, 258 cid six, and on Liftbacks, the 304 V-8. A four-speed transmission was standard as well. The company had a two-tier pricing policy this year, with cars sold in western states priced $120 less than the rest of the country. It was an attempt to build some volume in import-loving California.

Concord returned for 1979 with a new waterfall grille, quad rectangular headlamps, and a new half vinyl top for the D/L four-door. This year Concord offered distinct

Base, D/L, and Limited models rather than utilizing option packages. A Sport or GT model would have been appreciated by dealers but was not offered. During the year the four-cylinder engine became available for Concord.

The Pacer was back for another try. The base model was dropped, and the Pacer now offered only D/L and Limited models. Equipment levels were hiked as well. AMC had built some four-cylinder-powered Pacers for testing, but the results were not encouraging—the increase in fuel economy wasn't enough to justify the markedly slower acceleration. The AMX returned, now using the new Spirit Liftback body, and it was a very nice machine, with wheel flares, big tires, and an optional V-8 engine. The Matador line was gone, cancelled because sales had fallen to an uneconomic level and there was no money to redesign them. AMC was now firmly, and solely, in the small-car market.

Jeep for 1979 had numerous small changes. CJs got a new soft top with much better fit, a new standard engine, the 258 cid six, and revisions to the Renegade package. Cherokee now offered the Golden Eagle package and boasted new chrome-plated aluminum bumpers, a new grille, and dual rectangular headlamps. Wagoneer and Grand Wagoneer got minor upgrades and also got the new bumpers, a new grille, and headlamps, as did the J-series trucks. The J-10 and J-20 interiors were upgraded.

As things turned out, the company handled the Spirit's launch badly. On announcement day dealers were short of cars or had ones that were loaded with expensive optional equipment and bore rather high price tags. Someone at AMC had overestimated how much extra expense the market would bear, so Spirit sales got off to a very slow start. By December the company realized it had a problem and addressed it by lowering base prices by $200, adding whitewall tires to base models and an AM radio to D/L models. And the factory started shipping more modestly equipped Spirits. Once those changes were put through Spirit sales began to climb.

This mock-up of a new Eagle coming in 1981 is dated March 21, 1979. At this stage most of the exterior styling details seem completed, but many would be changed before production. Note the mock-up still wears the name Spirit 4x4, which is what it was called during development.

Financially, the year started out extremely well. Sales and earnings in the first quarter were the best for that period in AMC's history. Car sales fell about 10 percent, but Jeep sales climbed an amazing 42 percent. Gerry Meyers announced that the company would convert part of its Kenosha complex to build 50,000 Jeep Cherokees and Wagoneers per year. Meyers also announced a two-year project to put in a new paint facility in Toledo that would yield a 50 percent increase in Jeep production there.

In January 1979 Renault and American Motors signed the deal to have AMC distribute Renault cars in the United States and Canada, except for French-speaking Quebec. It was the first of what would be several agreements. Under these arrangements AMC would sell LeCar and 18i and by 1983 would be building an all-new Renault World Car that was still on the drawing boards. Unnamed as yet, under development it would come to be known as the X42. The announcement made clear that Renault would have no ownership in American Motors, nor was any planned.

The company continued to expand its overseas operations. In February 1979 AMC signed an agreement with Beijing Automotive Industrial Corporation to study the feasibility of producing Jeep vehicles in China. At the time Beijing AIC was producing a badly outdated four-wheel-drive vehicle based on an obsolete Russian design.

AMC's second quarter was even better—sales and earnings set new records, with the company reporting net earnings to that point of $58.2 million. Jeep sales were on fire, and that was fueling those profits. Cars, in the meantime, continued to fall, though Spirit sales were beginning to increase.

Top: The other new Eagle for 1981 was the Kammback, built on the Gremlin/Spirit sedan body shell. The Eagle Kammback sold poorly, mainly because most dealers—and the factory—didn't get behind it. Dealers who stocked the Kammback usually noticed that it sold well, mainly because of its low price and strong list of standard equipment.

Bottom: Here is the production version of the new for 1981 AMC Eagle SX/4. This small Eagle, dubbed the Eaglet by some members of the press, was popular among younger people.

In April 1979 Jeep unveiled a special Silver Anniversary CJ-5 to celebrate 25 years of CJ-5 production. It featured a unique silver paint job and stripes, special interior, and a dashboard badge. A Silver Anniversary Concord was also built, to celebrate the 25th anniversary of AMC's founding. Also in April, AMC officially began selling Renault cars.

In the third quarter of 1979 operating earnings for the nine months were the highest in the company's history. But there was a shadow over this. . Although in the third quarter AMC passenger car sales were essentially the same as the prior year—they had a strong third quarter and now included 7,327 Renault cars shipped to dealers—Jeep sales actually fell. Although the drop in Jeep sales was fewer than 500 units, it must have been surprising to AMC executives who'd come to rely on ever-increasing Jeep sales.

The reason for the increased car sales and reduced Jeep sales was the second fuel crisis to hit America. It began early in 1979 after the Shah of Iran fled his country, leaving it in the hands of extremists led by the Ayatollah Khomeini. Violent revolution had broken out in Iran, causing oil production to drop, which led to high prices and long gas lines in America. Almost overnight gasoline prices jumped 50 percent.

Once more AMC's reputation for fuel economy came to its rescue as buyers began to flock to AMC showrooms. AMC didn't offer the highest fuel economy, but the Concord and Spirit were very appealing cars, and after all, they did get fairly good gas mileage. But Jeep buyers were backing off, especially buyers who ordinarily would purchase Cherokees. This was a concern for AMC because the company relied greatly on the Cherokee's high-volume sales and high profit margin.

The fiscal year ended September 30, as always, and overall it had been a very good year indeed. Total revenues were $3.1 billion, a new record, and a net profit of $83.9 million was recorded. Operating earnings were the highest in AMC history. Working capital rose to $235.8 million. The company sold 184,456 cars in the United States and Canada along with 23,101 overseas. Jeep sales set a new record at 175,647 in the United States and Canada, 31,995 overseas. In total AMC sold 415,199 vehicles, and sales and earnings set all-time records. For the first time Jeep vehicles outsold AMC cars.

Among Eagle sedans, this senior-series four-door sedan was the more popular. Standard equipment on all Eagles included power steering, power disc brakes, and 15-inch radial tires.

International business was especially good. The company announced new Jeep assembly operations in Malaysia and Indonesia, along with a new sales effort in Australia. In Mexico VAM had sold 20,000 AMC cars and 4,500 Jeep vehicles. In Iran, however, production of Jeeps was affected by the violent uprising. For a time, American longshoremen refused to load any shipments that were headed to that country.

AM General returned to profitability, earning a meager $3.4 million on a half-billion dollars in sales. AMC's nonautomotive subsidiaries had another record year of sales and were very profitable.

But any idea that this prosperity would last was illusory. In the fourth quarter Jeep sales continued to be soft. It was a result of the turmoil in world oil markets as well as high inflation in the United States. Auto loan interest rates were climbing and that was having an effect on sales. In 1980 it would be worse.

For 1980 there was yet another new AMC automobile introduced. Like its stable mates the new Eagle line of four-wheel-drive automobiles was based on an existing car line—in this case the Concord. It was offered in two- and four-door sedans and a station wagon model. The Eagle was envisioned around 1977 by Product Engineering VP Roy Lunn while working on a new, more fuel-efficient transfer case for Jeeps. Lunn realized that AMC's unique passenger car front suspension would allow him to convert the Hornet to full-time four-wheel drive with relative ease and that this new transfer case would give much smoother performance than models he'd built earlier. He mocked up a running concept model and found it delivered outstanding four-wheel-drive performance along with a smooth, steady ride.

The Eagle was the first four-wheel-drive car from an American producer. Right from the start it was pitched as a premium product with automatic transmission, power steering and brakes, D/L level interior fittings, and six-cylinder engine all standard equipment.

The Concord and Spirit returned for 1980 with a new GM-sourced 'Iron Duke' 2.5-liter four-cylinder engine standard. The program for the 2.0-liter engine and plant had to be canceled to save the millions in tooling expense it would have cost. Fuel economy on the optional sixes, which was vitally important this year as gas prices soared, was increased by means of carburetor improvements. A lock-up torque converter for automatic transmissions also debuted. In addition, all cars now featured expanded use of one-sided galvanized steel, plastic inner front fender liners, and a battery of rust-inhibiting coatings. This was all part of a rust prevention program AMC called the Ziebart Factory-Rust Protection, which came with a full five-year warranty against rust-through. AMC was the only company in America to offer such advanced protection. In addition, a new aluminized exhaust system was designed to last years longer.

Equipment was upgraded. Spirits got new premium front seats for D/L and Limited models. The 258 cid six-powered AMX returned with minor improvements, but no longer offered a V-8 engine. In fact, no AMC cars offered the V-8 this year. Fuel economy rules were tightening, and AMC wanted to boost its corporate average fuel economy (CAFE). Concord got a new grille, a new landau vinyl top, and opera windows for two-door D/L and Limiteds, and a full vinyl top with quarter windows on DL and LTD four-door sedans. Concords now offered optional power windows and power seats as well. Because of very low sales the hatchback Concord was dropped. The Pacer returned with little change other than not offering the V-8 this year; sales had sunk to an uneconomic level, and its demise was expected soon.

For 1980 Jeeps got a lot of changes and improvements, much of it aimed at improving Jeep's less-than-stellar fuel economy. CJs now offered the GM four-cylinder engine as standard equipment, along with a four-speed transmission and free-wheeling hubs. It was the first conventional four-wheel-drive vehicle to attain 20 miles per gallon of gas, with an EPA rating of 21 miles per gallon city and 24 miles per gallon highway. New top-line Laredo models were available in CJ, Cherokee Wide-Wheel, and J-10 pickups. An all-new lighter and more efficient Quadra-Trac system debuted on senior Jeeps.

The 1980 Renault LeCar, sold now through hundreds of AMC dealerships, got a bigger engine and better fuel economy, now rated at 30 miles per gallon city and 40 miles per gallon highway.

In the third month of the 1980 model year (December 1979) industry sales suddenly took a huge drop. The combination of fuel concerns, unemployment, high inflation, and a stagnant economy were dragging everything down. Jeep sales continued to be soft though passenger cars were on an upswing.

The perennial best-selling Eagle was the station wagon, which offered good interior room and great utility. These cars appealed to many people who felt uneasy driving in winter in an ordinary car.

Before year-end a concerned and cash-strapped AMC found it had to turn to Renault for capital. The money was needed to fund development and tooling for all-new automobiles including the new X42, plus development of new fuel-efficient Jeeps. Renault obligingly coughed up $150 million to finance work to bring production of the new Renault car to Kenosha. Engines and transaxles would come from France, but sheet metal and assembly would be done in Wisconsin, and it would cost a lot of money to bring that to fruition. Renault bought stock and subordinated notes and a subordinated debenture giving it roughly a 22.5 percent share of the company, if full conversion of convertible debt were done. Neither AMC nor Renault wanted to see the French company own stock in AMC, but with

Left: The first Eagle that the author sold as an AMC salesman, which may have been the first Eagle sold in Connecticut, was an Eagle two-door sedan, sold to an elderly couple who lived on a steep hill and were terrified of winter driving. They owned the Eagle for many years and were extremely pleased with its performance and quality.

Below: Notice the lovely wire wheel covers on this Concord Limited two-door for 1981. Limited models included leather upholstery and thick carpeting and were as nice inside as a Lincoln or Cadillac. Unfortunately the auto market had another off year in 1981.

a soft four-wheel-drive market, there was no other choice. Money was tight and banks would not lend it to American Motors when it was clearly sailing into rough seas.

There was some good news. The new Eagle was met with instant acceptance. Magazine writers who customarily denigrated AMC wrote glowing articles full of praise for the revolutionary new car. Demand was strong, but once again AMC had been too conservative in estimating the sales appeal of a new product and in December the company announced a 60 percent increase in Eagle production, to 80,000 annually. At the same time it was announced that Pacer production was ending; management said it was to free up plant space for Eagle production, but it was really because it wasn't selling. The last Pacer would be built on December 3, so all 1980 Pacers were actually built in 1979.

In February 1980 VAM, AMC's Mexico affiliate, announced it would begin producing Renaults as soon as the all-new Renault world car was ready. AMC's Kenosha operations would supply the sheet metal.

American Motors was profitable in the second quarter of the 1980 fiscal year, though profits were down 32 percent to $12.8 million despite a 3 percent rise in unit sales of cars and Jeeps. The rest of the auto industry was experiencing sales declines. Paul Tippett noted that all car lines were profitable and Eagle was adding incremental sales. He told a reporter, "Now we're in a position where we can take some lumps and not get in the soup."

The 1982 Eagle SX/4. This year all Eagles came with the 2.5-liter engine as standard equipment, offering excellent fuel economy, and rather tame performance. For anyone looking for more power the 4.2-liter six was available.

But the third quarter brought a major loss. Car and Jeep sales fell to 74,387 compared with 111,988 the prior year and American Motors lost an astonishing $85 million on dollar volume that fell 32 percent to $542.7 million. The loss offset earlier profitability for the year and left AMC with a nine-month loss of more than $70 million. Trying to put the best face possible on the situation Gerry Meyers said that AMC had "performed substantially better than the rest of the industry" in the earlier months but that the "current economic downturn" finally took its toll. The economy was a mess, and the U.S. auto industry was entering a period that would bring it to its knees.

November 1980 brought another huge shock to AMC's stockholders. The company's management revealed that AMC was still incurring heavy losses and had to turn to Renault, once again, for help. A proposed new deal would see Renault buy $122.5 million of stock and convert a $45 million note to common stock, giving AMC a fast cash injection and giving Renault 46.4 percent ownership of the company. It could easily lead to Renault owning a majority interest but that company promised to keep its investments to no more than the 46.4 percent ownership. Amazingly, AMC told its stockholders that if they did not approve the deal the company would go into *voluntary or involuntary bankruptcy*—this less than a year after closing the books on its most profitable year ever. AMC also disclosed that Gerry Meyers would get a four-year employment contract, which smacked of a potential golden parachute.

At the same time Paul Tippett announced that American Motors would introduce a new model every six months for the next six years. He refused to say what share of that would be AMC-branded cars.

In December 1980 Gerry Meyers announced that AMC was changing its fiscal year to a calendar year basis, January 1–December 31. Thus quarterly reports would reflect the calendar year as well and be in line with what the Big Three did.

For the 1980 calendar year/fiscal year AMC lost an incredible $208 million. If the fiscal year still ended on September 30, as it always had, the loss for the year still would have been $159.7 million. Net sales for the calendar year fell by more than $600 million, to $2.55 billion. Working capital was $206 million. During the 12 months of 1980 AMC passenger car sales in the United States and Canada were 203,251, (including Renault); essentially the same as the prior year, (and actually rose to 25,686 in overseas markets). U.S. and Canadian Jeep sales, however, were just 67,312 a drop of 57 percent and an unadulterated disaster, for that was where AMC's profits came from. Adding in the 57,245 Jeeps and cars that were sold in overseas markets, AMC sold a total of 327,808 vehicles, a drop of 93,396 units—and essentially all of them were high-profit Jeep vehicles. It was a debacle. Analysts noted that AMC cars outsold Jeeps by more than double!

Sales at AMC's subsidiary companies fell to $73.9 million, and the segment lost money for the first time, a small loss of only $500,000. AM General, on the other hand, had another good year. Though sales fell to $374 million, profits rose to $19.1 million.

In fairness to Meyers and Tippett, AMC wasn't alone in its problems. U.S. auto sales were down dramatically, and the industry lost a total of more than $4 billion for the year. A nearly bankrupt Chrysler went to the government for a bailout and got loan guarantees that kept it afloat until it could redesign its entire lineup.

However, Bill McNealy had warned against waiting too long to address Jeep's fuel economy problems, and if the company had started redesigning the entire Jeep line when he proposed it, it would be closer to a solution than it was just now. As it was, the new cars wouldn't arrive until the 1983 model year and the Jeeps in the 1984 model year. That was a long time to wait for a company that was rapidly bleeding to death.

The 1981 model year started out fairly good so far as AMC passenger cars were concerned. The 258 cid six-cylinder was redesigned this year leaving it 90 pounds lighter, which aided fuel economy. The use of galvanized steel in car bodies was now 100 percent of exterior sheet metal—only Porsche and Rolls-Royce matched that. There were two new AMC models unveiled, the Eagle SX/4, which mated Eagle's four-wheel drive with a Spirit Liftback body, and the Eagle Kammback, which used the Spirit Sedan body. Unlike the senior Eagles, the new ones offered a Base level trim as well as a D/L trim. SX/4 could also be ordered in Sport trim via an option package.

This year all Eagles came standard with the 2.5-liter four-cylinder engine and four-speed manual transmission, which greatly improved fuel economy. Automatic transmission was an option on the smaller Eagles with either engine, as well as the larger ones equipped with the optional six. All Eagles also got a new egg crate grille.

Spirit returned this year, though the slow-selling Limited models were dropped. Spirit got a new grille, wheel covers and rally stripes

The Spirit Sedan and Spirit Liftback had little change for 1981 other than a new grille, some very stylish wheel covers and new stripes. The Spirit Limited models were dropped due to low sales.

Top left: Here we see a previously unknown proposal by AMC stylists. Dated August, 29, 1979, it depicts a possible Concord with a convertible-like top. This may have been a proposed optional vinyl roof, or it may be a study of a possible Concord convertible; the company was toying with the idea at the time, just as they were considering a Spirit convertible.

Top right: This is the Spirit GT Liftback for 1982. As you can see, the styling has held up well, and this is still an exciting car. The wheels shown here were optional; spoke-style wheels came standard. The Spirit was one small sporty car that offered performance to match its good looks.

Bottom: The year 1982 was the final one for the Eagle Kammback, a pity because it had great potential to be a volume seller. When properly equipped it was attractive and still offered a low price tag.

but otherwise was nearly the same as the prior year. Concord also got a new grille, and was again offered in Base, D/L, and Limited models.

Senior Jeep vehicles got the new lightweight six as standard equipment, and it was optional on the CJ line. They also benefited from a fuel-saving lower ride height, courtesy of redesigned springs. Trucks lost their trademark rooftop brow and now had a smooth roof. There were many mechanical changes, most of which were to improve real-world fuel economy. It was on everybody's mind.

Renault had some news for 1981. The new 18i model debuted in the United States after two years of engineering and design work to make it more appealing to Americans. Available in two body styles, four-door sedan and wagon, the 18i offered top fuel economy of around 26 miles per gallon city and 37 miles per gallon highway. It had all the things people said they wanted in a smaller car—room, excellent ride, tight handling, and superior fuel economy. And it was very attractive. It was available in Base and Deluxe trim, with prices starting at $7,398.

Early in the year a small company called Griffith in Ft. Lauderdale, Florida, announced the availability of custom-built Concord and Eagle convertibles dubbed Sundancer. The conversion retailed for $3,750, plus the price of the car.

During the year inflation ran rampant and costly marketing efforts were eroding margins, so like other automakers, AMC put through hefty price increases. AMC also put through a 10 percent rebate program that got a fair response. But overall sales remained slow, and the higher stickers certainly made it harder to move the iron.

In March Jeep unveiled another new product, the Scrambler pickup, a CJ-style vehicle on an extended chassis. It was the first domestically produced small pickup.

That June Gerry Meyers surprised many people when he told a reporter that AMC engineers would no longer design cars for AMC; Renault would handle all passenger car design: "We're not planning on designing all-new automobiles in addition to and aside from what Renault has already designed." This sounded like surrendering the passenger car business and left many dealers to wonder what happened to the small AMC station wagon and AMC-branded small cars that Meyers earlier said were coming in the future.

During the year Jeep started up assembly operations at a plant in Brisbane, Australia. It was to build Jeep Cherokees and J-20 trucks.

As the months rolled on the company got many questions about the upcoming X42. "Let's not refer to it as X42," said marketing manager Dave Van Peursem. "That isn't going to be the name." When asked if it would be badged an AMC or a Renault, Van Peursem replied, "Nothing's finally decided on that yet." He did say the new car would combine French technology, American durability, and Japanese quality—and that it was going to be spectacular. Some months later a hand-built prototype was photographed wearing both Renault Alliance and AMC badges.

During the year the company initiated cost cutting that saw 13 percent of its salaried workforce laid off. And the new $30 million Jeep paint facility came on line, though of course the extra capacity was no longer needed.

Gerry Meyers knew all along that 1981 was not going to see a turnaround, but at least the company was able to cut its losses somewhat. For the fiscal year AMC lost $136.5 million on dollar volume of $2.58 billion. Working capital dropped to $154 million. U.S. and Canadian car sales fell to 179,834, and Jeep sales sank further to just 63,216 units. In overseas markets car sales increased to 26,907—down in Mexico VAM was having another good year—and 41,412 Jeeps. So the grand total was 311,369 cars and Jeeps—or roughly 200,000 fewer than just Rambler alone had sold in 1963. AM General earned $13.2 million for the year on sales of $275.6 million while the non-auto subsidiaries lost $400,000.

One thing that was a bit ominous—the Renault 18i bombed on the market. For what reason is hard to say. It had everything going for it but the public just didn't seem to want to buy it. It didn't bode well for future Renault introductions.

Things were getting desperate. That November AMC went to its union to propose a way they could help the struggling company. The proposal was for hourly and

Top: The year 1982 was the final one for the Spirit Sedan, as it was dropped from the line midyear. Although it never sold in high volume it was missed by dealers, as the AMC car line was slowly being whittled down.

Bottom: This 1982 Concord D/L sedan has the standard full-styled wheel covers that came with Concord D/L models and were optional on Concord base models. To date, no photos of base model Concords have ever been found by the author, though they must have been taken for illustration purposes.

salary employees to forgo about 10 percent of their wages to bring down overhead. The company was trying to stem some of the bleeding so it could hold on until the X42 came to market. With great reluctance and hard feelings the union agreed to AMC's request but demanded certain guarantees of when payback would come and how much interest they would earn.

Also in November AMC announced plans to—at last—build its own four-cylinder engine, essentially a cut-down version of its inline six. This was a smart move because it was going to be the volume engine in the new downsized Jeeps, but it was a major expense just when the company could least afford it. The new engine would debut in about two years, AMC said.

For 1982 American Motors had nothing new to show in the way of AMC-badged automobiles, but it refined what it had as much as it could. All cars could now be ordered with an optional Borg-Warner five-speed transmission, something they should have had at least three years earlier. A wide-ratio automatic transmission debuted for six-cylinder cars that permitted lower axle ratios for better fuel economy. Eagles now had Select-Drive, which allowed one to disengage the fulltime four-wheel drive to save gas—it actually debuted in late 1981. All cars now came with low-drag disc brakes.

Jeep debuted a new CJ-7 Limited with luxury interior and a smoother ride. Most Jeep models could be ordered with the new five-speed. A new mid-level Wagoneer Brougham appeared. During the year a special Jamboree CJ was offered.

January 1982 brought a blockbuster of a shock—AMC chairman Gerry Meyers was leaving the firm and was replaced as CEO by Paul Tippett. Speculation about the change was that the board wanted a marketing man at the top, not an engineer/product planner like Meyers. Jose Dedeurwaerder, a Renault executive who'd joined AMC just four months earlier, was elevated to president and COO, so the French now had a tighter grip on the company. Tippett later told a reporter that plans were to discontinue building the Spirit and Concord in 1985 so AMC could concentrate on front and four-wheel drive vehicles. He also projected that a stream of X42 derivatives would be the key to raising sales volume.

One model that had gotten no support from the dealers or the company was the Eagle Kammback, despite its attractive price tag. In March 1982 the company notified dealers it was discontinuing the Kammback and the Spirit Sedan, retiring a body shell that dated to 1970. Also in March the new Renault Fuego sports coupe debuted. This was an attractive four-seater with decent styling and performance along with great gas mileage. Offered in turbo and non-turbo versions, expectations were that 20,000–30,000 would be sold in the model year.

In an interview in May 1982 AMC's new marketing VP Joseph Cappy, a former Lincoln-Mercury executive, let slip that long-term plans called for no AMC cars at all—just Renault and Jeep. He said Spirit and Concord would remain in production through 1985 before they were dropped. After that the Eagles would be marketed as Jeep vehicles. In July James Tolley, AMC's much-valued vice president of public affairs, left for greener pastures.

Top: The Eagle wagon for 1982. The company also offered a stripped Fleet Eagle available in all three body styles and a Sedan Delivery package that converted the wagon into a small window van with no back seat, just a wooden load floor. All senior Eagles could be ordered with special trailer hitches to haul boats or trailers and were popular with sportsmen. For those more interested in fuel economy, a four-cylinder engine and five-speed transmission offered fuel economy of up to 32 miles per gallon on the highway.

Bottom: This attractive Concord station wagon is a 1982 model. Notice how the optional spoke-style wheels add a touch of sportiness to the car. These wheels were standard on the Spirit GT package, and optional for all other Spirit and Concord models. The Concord also offered a Sedan Delivery Package like the Eagle's.

September 1982 brought—at last—the new Renault car that AMC was pinning its future on—the 1983 Renault Alliance. It was a remarkable product with room for five, a very stylish body, radial tires, disc brakes, front-wheel drive, and fuel injection all standard and an EPA rating of 37 miles per gallon in the city and 52 highway. Acceleration was good, the ride was outstanding, and the price was right—just $5,595 for the base two-door model. The car could also be had in L, D/L, and Limited two- or four-door models. The Alliance percentage of local-parts content was 74 percent—excellent for such a new product. Executives predicted the company would sell 100,000 Alliances in the first year. They would be needed, because AMC car sales were still dropping.

Branding remained a touchy subject. Disappointingly, the new Alliance was badged as a Renault, not an AMC or AMC-Renault as dealers had hoped. In a last minute nod to loyal owners and dealers an AMC badge was placed on the deck lid opposite the Renault Alliance badge. In interviews chairman Tippett still referred to the car as the Renault-AMC Alliance but in all other respects—brochures, commercials, and press releases Renault was clearly the brand name. What did this mean for the AMC brand?

There were disappointments in financial results for 1982. Total sales climbed to $2.87 billion but, dishearteningly, losses also climbed, to $153.4 million. And though car sales, boosted by early sales of the Alliance, rose to 186,957 in the United States and Canada they perversely fell to a mere 8,834 internationally, as the Mexican economy, and many others, went into free fall. Jeep vehicles sales also rose in the United States and Canada, to 67,646 as the four-wheel-drive market gradually came back, but overseas they dropped to 23,083—the worst showing in years. For the year AMC sold a total of just 286,520 vehicles, a drop of 25,000 from 1981's discouraging numbers. Working capital sank to $73.7 million. The situation was grim.

Above: This is the Concord Limited two-door for 1982. Concord Limited models came with wire wheel covers as standard equipment. The wire caps were available on all other Concord and Spirit models as an option. This attractive two-tone combination was popular with buyers.

Left: This mock-up, dated February 5, 1980, shows an alternative design for the Concord D/L two-door landau top that might have debuted in 1983. It's rather attractive, and we can't help but wonder what the public would have thought of it.

Here we see *Motor Trend* magazine's Bob Brown (left) present the Car of the Year award to AMC president Paul Tippett. The award was for the Alliance, possibly the best subcompact in the world at the time.

1983–1984
THE COMEBACK

AMERICAN MOTORS RECEIVED a tremendous honor when the new Alliance was named *Motor Trend* 1983 Car of the Year, and it was entirely appropriate because the Alliance was a really extraordinary car. It was also the first AMC product to win that award since 1963. What was especially gratifying was how the Alliance scored so much higher than its competitors in nearly every category—there was no question of legitimacy; it was the first choice of every judge, and quality was listed as an especial strong point. To celebrate AMC put together a special limited edition Alliance MT model with special paint, wheels, and stripes. Just 3,000 were built.

Eagles received a minimum of refinements or improvements this year, as did the Concord/Spirit. The base Spirits were dropped but one new model was added: a very well-equipped Spirit GT, a separate model now rather than an option package, and a very nice machine all around. Little did anyone know that it would be the last new AMC-branded model ever. And once again the company underestimated demand as loyal AMC enthusiasts went to their local dealers for one last purchase and often did not find a GT there, not even to test-drive.

There was not much new in the 1983 Jeep line; the company was just counting time, waiting for the all-new lightweight Jeep XJs to debut, now less than a year away.

Early 1983 brought the sad news that the Concord and Spirit were being dropped after the 1983 model—not 1985 as had been promised and

The car that was supposed to save American Motors was the Renault Alliance. Introduced in the 1983 model year it was a remarkable small car, with fuel injection, disc brakes, and a choice of four- or five-speed overdrive transmissions combined with outstanding ride and handling. In its first year it sold very well.

despite the fact that the company had already created a very attractive restyling of the Concord, ready for production. The only reason given for dropping the Spirit/Concord was to reduce complexity in the factory. Now the only AMC-branded cars left would be the Eagle line.

In March 1983 came surprising news. First, it was announced that the Renault LeCar and 18i sedan were being dropped at the end of the model year. The 18i announcement wasn't a complete surprise; the car was an admitted flop. But LeCar had been selling at a yearly rate of about 20,000 units and people liked it. The 18i wagon would continue to be sold, with the name changed to Renault Sport Wagon.

Left: AM General was the world's largest producer of tactical wheeled vehicles and was busy producing the M939 series trucks during 1983. This company still exists and builds the Humvee for the U.S. military, as well as some overseas customers.

Below: As in the United States the VAM two-wheel-drive AMC cars came to an end after 1983. This 1983 VAM American wears a unique grille that was developed in Mexico for the local market. This is a base model; note the lack of opera windows and vinyl top.

More surprising news—AMC put the highly profitable AM General up for sale. The excuse given was a need to focus on its core auto business, but the real reason was the company desperately needed money and selling assets was probably the only way it could get it—Renault was becoming tired of pumping funds into its money-losing AMC operation. AM General had just won the first big contract to build the Hummer, an AMC-designed military 1¼-ton truck, so there was an excellent chance the company would get a good price for the firm. The sale went through in August for $170 million cash plus a dividend of $20 million from AM General—for a total of $190 million, roughly $120 million more than AMC paid for AM General *and* Jeep when they were one company.

Rumors abounded during the year that future Eagles would be based on Renault bodies beginning in 1985; it was later changed to 1988. According to the rumors, the first one, on an Alliance chassis, would

Top: In Mexico, AMC affiliate VAM produced a unique series called the Lerma, named for the city where the company had an engine plant. The Lerma was basically a stretched Spirit D/L on a Concord wheelbase, giving it sporty, almost luxurious looks with excellent interior room as well. Too bad we didn't see this in the United States.

Bottom: This unusual vehicle is an engineering prototype of the upcoming Jeep XJ models—the Cherokee and Wagoneer scheduled for 1984 introduction. This vehicle is disguised; the production styling had already been settled by the time this Jeep was photographed.

be targeted at buyers who ordinarily would buy a Subaru.

In May 1983 the company announced it had reached an agreement with Beijing Automotive Works to build Jeeps in China. This was China's first automotive venture since before World War II and the biggest industrial joint venture in the country. Initially vehicles would be built solely for the Chinese market, but the hope was that eventually Chinese Jeeps could be exported to other Asian countries, including Japan, where the 60-cents-per-hour Chinese labor rate would give Jeep a pricing advantage.

But back home, losses continued. By the end of the second quarter of 1983 AMC had already lost $145 million despite a 42 percent increase in vehicle sales. The reason was the cost of tooling for the new Jeeps, now just months away, along with tooling for another line of Renault small cars from Kenosha. What was of concern was that the U.S. market was beginning to shift its preference back to big cars—and AMC had none, nor were any on the way anytime soon.

Shown here are two Jeeps: the production Cherokee Chief on the right and a prototype Cherokee XJ on the left. Although this photo is dated May 5, 1981, it shows that by that point the XJ production styling was pretty well settled.

Because of stronger demand for larger cars the Big Three makes had become profitably again, while AMC was still bleeding profusely. But Renault declared that the big Renault R-25 sedan was not coming to America, not even as an import.

That July saw the 100,000th Alliance sold, a happy event occurring less than a year after production began. But August brought news that AMC was selling its fine new Southfield, Michigan, headquarters building, opened in 1976, by year-end. It was another asset sale, and not the last. During the year Wheel Horse was sold as well for $8 million. In other news Renault took over a faltering VAM. Exactly what it was going to do with it—merge it with Renault de Mexico and build Renaults there or continue building AMC cars—was left unsaid.

The balance of the year was quieter, though company engineers and planners were working frantically to get the new 1984 Jeep Wagoneer and Cherokee into production for the fall of 1983. A new line of Renault cars, the Encore series, would also begin production.

A new company, Renault/Jeep Sport was added to the corporate roster. It was a small skunk-works-type firm headed by AMC's talented engineer Roy Lunn, with a goal of increasing AMC's presence in racing. One of the first goals was to build a sports racing car kit that could be put together for less

Top: Seen in the Styling Studios is this Spirit Sedan with an unusual stripe on its side that flows onto the roof panel. Might this be what the 1983 Spirit Sedan was to wear?

Center: This proposal, photographed in September 1979, shows an obvious attempt at recreating the classic AMX look on the Spirit Liftback body. Although it looks nice, the front-end styling doesn't really match up to the rear, so AMC likely would have had to redo the entire body.

Bottom right: Jeep vehicles continued to be popular in world markets. This photo shows a Jeep CJ-10 pickup truck, which was designed for international markets. The CJ-10 was sold mainly in Australia.

than $10,000. The very capable Lunn had no trouble accomplishing that. The Sports Renault race car was an immediate hit.

In the fourth quarter of 1983 American Motors actually showed a profit, a small one of just $7.4 million, but a profit nonetheless—and they made it selling cars and the new Jeep XJ wagons. It showed a positive direction—for the prior 14 quarters the company had reported losses. During the year the company sold 265,999 cars in the United States and Canada, up about 80,000 units, and 93,169 Jeeps, up some 25,523 units. Overseas markets were down again because the rest of the world was suffering through the same high inflation, unemployment, and recession as was the United States. Only 4,020 AMC cars were sold overseas along with 20,274 Jeeps. For the year AMC sold a total of 383,462 vehicles, a sharp increase from 1982. But the company reported yet another loss, this one gigantic—$258.3 million on net sales of $3,271,720,000. The company had shown a positive turnaround on vehicle sales; now it needed more than anything to have a turnaround in finances. With a hopeful eye AMC management began the 1984 model year.

The omens were both good and bad as the 1984 model year began. The bad news was that the subcompact market was shrinking rapidly and that was essentially the only part of the car market where AMC

The three men most responsible for styling the 1984 Jeep XJ series were (left to right) Styling Vice President Dick Teague, Interior Design executive Vince Geraci, and Exterior Design chief Bob Nixon. Teague has passed away. The author counts Geraci and Nixon among his best friends to this day.

had volume contenders, and the good news was that the new Jeep XJ Cherokee and Wagoneer's were finally unveiled.

The new Jeep wagons were bold, innovative machines, loaded with new technology and engineering, and so far advanced from their competitors as to make comparisons meaningless. The basic platform, designed by Roy Lunn and his engineering team, featured an advanced type of unitized construction called Uniframe, which provided superior strength in a lightweight package, an advanced new front suspension system that utilized a solid front axle for strength but gave the ride and handling of an independent suspension, and a choice of Command-Trac or Selec-Trac shift-on-the-fly four-wheel-drive systems. The new Jeeps weighed 1,000 pounds less than the old ones yet retained 90 percent of the interior

Here's a production model Cherokee Chief XJ. The new Jeep was a wonder of innovation and extremely well designed. The new Jeeps were years ahead of their competitors.

space and offered fuel economy of 24 miles per gallon city and 33 miles per gallon highway. The styling, created by a team led by Bob Nixon, was perfection itself; American in nature with an aura of European sophistication. The interior design team was headed by Vince Geraci. Their efforts yielded the best-looking interior of any compact four-wheel-drive vehicle. The new Cherokee and Wagoneer were masterpieces of the automakers art.

Alliance had little change for 1984, other than a higher price, and was joined by the new Renault Encore, a hatchback version of the Alliance. The Encore was a good car, every bit as competent as the award-winning Alliance, and AMC had hopes that it would sell in similar volumes. But the problem was that Encore really wasn't very much different from Alliance, so it appealed to basically the same people. Also, the four-door hatchback was a bit odd-looking and in the end the public didn't swing to Encore with

Top: The Eagle sedan for 1984. The photo illustrates the sort of off-road driving the Eagle was suited for—running up sandy hills, crossing muddy fields, and going anyplace where traction and good ground clearance were needed.

Bottom: Also arriving in 1984 was the new Renault Encore, essentially an Alliance with a hatchback. Although they sold decently in the first year, sales of the Encore began to slacken in its second model year.

Top: Here is the Eagle wagon for 1984. Although the base Eagle's didn't carry D/L badges, they were often referred to as D/Ls in memos to dealers and in-house because their interior and exterior trim was roughly the same as a Concord D/L.

Bottom: Have you ever wondered what the 1984 AMC Concord might have looked like? This design, photographed in November 1979, shows the styling progression designers felt could be achieved with the Concord to keep it fresh and salable through the 1980s. Even without a vinyl top this is a luxurious-looking car and probably would have sold well.

anywhere near the vigor they had shown Alliance. Meanwhile, the subcompact market continued to decline.

Eagles for 1984 were essentially unchanged. The new 150 cid (2.5-liter) AMC four-cylinder engine, mainstay of the Cherokee/Wagoneer, was now the standard engine on Eagles. A new standard wheel cover debuted.

In August it was announced that AMC's legendary design chief Dick Teague was retiring. He was the man Ed Anderson had hired back in the late 1950s when Bill Reddig moved over to Kelvinator, and he had done a pretty good job over the years. It's hard to fault him or any designer for the Matador coupe or Pacer because the programs were laid out by management and those managers were the ones who dictated that each car have its own unique body, one not that could be shared with any other car. It was a stupid, tragic program that went against all the lessons AMC had learned in the beginning, but no fault of the designers.

Top: Here we see the same styling theme, but on the two-door Concord this time. The two-door and four-door models probably shared the same roof panel to cut tooling cost, as had been done on the original Hornet.

Bottom: This model wears the sporty wheel covers from the Eagle and appears to be jacked up a little higher. However, a close look shows it wears a Concord D/L nameplate and what appears to be a Limited badge.

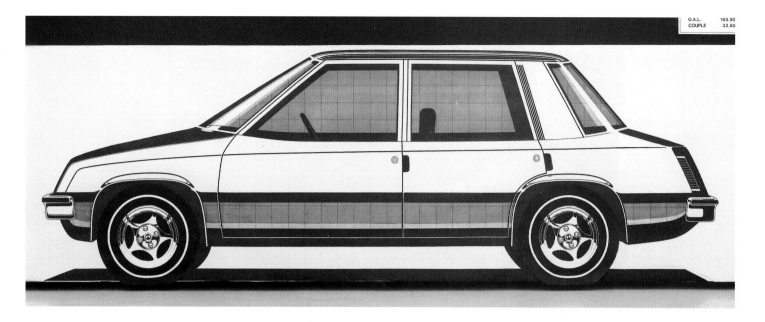

O.A.L. 163.50
COUPLE 32.50

Top: Here is one of the designs created by American Motors stylists, a four-door sedan on a 100.4-inch wheelbase. This was one of what was supposed to be a line of models, had it been approved for production.

Bottom: This photo, taken in the AMC Styling studios, shows a proposal for a small car to replace the Gremlin/Spirit sedan. This is a full-size clay, indicating that the company had strong interest in doing something like it.

Replacing Teague was Tom Scott, who came from Ford. Rather than being a VP, he was named director of Styling.

That September AMC purchased 250 acres in Brampton, Ontario, from Bramalea Ltd. of Toronto, where it would build a new assembly plant for an all-new intermediate size car to be co-designed by Renault and AMC designers. The plant would come to be known as the Bramalea plant.

In November 1984 the company announced it would be adding the Renault Espace minivan to its U.S. offerings beginning in 1986. This move seemed pointless because the stylish Espace, built by Matra for Renault, was a very low-volume fiberglass-bodied van—only 11,000 were built in 1983—with a high price tag and no chance of large sales potential. Also coming was the high-performance Renault Alpine sports car.

That same November the company notified the local UAW that the future of the Kenosha plant was tied to labor costs—and they would have to come down significantly. As before, AMC's hourly wages were higher than at GM or Ford when they should have been much lower. But the union had always kept AMC management over a barrel, knowing the company couldn't afford a strike. Even more important than the wage disparity was the problem of work rules. Kenosha had one steward for every 25 shop workers, whereas Ford had one for every 193 workers, and GM one for every 169 workers. This was costing AMC a fortune. The company asked the local to help it by reducing the number of stewards, and, typically, the union refused. Not even the offer of a 25-cent-per-hour raise could get the union to cooperate. The militant, all-for-us attitude the Kenosha local had shown so many times was still in play. Now, AMC was seeking some $2 per hour in concessions, fewer job categories, and fewer stewards. The threat was real; with the new Canadian plant the company had another source for automobiles. AMC would only guarantee work for Kenosha through the life cycle of the Alliance/Encore, expected to be about 1989.

The year ended on a good note. Sales volume rose to $4.2 billion, and the company crossed into profitability, though only marginally. The net profit for 1984 was $15,469,000. In the United States and Canada 237,309 cars were wholesaled (down about 29,000) along with 171,036 Jeeps, while overseas saw 11,646 cars and 22,392 Jeeps. In total, AMC sold to its dealers 442,383 vehicles, up 59,000 units. There were hopes that 1985 would be even better.

Top: Another small-car proposal, this one for a two-door hatchback. This model appears to be related to the previous clay shown.

Bottom: This photo, dated April 2, 1976, shows a small van-type car on a subcompact wheelbase of only 86 inches. This likely was planned as a new small car targeted below the Pacer.

10

1985–1987
THE FINAL STRUGGLE

IN EARLY 1984 PAUL TIPPETT TOLD A REPORTER that there would be a new Renault car for 1985. Playing coy, the AMC chairman wouldn't say exactly what it would be but speculated it might be a station wagon. However, when the 1985 Renaults were unveiled the new product proved to be a minor new model—an Alliance convertible. Convertibles, long out of favor with the public, were seeing a resurgence in popularity, and every automaker wanted to have one in its lineup. Tippett was no different, but in this case the decision to bring out the ragtop rather than a station wagon was a serious mistake. In the U.S. market convertibles are generally low-volume products; station wagons, on the other hand, are usually higher-volume sellers and have been since the early 1950s. Alliance needed something to prop up its volume. Why AMC failed to introduce an Alliance wagon is mystifying.

For 1985 Alliance and Encore got a new 1.7-liter engine, standard on Encore GS and Alliance Limited and the convertible and optional on other Encore and Alliance models. The rest of the Renault line was mostly carryover. Likewise, Jeeps were also mostly carryover, though the company now offered a two-wheel-drive version of the Cherokee, as well as an optional turbo-diesel engine for maximum fuel economy and towing power.

AMC's Eagle soldiered on with a minor facelift—stylists added the SX/4 hood and grille surround. The 258-cid six was once again the standard engine, the four being confined now to Jeep products, and shift-on-the-fly was now standard as well. The standard transmission was a five-speed stick. Wire

For 1985 American Motors introduced the new Alliance convertible. Although it was an attractive car, convertibles rarely sell in high volume. The company would have been much better off introducing a new Alliance station wagon.

THE 2-WHEEL/4-WHEEL DRIVE AMERICAN EAGLE
AVAILABLE FOR PURCHASE OR LEASE AT PARTICIPATING AMC DEALERS
SEAT BELTS SAVE LIVES

Above: The 1985 Eagle got a no-cost facelift when AMC decided to use the SX/4 hood and grille surround on all Eagles.

Below right: For its own AMC brand American Motors usually focused what little advertising it could afford on the Eagle wagon, which was the best-selling model. Note how this Eagle handles the snow with ease. The Eagle's higher ground clearance made it superior to the Subaru.

wheel covers were standard on the Eagle Limited, optional on the other Eagles.

But the noose was slowly tightening on AMC. Renault was having severe financial problems at home and was looking for ways to bail itself out. Bernard Hanon, the Renault executive who fought so hard for the AMC-Renault collaboration, was ousted as board chairman, replaced by Georges Besse. Known for his relentless efforts to cut costs, Besse began reviewing all the company's world-wide operations, looking to slash overhead. One of the first places he looked at was the money-losing American operation.

In addition, AMC's union was up in arms over the payback deal they had signed three years earlier. AMC was in the process of returning some of the money to them, albeit in a small way. The company set aside $5.4 million this year to begin the payback. But AMC employees wanted the company to use an alternative method that was part of the original agreement—a so-called wheel tax of $100 per vehicle built up to 200,000 units and $150 per car for every unit over that. AMC simply couldn't pay it, and in the end the only way the company could get the union to back off on its demands was to tell it that if it insisted on the higher payment the Kenosha plant would be closed and everyone laid off as soon as the Alliance/Encore program ended. That finally brought the Kenosha union people around, and they settled for the much smaller payment schedule. Down in Toledo union members pushed back with acts of vandalism, damaging Jeep vehicles, denting bodies, and pouring sugar in fuel tanks to render the Jeeps useless. It was a

Above: A good photo of some of the most important AMC executives; left to right they are Dale Dawkins, VP marketing; Roy Lunn, VP engineering; Keith Ebersol, VP purchasing; Dick Teague, VP styling; and George Maddox, VP manufacturing.

Left: The Eagle for 1986 looked the same as all Eagle wagons that came before, with the exception of a few minor items.

shameful and cowardly reaction to the very real and perilous situation AMC was in, but in the end AMC had to pay them the higher formula. In any event, the debt had to be paid back by 1988.

Meanwhile, rumors circulated that Renault was about to pull the plug on its partnership with AMC. The industry trade paper *Automotive News* predicted that a day of reckoning might be at hand.

Unfortunately, after five consecutive quarters of profits AMC slid into losses again in the first quarter of 1985. Across-the-board budget cuts were instituted, though by now there was very little fat left in the white-collar ranks. One prominent executive to feel the heat was Paul Tippett, who stepped down as a full-time employee of AMC, becoming a part-time chairman. This unusual situation left Jose Dedeurwaerder in charge.

Down in Mexico VAM's passenger car business had dried up after the Mexican government devalued the peso in 1982. Subsequently VAM was sold to Renault de Mexico. As in the United States, Renault trimmed down the VAM model range, and eventually production of cars was ceased after fewer than 2,000 1983 models were produced. Just as in the United States, Renault in Mexico had no interest in building AMC cars. The company did build a plant to produce 1.7-liter engines for Alliance/Encore and also began producing the Alliance for the Mexican market, though the car proved a complete flop there.

In 1986 AMC discontinued the Jeep CJ series, replacing it with the all-new Wrangler. Here we see freshly built CJs, some of the final ones produced, waiting to be shipped to dealers. This photo is dated January 1986.

The Kenosha union agreed in mid-May 1985 to contract concessions that cut wages by 37 cents per hour and reduced vacation and paid days off, saving the company millions. Joe Cappy said, "For the first time in 35 years [we have] a competitive labor contract." The concessions would go a long way toward returning AMC to profitability.

During 1985 the subcompact market was weak in both the United States and Canada, and Alliance/Encore sales dropped by 100,000 units to 136,989, ruining any chance for AMC to earn a profit even though Jeep sales rose to 217,806 units, a new record. In the international market car sales rose to 14,492, and Jeep sales climbed to 22,482. For the year AMC sold a total of 391,769 vehicles, a net drop of more than 50,000 units. Total sales volume was $4,039,901, and a loss of $125 million was recorded. As usual, in the annual report to stockholders management talked mainly about the future, which they said looked rosy, rather than the present, which was black. Dedeurwaerder spoke of the new plant being built in Canada to produce an all-new midsize car for 1988, and he gave a glimpse of that car along with the upcoming Renault Alpine sports car and a new Renault compact that was going to be imported in 1987.

December 1985 brought a small flurry of management changes. Joseph E. Cappy, executive vice president, was made chief operating officer, and Paul Tippet left the company to become president of Springs Industries. He remained a board member. Pierre Semerena, executive vice president of Renault, was named chairman of the board of American Motors. Leaving the board was Bernard Hanon. He had been largely responsible for the linkup of AMC and Renault, and right now his masters were not happy with him.

In a late-1985 interview Jose Dedeurwaerder revealed that the Alpine sports car project had been pushed back to mid-1987 and that the Espace Van deal was dead; the high cost of the Renault minivan priced it out of contention in the United States. He also stated that he had a good replacement for the Eagle coming in 1988—the R-19, a small Renault subcompact with four-wheel drive (the R-19 eventually replaced the R-9/Alliance outside the United States). That meant that the days of the present-day AMC Eagle were running out; Dedeurwaerder didn't say if the R-19 4x4 would be badged as an Eagle or a Renault, but

Left: Here's something you've probably never seen; inside the lobby of American Motors headquarters in the American Center, Southfield, Michigan. The new Wrangler is on display along with what appears to be a 1909 Hudson in the background. The photo is dated March 1987.

Right: This is the man who became the last president of American Motors, Joe Cappy. Cappy started out in Marketing at American Motors before becoming president. Under Cappy labor costs and overhead were cut drastically.

Top: The new Jeep model for 1987 was the Comanche SporTruck, a low-priced entry in the popular small two-wheel-drive truck market. With Comanche AMC had an entry that was better than the Japanese trucks and could compete with them on price as well.

Bottom: The new Renault GTA was a neat package but arrived during the merger negotiations and never caught on. Notice the ground effects body cladding, unique grille.

history would suggest that Renault would be the name. He also noted that 1986 was going to be a difficult one for AMC because it had nothing new to offer in its passenger car lines. "It's going to be a very tough year for us," Dedeurwaerder said.

As stated, nothing was new in the 1986 Renault or AMC lineup. The three Eagle models—sedan, wagon, and Limited wagon—had virtually nothing new for salesmen to talk about. Alliance and Encore were essentially the same as before, though they had new instrument panels and grilles. Encore also had a new Electronic model that boasted an electronic digital instrument panel. Alliance added a Base four-door sedan.

Jeep had big news—a new compact pickup truck called Comanche. It was based on the Cherokee platform and offered both two- and four-wheel-drive models. The company hoped to sell 50,000 of them in its first year. In May 1986 the new Wrangler, a completely new vehicle designed to replace the CJ-7, debuted to great acclaim. It was considered an early 1987 model. The new Wrangler, though still tough as iron, was a more civilized vehicle that closely resembled the beloved CJ.

In March 1986 Joe Cappy was named president and CEO of American Motors, with Jose Dedeurwaerder elevated to vice chairman and Pierre Semerena remaining as chairman. Cappy told a reporter that AMC was on the verge of a great turnaround. His belief was based on the many new cars he had in the pipeline—the new Wrangler, followed in the fall by a new performance subcompact Renault GTA, followed in January 1987 with the new R-21 (Medallion) compact, later by the Alpine sports car, and, in the fall of 1987, the new X-58 mid-size sedan. He didn't mention that he also had a coupe version of the X-58—called the X-59—which would debut as a 1989 model, and an all-new midsize Jeep SUV code-named the ZJ coming for 1990. Cappy did

The new Renault Medallion, which was to be the company's entry into the compact market, was likewise lost in the shuffle when AMC and Chrysler agreed to merge. It was renamed the Eagle Medallion and sold for a time, though it never proved popular.

Right: This photo, dated August 1987, shows a temporary sign being installed over the existing AMC dealer sign. This dealership, TelTwelve AMC/Jeep, was within eyesight of AMC headquarters. It would be months before permanent signs would be available.

Below: The all-new 1988 Renault Premier was launched in 1987 to great acclaim, right in the middle of the merger. It was quickly renamed the Eagle Premier and sold for several years under that name. Too bad it wasn't branded as an AMC product—it would have revived the brand.

reveal that the company was also searching for a low-priced Asian-sourced car to sell.

AMC had a great many things going on at that point, including some that were rather startling. During March 1986, AMC board member Felix Royhatyn, who had helped rescue Chrysler years earlier, introduced Chrysler CEO Lee Iacocca to Renault's Georges Besse over lunch in a private New York club. There was no buy-out talk then, but twice during the spring of 1986 Iacocca met quietly with Besse to talk about possible cooperative ventures between the two firms. Results were soon forthcoming—in July AMC signed an agreement to assemble Chrysler's M-body cars in the Kenosha plant. The M-body vehicles were the very popular midsize Dodge Diplomat, Plymouth Grand Fury, and Chrysler Fifth Avenue. Chrysler had intended to phase out these cars, but because of their continuing popularity the company now wanted to keep selling them. And because the plant where the M-bodies had been built was already ticketed for another product Chrysler decided to ask AMC if it would put some of its unused capacity to work building the cars. AMC's union had to agree to cut job classifications from a ridiculous 166 to a more manageable 46. Production would begin in February 1987. The company later had discussions about also building Chrysler's L-body subcompacts, Dodge Omni and Plymouth Horizon, in Kenosha. It could go a long way toward offsetting some of AMC's fixed costs. Joe Cappy scoffed at rumors that a bigger deal was brewing.

Also in July American Motors sent out a preliminary prospectus for 8 million shares of Cumulative Convertible Preferred Stock, hoping to raise $200 million (net $187 million). AMC was once again in the position of needing a cash infusion, and this was about the only way left to get it. The prospectus stated that "the company is in a very tight cash position. The Company's working capital decreased . . . to $3 million on December 31, 1985. It was now at a negative $21 million as of March 1, 1986."

There it was in black and white, the effect of the continuing losses that AMC hadn't been able to offset completely by the continued borrowings to this point. In 1979, AMC's best year, working capital stood at $235.8 million. In calendar 1980 it fell to $206 million ($94.6 as of September 30, 1980). It fell again to $164.5 million in 1981 and then to $73.7 million in 1982. In 1983 working capital was a mere $6.4 million, and in 1984 it was a negative $16 million, which rose to $3 million in 1985. Now it stood at a negative $21 million, when a company the size of AMC should have had working capital of at least $200 million. AMC also had long-term debt of $947 million and expected borrowings to increase from 1986–1989. Now it was time to borrow again. The noose continued to tighten.

And so it was in the fall of 1986 that a concerned Roy D. Chapin Jr. began to hear rumors that American Motors might be sold. He queried his Renault contacts, who reassured him that no such deal was being contemplated. Certainly, they said, if such a move were being considered, they'd let him know. An uneasy Chapin had to settle for that. But the truth is by that point Iacocca's plans had moved well beyond a mere cooperative venture—in secret meetings he'd discussed buying Jeep from Renault. Besse, however, refused to consider it. He was only interested in selling the entire AMC package—wanting to cut his losses and get some money back from all that his company had put into AMC. Slowly an agreement began to take shape.

For 1986 AMC reported total sales of $3.46 billion and a net loss of $91.3 million. What was remarkable about the loss was that it was so much lower than the prior year despite the fact that wholesalesales to dealers fell to 50,041 cars (which curiously included one AMC two-wheel-drive car) in the United States. Domestic Jeep sales fell to 183,987 units. In overseas markets (which for this year's reporting now included Canada) 16,331 cars and 37,375 Jeeps were sold, for a grand total of 287,734 cars and Jeeps worldwide—a drop of more than 100,000 units. It was quite impressive that AMC was able to reduce its losses so dramatically

The final AMC cars were the 1988 Eagles. By this time only the station wagon was offered and only in one model, which had most major options, air conditioning, AM/FM radio, etc., as standard equipment. All were built before the end of 1987.

in the face of such an enormous drop in sales—remarkable, really. Even more germane, American Motors had actually turned a profit in the fourth quarter of 1986. And things were looking good for the first quarter of 1987.

Iacocca still lurked in the background. The plan to transfer AMC to Chrysler was now code-named "Project Titan." Talks continued until November 17, 1986, when Georges Besse was murdered in Paris by French terrorists for no other reason than they saw him as a symbol of hated capitalism. After that talks stalled for a time until they were revived by Besse's replacement, Raymond Levy, in February 1987.

In December 1986 Joe Cappy complained to industry magazine *Ward's AutoWorld* about the wheel tax deal the Toledo union had forced on him, as well the Jeep plant's generally uncompetitive labor practices. He told *Ward's*, "[O]nly a stupid person would do business down in Toledo if they don't have a competitive contract. I may be many things, but my mother didn't raise a stupid child."

Under Cappy's watch, AMC's Jesus Peon, manufacturing VP, slashed dozens of layers of management and cut about $120 million in cost from AMC manufacturing. Cappy had AMC's sourcing operations streamlined, saving millions, and made the decision to keep inventories of Jeep vehicles tight by not overproducing, "Maybe I'm missing a few sales, but the results in profitability have been phenomenal," he told *Automotive Industries* magazine.

Meanwhile the 1987 products of American Motors were announced. Jeep had some big news that almost went unnoticed in the whirlwind of AMC news that year. Comanche, previously available only as a long-bed truck, introduced a new short-bed SporTruck priced at only $6,495, undercutting the competition with a better-equipped truck at a lower price. Cherokee introduced a new Limited luxury model that quickly became one of the hottest-selling vehicles on the market—and a favorite of car thieves due to its incredible popularity. And an especially important new engine debuted—the Jeep 4.0-liter Power-Tech Six. Based on the AMC six-cylinder block the new fuel-injected 4.0 liter (242 cid) was smaller than the old 258 cid (4.2-liter) engine but much more powerful; 173 horsepower versus 112 horsepower. In fact, the new Power-Tech Jeep six was the most powerful engine in its class by far. In power and acceleration Jeep Cherokee, Wagoneer, and Comanche simply blew away the competition. Equally important was the fact that AMC made much more profit on Jeep's equipped with the 4.0 liter than it had when it used the GM six. It would greatly enhance AMC's bottom line, as it would be the highest volume engine in the highest volume products. Also debuting was a new Aisin-Seiki four-speed automatic overdrive transmission.

The new Renault GTA performance car debuted in two-door sedan and convertible models—two body styles not offered by competing so-called hot subcompacts like VW GTI. The GTA was an Alliance powered by a 2.0-liter engine and boasting ground-effects body cladding. It could do 0 to 60 in less than 10 seconds.

This would have been the next new car coming from AMC; the Renault (or Eagle) Allure. The Allure was a two-door coupe version of the Premier and was designed to sell in the higher price ranges. Chrysler cancelled it soon after taking over AMC despite the large amount of work that had been done to bring it to production.

The Renault Encore name was dropped because sales of that model had fallen to an uneconomic level. The hatchback body styles were kept in production but renamed Alliance Hatchback. The Alpine sports car was pushed back to an April or May introduction.

There was no change—again—in the Eagle line. Why the new 4.0-liter six and four-speed automatic transmission were not introduced to the Eagle is unknown, other than perhaps a total lack of interest by Renault in saving the AMC brand. A new drive-train certainly would have revived Eagle's fortunes. As things stood it was dying from sheer neglect.

In February 1987 talks resumed between Chrysler and Renault over a possible sale of AMC to Chrysler. Within a month the framework of an agreement was agreed on, followed by negotiations to settle some fine points, and all this time Joe Cappy and AMC were left in the dark. In Paris on March 9, 1987, after all-night negotiations, Renault and Chrysler entered into a formal letter of intent, which contemplated that definitive agreements would be negotiated under which Chrysler would purchase all of the AMC securities and equity in AMC held by Renault. It was still early morning in America, and at 7:00 a.m. Joe Cappy was finally told. At 9:15 a.m. that day the rest of the world heard the announcement.

As plans became known, it was revealed that AMC initially would be a free-standing subsidiary of Chrysler. However, as Chrysler vice chairman Ben Bidwell quickly explained, "The free-standing concept will only be transitory." It was Chrysler's plan to dismantle AMC, get rid of what it didn't want, and meld the rest into the parent corporation.

The main reason why Iacocca was buying AMC was to capture Jeep Corporation, highly profitable and the best-known vehicle brand in the world. He was also getting the brand-new Bramalea plant that AMC had built for a bargain $340 million, but which was now worth about $600–$800 million. Besides all that he was gaining a dealer network of nearly 1,500 dealers who were battle-toughened and ready for a comeback. He had no intention of keeping the AMC brand alive.

Over in AMC Styling, design chief Tom Scott realized he probably soon be demoted or possibly terminated when the merger was completed, so he quietly went back to Ford. Ever-loyal Vince Geraci was named as his replacement and thus became the last head of AMC Styling.

It was a strange time for Renault to bail out. American Motors earned a profit of more than $20 million in the last quarter of 1986 and went on to earn $23.4 million in the first quarter

Top: This photo is undated but probably related to the very similar four-door car shown in the previous chapter. Unlike the Renault products, this was designed entirely by American Motors stylists in Detroit and seems a good deal more handsome than the Renault products.

Bottom: A glimpse of a possible future. The small sedan shown here in a photo dated May 6, 1975, is a proposal for a Gremlin replacement for the 1980s. The windows are too big to be rolled completely into the doors, so they had to be split in the middle to allow the lower portion to be rolled down.

of 1987 as U.S. wholesale sales of cars and Jeeps continued to improve. Second quarter profits set a record for that period—something on the order of $26 million—when Jeep sales took off. Joe Cappy bragged to *Ward's AutoWorld* about the $50 million first-half profit and how easily he'd sold that $200 million in bonds. So clearly now the company was coming out of the woods. It's the opinion of many analysts that AMC, which finally had a competitive labor contract, streamlined production and sourcing, tremendous sales of Jeep vehicles (and using its own engines in them again) plus money-making contract assembly of Chrysler cars at its Kenosha plant, was on the way to record-setting profits. In fact, a later informal study by Chrysler staffers revealed a pro forma profit of $200 million for 1987—a new record—if AMC had remained independent. It was as if, one executive said, Renault decided after nine months that it didn't want to be pregnant.

Chrysler used part of those 1987 AMC profits to write off launch costs for the Premier and development costs for the X59 coupe—the latter of which was then cancelled. It would have been called the Renault Allure if Renault had stayed on or the Eagle Allure if Chrysler hadn't killed it. The Alpine sports car was pushed back once again and finally cancelled.

Chrysler bought out all of AMC's stockholders for an offer of $4.50 per share, in cash or stock. The cost was $518 million of Chrysler stock plus $200 million cash. As part of the deal Chrysler also agreed to pay Renault up to a total of $350 million in additional payments depending on the volume of Premier production, which used a Renault-supplied transmission and V-6 engine. Chrysler had to guarantee a certain production level or pay a penalty to Renault. Chrysler also agreed to assume AMC liabilities of approximately $900 million, of which more than a third were pending lawsuits attributable to Jeep CJ rollover accidents. In addition, Chrysler assumed AMC's pension liabilities of $600 million.

The net cost, not counting liabilities, was reported in the press as $1.1 billion. But it was well worth it. The Jeep brand alone was worth at least that amount. The AMC/Jeep retail channel was worth another $1 billion, and the Bramalea plant, Kenosha plant, and in-house supplier plants were worth still another $1 billion or more. In addition, Chrysler inherited about $425 million in net operating loss (NOL) and tax credit carry-forwards. These were usable through 2002 to reduce the company's tax burden. Chrysler had cut itself a great deal.

Top: Here we see another full-size clay model of a proposed small sedan for the 1980s or later. Notice how the rear window is shaped like the Gremlin's and how much higher the belt line is than in the prior photo. This car is more production ready than some of the other ideas.

Bottom left: Even in 1966 AMC stylists were looking far into the future at possible small-car designs for the fuel-short world to come. This small three-wheel runabout was drawn by AMC designer Bob Nixon.

Bottom right: This mock-up of a small van was created about seven months after the Pacer was introduced. It looks similar to the Concept AM Van and may indeed be related to it.

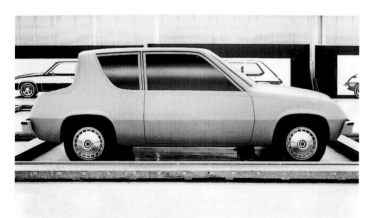

It was left to Joe Cappy to give the final pronouncement on Renault's future in North America. Never one to mince words, he said "I don't think Renault will ever come back to the U.S. market. They're finished in America—at least for my lifetime."

During the fall of 1987 workers at the old Brampton plant assembled the final AMC cars to be built—the 1988 Eagle wagon. It was whittled down to a single model with air conditioning, roof rack, and many other former options as standard equipment. Rather than have a separate Limited model they made wire wheel covers standard and leather optional at $201. Though technically the cars weren't AMC's because that company no longer existed, the last Eagles wore the AMC name and badges and even the ordering guides were issued under the American Motors name. Production ended for good on December 14, 1987. The AMC brand went out of being.

As far as the rest of the cars, Chrysler had already dropped the Renault badge and renamed the line Eagle. This was a management decision, and it was probably the biggest mistake Lee Iacocca made in his entire career. It's a basic truth of automobile marketing that it's easier to revive a weak brand than it is to try to launch a new brand. Eagle as a brand name was new and thus unknown to 100 percent of the population. AMC, on the other hand, had sold millions of cars over the years, it had millions of owners as a base, and its dealers were well-known in their communities. Certainly, the AMC brand would need to be relaunched because it had been given no new products for so many years, but this could have been done and for less money than the company spent trying to get the Eagle brand established. Naturally, to this day Chrysler's former management still claims that introducing Eagle as a replacement for AMC was the right move. But how right a move was it? The history of the Eagle brand was one of struggling for 11 years trying to establish itself before finally giving up. Chrysler discontinued the brand after 1998.

The shame of it is that Chrysler could have relaunched AMC as a builder of four-wheel-drive cars. It would have taken a few years to develop a product line but it would give AMC a definite niche in the market—one held today by Subaru.

Kenosha eventually got to build the L-body cars and employment shot up as workers returned to the job. But then in January 1988 Chrysler announced it would close the Kenosha complex for good by September of that same year. Rudy Kuzel, the highly militant union leader of Kenosha's UAW Local 72, took a tough stance. According to published accounts, rather than appeal to Iacocca's sense of fairness, Kuzel instead threatened to "make the plant closing the most expensive in history if Chrysler did not reconsider." This was the caliber of labor representative AMC had to struggle with all those years as it tried to squeeze a profit out of building cars. Is it any wonder Chrysler wanted out? In the end Chrysler came up with

Top: Another small van idea, probably from the mid-1970s. This is larger and squarer than the others and bears a resemblance to the Chrysler minivans. We wonder why AMC didn't produce it.

Bottom: Designed by Roy Lunn, the R-Car was an idea for a 50 miles-per-gallon commuter car.

a reasonable compensation package and also promised to keep L-body production going through January 1989. It was the best deal Kenosha could get. The former AMC assembly plants were later torn down.

Chrysler took fairly good care of AMC's white-collar workers, transferring many of them to higher positions at Chrysler, where many of them thrived. When Chrysler itself ran into financial troubles it ended up laying off quite a number of people, and many feel that former lower-level AMC people took the brunt of it. But the fact remains that even today many former AMC employees are working for Chrysler, and many more are living on a Chrysler-funded pension.

But the fact remains that Chrysler shut down the AMC brand even though American Motors had a bright future ahead of it. Ironically, AMC was closed down just as it finally turned profitable and was on the road to new glory. Plans were to introduce the Allure coupe for 1989, the new Jeep ZJ—which became the Grand Cherokee—for 1990 while work continued on a new small Jeep JJ suited for world markets. Additional production capacity was planned for the new Bramalea plant to support a new Jeep product. Memos also indicate work was proceeding on a 4x4 Alliance replacement- (possibly the Renault 19) and a U.S.-designed passenger van. Who can say how far AMC might have climbed?

The last AMC product to enter production was the 1993 Jeep Grand Cherokee. It was entirely designed and engineered by AMC engineers and stylists well before the Chrysler takeover, and once Chrysler assumed control of AMC those same designers completed the initial prototypes. Only cash shortages kept Chrysler from introducing it until 1992.

Parts of AMC are still around. Since 1987 Jeep had grown and thrived, becoming more successful than ever before and growing on the worldwide stage. In 2012 Jeep sold more than 700,000 vehicles worldwide. Up in Canada Chrysler cars are built in the Bramalea plant, and engines are still built in Kenosha. Many of AMC's former overseas affiliates are still operating, selling Jeep and Chrysler products. The Jeep plants in Egypt and Venezuela are still building new Jeeps. Many people are doing well under the Chrysler regime.

But the rest of us, the people who bought or sold or serviced AMC cars and who loved owning an independent make, we are not better off than before. Our choice in the market is less now than it used to be, and our automobile market is becoming dominated by Korean and Japanese makes, cars and SUVs from countries that are notoriously reluctant to open up their markets to U.S. cars. You and I don't have the opportunity to purchase a new American Motors car anymore, and nothing can be done to change that.

Designer Vince Geraci perhaps put it best when he said " There will never be another company like American Motors."

He's right, of course; there won't. And that is one of the saddest statements anyone can make.

Top: In 1985 AMC was interested in getting into the minivan market in the near future, and reliable Bob Nixon sketched out this idea for a handsome van that probably would have sold well.

Bottom: The final design we have found thus far from AMC Styling is this 1986 proposal for a new AMX sport coupe using the chassis of the AM Motorsport racecar platform along with its drivetrain components. Was this Bob Nixon design the last AMX drawing produced?

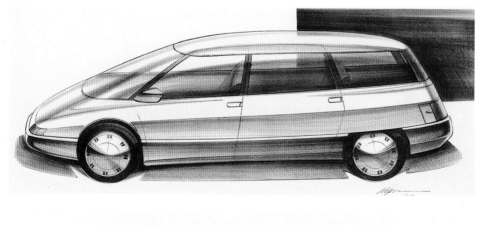

INDEX

A Mark, 105
ABC, 21
Abernethy, Roy, 31, 52, 55, 66–67, 70, 71, 73, 75, 79, 80, 82, 83–87, 90, 92, 105, 126
Adams, Charlie, 97
Advance Unit-Body Construction, 70
Aisin-Seiki, 200
Alexander, Jim, 102, 141, 143
Allstate Insurance, 152
AM General Corporation, 115, 117, 122, 124, 127, 128, 131, 141, 142, 146, 147, 150, 151, 163, 167, 170–171, 173, 179
Ambassador, 40, 90, 92, 93, 96, 99, 102, 110, 113, 115, 121, 122–123, 125, 126, 128, 132–133, 134, 136
    Brougham series, 123, 125, 128
    DPL, 118
    SST, 94–95, 107
American International Racers, 104
American Motors Engineering, 92
American Motors Export, 60
Amigo, 131
Amitron show car, 90, 149, 150
Amoroso, Eugene, 148
AMX, 85, 91, 98, 99–100, 102, 105, 107, 110, 111, 114, 115, 131, 147, 148, 159, 165, 168, 182, 204
    GT, 101, 103
    II, 87, 91
AMX/2, 106
AMX/3, 106
Anderson, Edmund E., 24, 26, 33, 36, 37, 40, 50–51, 53–54, 58, 61, 62, 63, 65, 67, 68–69, 75, 84–85, 187
Anderson, Helen, 62
Anderson, Ian, 160
Angers, Jim, 121
A-OK Quality Workmanship campaign, 60
Apache, Ambassador, 74–75
Arab-American Vehicles Company, 152, 154
Arbib, Richard, 38, 40
Auburn, 14
Audi, 141, 146
Automotive Industries, 200
Automotive News, 148, 194

Baja 500, 104
Bantam, 14
Barit, A. E., 20, 22
Beijing Automotive Industrial Corporation, 166
Beijing Automotive Works, 180
Besse, Georges, 192, 198, 199, 200
Bidwell, Ben, 201
Big Bad colors, 101, 102, 104
Boch Motors, 35
Boe, Archie, 152

Bold Look, 38
Booth, Wally, 135
Borg-Warner, 48, 118, 174
Bramalea Ltd., 188, 201, 202, 204
Brampton, Ontario, 60, 129, 130, 156, 160, 188, 203
Breedlove, Craig and Lee, 100
Brisbane, Australia, 172
British Motors Company (BMC), 55
Brougham series, 115
Brown, Bob, 176–177
Brush, 14
Buick, 18, 127, 130
    Riviera, 70
Buyer Protection Plan, 118, 148

Cadillac, 65, 139
Camaro, 96, 97
Canadian Fabricated Products, 108
Canadian Postal Service, 128
Cappy, Joseph E., 174, 195, 196, 198, 199, 200, 201–202, 203
Car and Driver, 119, 140
Car Life, 38, 59
Card, Carol, 33
Cardin, Pierre, 118, 121
Carib, 67
Carousel, 81
Cassini, Oleg, 128
Cavalier, 88, 91
Chakmakian, Carl, 100
Chapin, Roy D., Jr., 10, 12, 13, 22–23, 38, 44, 55–56, 57, 60, 65, 66, 90, 91, 93, 94, 95, 97, 100, 101, 105, 106, 108, 110, 112–113, 117, 120, 121, 124, 125, 126, 129, 130–131, 133, 139–140, 141, 143, 144, 145, 146, 148, 149, 152, 154, 157, 163
Chapman, Bernard, 55
Checker, 16
Chevrolet, 16, 17, 18, 27, 31, 49, 56, 102, 127, 163
    Blazer, 128
    Chevelle, 79–80
    Chevette, 114
    Corvair, 52
    Corvette, 98, 100
    Corvette Stingray, 70
    Malibu, 79–80
    Malibu SS, 83
Chicago Auto Show, 37, 68
Chilson, Gordy, 101
Chrysler, 18, 44, 45, 50, 52–53, 56, 112, 116, 118, 127, 171, 197, 198, 200, 201, 202, 203–204
    Fifth Avenue, 198
    Turbine, 77
    Valiant, 52

Chrysler Corporation, 14
Coast-to-Coast Economy Run, 56
Cole, Ed, 138
Coleman Products Company, 124
Command-Trac, 184
Concept '80, 149, 150, 151
Concept AM Van, 149, 154, 202
Concept Electron, 149, 150
Concept Gran Touring, 149
Concept Grand Touring, 154
Concept Jeep II, 149, 151
Concept One, 149
Concept Two, 149
Concord, 152–153, 157–159, 161, 162, 164–165, 167, 168, 172, 174, 177–178, 180, 187
    D/L, 151, 155, 158, 163, 164–165, 168, 173, 175, 186, 187
    Hatchback, 162
    Limited, 165, 168, 169, 175
    Sedan Delivery Package, 174
    Silver Anniversary, 166
    Touring Wagon, 160
Conde, John, 73
Cord, 14
Cowboy, 127
Crosley, 16
Cross, Richard, 66–67, 91
Crown Pacer, 160
Cumulative Convertible Preferred Stock, 198
Cunningham and Walsh, 120

Dallas car, 139, 140
Dawkins, Dale, 148, 193
Daytona Beach, 40
Daytona Speedway, 70, 88
Dealer Volume Investment Fund, 37
Deduerwaerder, Jose, 174, 194, 195–196
Deep-Dip Rustproofing system, 57
DeLorean, John Z., 154
DeLorean Motor Company, 154
Detroit, 23, 28, 39
Dodge, 127
    Charger, 85
    Dart, 70
    Diplomat, 198
    Omni, 198
Donohue, Mark, 110, 111, 114, 134, 138
Doss, H. C., 28
Ducks Unlimited, 19
Duesenberg, 14

Eagle, 160, 161, 162, 165, 166, 167, 168, 169, 172, 174, 177–178, 179–180, 185, 186, 187, 190, 192, 193, 195–196, 199, 201, 203

Allure, 202
    Kammback, 166, 171, 172, 174
    Limited, 13, 192
    Medallion, 197
    Premier, 198
    SX/4, 170, 171
Ebersol, Keith, 193
Eisenhower, Dwight, 66
El Segundo, California, 27, 39
Evans, Robert B., 84, 85, 91, 93, 97
Evart Plastics, 129
Evart Products, 108

Fashion-Tone paint combination, 27, 28
Flyer Industries, 115
Follmer, George, 97, 98
Forbes, 91
Ford, 14, 16–17, 18, 27, 31, 49, 52–53, 56, 93, 102,
    112, 113, 116, 127, 163, 188–189, 201
    Bronco, 128
    Fairlane, 70, 80
    Falcon, 52, 85
    Galaxie 500, 83
    Granada, 158
    GT 40, 113
    Maverick, 110
    Mustang, 82, 85–86, 96, 97
Ford, Henry, II, 16
Franklin, 14

Garner, James, 104
General Electric, 130
General Motors, 12, 14, 18, 52–53, 112, 113, 116, 138,
    154, 168, 188–189, 200
General Products Division, 108, 113, 115
Geraci, Vince, 58, 85, 112, 118, 140, 183, 185, 201, 204
Geyer, 39
Gilchrist, Ronald, 148
Gould Incorporated, 128
Graham-Paige, 14, 16
Gran Touring, 100
Grant Rebel SST, 97
Gremlin, 103, 110, 112, 113–114, 117, 120, 121, 126,
    127, 128, 131, 133–134, 135, 136, 137, 138, 139,
    141, 142–143, 146, 148, 149, 150, 151, 156, 157,
    158, 159, 162, 163, 164, 166, 188, 201, 202
    CJ-5, 122
    Custom, 142, 143, 146–147, 149, 163–164
    D/L woody, 117
    G-II, 129, 163
    GT, 156, 159, 160
    Rallye-Pac, 128
    Renegade, 122
    X, 117, 128, 137, 143, 156, 159
    XP, 121
Grey Advertising, 161
Griffith, 172
Gucci, Aldo, 120

Gulton Industries, 90

Hanon, Bernard, 160, 192, 195
Hellcat, 131
Holden, William, 25
Holmes Foundry Ltd., 108, 113
Honda, 148
Hornet, 28, 35, 40, 88, 108, 110, 112, 114, 126, 128,
    129, 130, 133–134, 139, 142, 143, 147, 150, 151,
    157, 158, 164, 187
    AMX, 147
    Cowboy, 141
    GT, 114, 126, 154
    Hatchback, 119, 122, 135, 136
    SC/360, 114, 120
    Sportabout, 114, 115, 118, 120, 122, 126, 154
    Touring option, 135
    Touring wagon, 160
Hudson, 8–9, 14, 15, 16, 17, 18, 19, 20, 22–23, 26–27,
    28, 29 30, 35 37, 39, 40, 48, 52, 93, 195
    Hollywood Hardtop, 20
    Hornet, 18, 20, 23, 24, 25, 31, 40, 41, 45, 48
    Hornet Hollywood, 37
    Hornet Special, 24, 42
    Italia, 15, 24
    Jet, 8–9, 24, 25, 26
    Metropolitan, 21, 24
    Rambler, 29
    Super Wasp, 23
    Wasp, 23, 24, 25
Hudson Motorcar Company, 12
Hummer, 179
Hurst, George, 104
Hurst Performance, 102, 105
Hyde, Larry, 163

Iacocca, Lee, 198, 200, 203
IKA-Renault of Argentina, 93
IMSA series, 145
Industrias Kaiser Argentina (IKA), 60
Iron River, Michigan, 129

Jaguar, 65
Javelin, 94–95, 96, 97, 99, 100, 102, 104, 105,
    107, 110, 111, 115, 117, 118, 120–121, 122,
    128, 131, 134
    AMX, 114, 115, 118, 122, 125, 128, 134
    Racing Team, 97
    SST, 118
    Trans-Am, 110
    Trans-Am Victory package, 121
Jeep, 56, 106, 117, 121–122, 123, 125, 129–130, 134,
    136, 141, 143–144, 145, 146, 147, 150–151, 156,
    159–161, 163, 165, 166–167, 168, 170, 171, 172,
    173, 175, 177, 179–180, 184–185, 189, 190, 192,
    199, 200, 202
    Cherokee, 126, 128–129, 136, 147, 160, 165, 166,
      167, 172, 180, 182, 185, 187, 190, 196, 200

Cherokee Chief, 136, 181
Cherokee Chief XJ, 184
Cherokee XJ, 181
CJ-5, 120, 121, 129, 137
CJ-5 Renegade II, 108–109, 116
CJ-6, 121, 143
CJ-7, 143, 174, 196
CJ-7 Golden Eagle, 148
CJ-10, 182
CJs, 136, 156, 160, 165, 168, 172, 194, 202
Comanche, 196, 200
Comanche SporTruck, 196, 200
Commando, 121, 128, 143
Dispatcher DJ-5, 127
DJ-SC Dispatcher, 128
DJ-SE Dispatcher, 128
Gladiator, 115
Golden Eagle, 147, 160, 165
Grand Cherokee, 204
Grand Wagoneer, 165
Honcho, 143–144, 147, 160
Hurst Jeepster, 116
J-20, 172
Jamboree CJ, 174
Jeepster Commando SC-1, 116
JJ, 204
J-series, 165
Laredo, 168
Pioneer, 136, 147
Quadra-Trac, 123–124, 128–129, 143, 168
Renegade, 121, 123, 129, 165
Renegade I, 108–109, 112
Scrambler, 172
Silver Anniversary CJ-5, 166
Sport, 182
Truck, 123
Universal, 115–116, 121
Wagoneer, 115, 121, 123, 126, 128–129, 136, 147,
    165, 166, 180, 182, 184, 185, 187, 200
Wagoneer Brougham, 174
Wagoneer Limited, 160
Wrangler, 194, 195, 196
XJs, 177, 180, 183
ZJ, 204
Jeep Corporation, 108–109, 112–113, 201
Jeffrey, Charles, 12
Jeffrey, Thomas B., 12
Jet, 35
Johnson, Amos, 145

Kaiser, 18, 21, 130
Kaiser, Edgar, 56
Kaiser, Henry J., 16
Kaiser Industries Corporation, 56, 60, 106
Kaiser Jeep Corporation, 82, 106, 108, 115, 121
Kaiser-Frazer, 16, 17
Kaiser-Frazer Corporation, 56
Kaiser-Willys, 19, 31

Karmann GmbH, 99, 101
Kelvinator, 12, 21, 23, 30, 50, 52, 60, 65, 82, 87, 92, 101, 187
Kennedy, Jackie, 128
Kenosha, Wisconsin, 27, 39, 78, 108, 110, 129, 130, 148, 156, 166, 168, 169, 180, 188–189, 192, 195, 198, 202, 203–204
Kenosha Lakeside Stadium, 42
Khomeini, Ayatollah, 166
Knox, 14
Knupp, Ike, 102
Kornmiller, Allan, 24, 27, 28, 48, 52
Kugler, Eric, 117
Kuzel, Rudy, 203

LaFayette, 14
L-bodies, 198, 203–204
Le Mans, 25, 26
LeCar, 166
Lehman Brothers, 156
Leonard, 21
Lerma, 180
Levy, Raymond, 200
Lincoln Cadillac, 169
Lincoln-Mercury, 174
Luneburg, William V., 93, 94, 95, 115, 125, 126, 145, 146, 149
Lunn, Roy, 113, 115, 160, 167, 182–183, 184, 193

M-151 MUTT, 142
M-915 trucks, 151
Maddox, George, 193
M.A.N. (Germany), 147
Mark Donohue Javelin, 110
Mark Donohue Javelin-AMX, 114
Marlin, 83, 85–86, 87, 88, 90, 92, 93, 96, 97, 99
Marmon, 14
Mashigan, Chuck, 115, 137, 140, 148
Mason, George W., 16, 19–20, 22, 23, 24, 27–28, 30, 31, 33
Matador, 115, 119, 121, 122, 123, 124, 126, 127, 128, 132–133, 134, 136, 139, 142, 143, 147, 150, 157, 165, 187
    Barcelona, 159
    Barcelona II, 147, 148
    Brougham series, 128, 134
    D/L package, 129
    Machine, 115
    Machine Go package, 121
    X, 128, 134
Matra, 188
    Alpine, 188
Mazda, 138
M-bodies, 198
McCahill, Tom, 49, 58–59, 70, 93
McGaughey, Bill, 44–45
McMahon, Ed, 144
McNealy, R. William, Jr., 145

McNealy, William "Bill", 97, 99, 104, 149, 152, 154, 156–157, 160, 171
Mechanix Illustrated, 58, 70, 93
Mercury, 127
Mercury Plastics Company, 124
Metropolitan, 34, 36, 41, 48, 49, 51, 54, 55, 60, 63, 65, 70
Metropolitan Transit Authority (Washington, DC), 115, 124
Meyers, Gerald C. "Gerry", 117, 121, 138, 139, 145, 149–150, 152, 154, 156–157, 160, 161, 163, 164, 166, 170–171, 172, 173, 174
Michigan International Speedway, 111
Mighty Mite, 41, 54, 62, 63, 71
Milwaukee, Wisconsin, 27, 156
Mobilgas Economy Run, 52, 54, 81
Moore, Meade, 34
Moss, Cruse, 115, 163
Motor Trend, 70, 85, 88, 140, 176–177
Motor Trend Car of the Year Award, 70, 177
Murray Corporation, 33
Muskrat, 63

Nance, James J., 20, 31, 33–34, 38
NASCAR racing, 134
Nash, 16, 17, 18, 19, 22–23, 26–27, 29–30, 39, 45, 48, 52, 93
    Ambassador, 24, 25, 40, 41, 43, 48, 52
    Ambassador Country Club hardtop, 30, 38
    Ambassador Custom Country Club hardtop, 43
    Ambassador Customs, 38
    Ambassador Special, 42
    Canadian Statesman, 32
    Metropolitan, 21, 24, 25
    Rambler, 22, 23, 24–25, 48, 58
    Statesman, 24, 25
    Statesman Super, 19, 38
Nash, Charles, 12
Nash Motors Company, 12
Nash-Healey, 25, 26, 35
Nash-Kelvinator Corporation, 12, 16, 19, 20–21, 34
National Association of Manufacturers, 39
Nixon, Bob, 58, 71, 105, 106, 112, 137, 140, 183, 185, 202, 204
Nixon, Richard, 66

Oldsmobile, 18, 127
OPEC (Organization of Petroleum Exporting Countries), 125
Ostrowsi, Norbert, 135

Pacer, 131, 135, 137–141, 142, 143, 144, 145, 147, 148, 150, 155, 157, 158, 159, 160, 165, 168, 169, 187, 189, 202
    D/L, 165
    Limited, 165
    Rally, 143
    Sundowner, 145

Packard, 14, 16, 17, 18, 19, 20, 26, 27, 31–33, 34, 63, 102
Pappas, Jim, 65
Pathfinder, 160, 161
Peerless, 14
Penske, Roger, 138
Peon, Jesus, 200
Peugeot, 156, 160, 161
Pininfarina, 39, 93
Plymouth, 31, 49, 102, 127
    Barracuda, 85
    Grand Fury, 198
    Horizon, 198
Pontiac, 18
Popular Science, 99
Porsche, 171
Porter, Sylvia, 44–45
Pow-R-Pak, 142
Premier, 202
Project IV, 85, 91
Pure Oil Economy Trials, 59

Ram-Air hood, 110
Rambler, 12, 17, 27, 29–30, 31, 34, 35–38, 39, 41, 45, 53–59, 65, 68–70, 78–79, 84, 103, 126, 137, 140, 148, 173
    Ambassador, 48, 50, 51, 52, 54, 59, 60, 61, 62, 63, 67–68, 69, 70–71, 72–73, 79–80, 83–84, 85, 86–87, 89
    Ambassador 880, 74–75, 83
    Ambassador 990, 74–75
    Ambassador Custom, 62, 68
    Ambassador DPL, 85
    Ambassador DPL hardtop, 88
    Ambassador Vegas, 68
    American, 48–49, 50, 51, 52, 54, 55, 56, 58, 60, 62–63, 65, 69, 70, 71, 72–73, 74, 75, 76, 77, 80, 81, 83, 85, 86, 87–88, 90–91, 95, 97, 99, 101–102, 105
    American 220, 77
    American 330, 77
    American 400, 63, 64
    American 440, 76, 77
    American Classic, 83
    American Custom, 63
    American Deluxe, 49, 63
    American Rogue, 93, 99
    American Rogue hardtop, 88
    Classic, 46–47, 63, 64, 67–68, 70–71, 72–73, 74, 79–80, 84, 86–87, 88, 90
    Classic 6, 57
    Classic 550, 83
    Classic 770, 74, 80, 82
    Classic Custom, 58
    Classic Rebel hardtop, 88
    Classic V-8, 57, 68, 70
    Country Club hardtop, 27
    Cross Country, 36

Custom, 39, 44, 54
Deliveryman, 59
Deluxe, 34
Deluxe Six, 52
Rebel, 40, 47, 50, 51, 74–75, 83, 91, 92–93, 102, 107, 110, 112, 115
Rebel 770, 96, 99
Rebel Custom, 55
Rebel II, 89
Rebel Machine, 92, 110, 112
Rebel SST hardtop, 92
Rebel V-8, 54, 57, 60
Rogue, 100
SC/Rambler, 102, 104, 105
Scrambler Rambler, 102
Six, 47, 50, 52, 54, 57, 60, 63
Sportster, 67
St. Moritz, 82
Typhoon, 79
Ranco, Inc., 21, 39
Reddig, Bill, 17, 26, 37, 39–40, 52, 62, 87, 187
Redisco, 30, 52, 66, 82, 92, 101
Renault, 10–11, 12–13, 60, 82, 160, 161, 166, 168–169, 170, 172, 173, 174, 179, 182, 188, 192, 194, 199, 202, 203
    18i, 166, 172, 173, 178
    Alliance, 173, 175, 176–177, 178, 182, 185, 187, 189, 194–195, 196, 200
    Alliance convertible, 190–191
    Alliance Hatchback, 201
    Alliance Limited, 190
    Alliance MT, 177
    Allure, 200, 202, 204
    Alpine, 195, 196, 201, 202
    Encore GS, 190
    Encore series, 182, 185, 187, 189, 194–195, 196, 201
    Espace, 10–11, 188
    Espace Van, 195
    Fuego, 174
    GTA, 196, 200
    LeCar, 168, 178
    Premier, 198, 200
    R-19, 195–196
    R-21 (Medallion), 196, 197
    R-25, 182
    Sport Wagon, 178
    World Car, 166
    X42, 166
    X-58, 196
    X-59, 196
Renault, Règie, 10
Renault de Mexico, 182, 194
Reuther, Walter, 59–60
Richmond, Indiana, 142
Richmond Rambler, 100
Riker, 14
Rockne, 14

Rogue hardtops, 85
Rolls-Royce, 65, 171
Romney, George W., 20, 22, 23, 27–28, 30–34, 36–37, 38–45, 47–49, 50, 51–57, 58, 59–60, 62, 63, 65, 66–67, 71, 73, 75, 77, 79, 80, 83, 84–85, 126
Royhatyn, Felix, 198

Sabrina, 25
Sceptre, 78
Scott, Tom, 188, 201
Sears-Roebuck, 152
Sebring, Florida, 98
Select-Drive, 174
Selec-Trac, 184
Semerena, Pierre, 195, 196
Shahan, Shirley, 138
Shahn, H. L., 138
Shaw, Dennis, 145
Shinjin Jeep Company, 129
Sick, Wilson, 163
Singer, 163
Small Cars, 140
Sneider, Jesse, 100
South Bend, Indiana, 130
South Charleston, West Virginia, 129, 148
Southfield, Michigan, 182, 195
Special Products division, 62
Speed Week, 40
Spirit, 157, 162, 163–164, 166, 167, 168, 174, 175, 177–178
    D/L, 164, 168, 180
    GT, 164, 174, 177
    GT Liftback, 172
    Liftback, 129, 158, 163, 164, 165, 171, 182
    Limited, 164, 168, 171–172
    Sedan, 163, 171, 173, 174, 182, 188
Sportabout, 110
Sports Renault, 183
Springs Industries, 195
Stevens, Brook, 105
Studebaker, 14, 16, 17, 19, 20, 23, 26, 31–32, 71, 83, 90, 130
    Lark, 51
Studebaker-Packard, 31, 33, 34, 38
Styling Studio, 58, 80
Subaru, 180, 192, 203
Sundancer, 172

Tarpon, 77, 78, 82, 83, 85
Teague, Dick, 58, 62, 63, 75, 77, 103, 106, 112, 115, 140, 183, 187–188, 193
T.E.A.M. (Technical Employees of American Motors), 102
Team Highball, Inc., 145
Teheran facility, 101
Thomas, 14
Thomas B. Jeffery Company, 12
Timpy, Jack, 33, 37, 39

Tippett, W. Paul, 163, 169–170, 174, 175, 176–177, 190, 194, 195
Toledo paint facility, 166
Tolley, James, 163, 174
Torino, 93
Torque Command 232 cid inline six-cylinder engine, 77–78, 83
Toyota, 134
Trans-Am racing, 97, 98, 100
Typhoon, 77–78

Ultramatic transmission, 27
Uniframe, 184
Uniside construction, 69, 70
United Auto Workers union, 59–60, 83, 87, 188–189, 203
U.S. Army, 151
U.S. Postal Service, 117, 124, 127, 128

Van Peursem, Dave, 173
Vehiculos Automores Mexicano (VAM), 146, 167, 169, 173, 179, 180, 182, 194
Viland, Les, 59, 62, 81
Vixen, 88, 91
Volkswagen, 34, 55, 141, 160
    Beetle, 90, 95
    GTL, 200
Volkswagen Manufacturing Corporation, 148
Volvo, 156
Voyageur, 130

Wankel, 138
Ward's Auto World, 143, 200, 202
Wasp, 35, 42
Wells, Mary, 97
Wells, Rich, Greene, 97, 102, 116, 119, 120
Wheel Horse Products, 130, 141, 146, 151, 182
White Consolidated Industries, 101
Wibel, A. M., 28
Willys, 14, 21
Willys Motors, 18, 56
Willys-Overland, 14, 16, 18, 51
Windsor Plastics, 108
Wisconsin Proving Grounds, 75
Wolfson, Louis, 40–41, 44–45

X42, 168, 173, 174
X59 coupe, 202

Ziebart Factory-Rust Protection, 168
Zug, Switzerland, 60